Tariffs, Quotas, and Trade: The Politics of Protectionism

TARIFFS, QUOTAS, AND TRADE: THE POLITICS OF PROTECTIONISM

Walter Adams

Ryan C. Amacher

Sven W. Arndt

Malcolm D. Bale

John T. Cuddington

Alan V. Deardorff

Joel B. Dirlam

Roger D. Hansen

H. Robert Heller

D. Gale Johnson

Robert O. Keohane

Michael W. Keran

Rachel McCulloch

Ronald I. McKinnon

Gordon W. Smith

Robert M. Stern

Richard James Sweeney

Robert D. Tollison

Thomas D. Willett

Institute for Contemporary Studies

San Francisco, California

Copies of this book may be purchased from the institute for $6.95. All inquiries, book orders, and catalog requests should be addressed to the Institute for Contemporary Studies, Suite 811, 260 California Street, San Francisco, California 94111—(415) 398-3010.

Library of Congress Catalog Number 78-66267
ISBN 0-917616-34-0

CONTENTS

V

Conclusion

CONTRIBUTORS

WALTER ADAMS
Distinguished University Professor, Professor of Economics, Michigan State University

RYAN C. AMACHER
Associate Professor, Chairman, Department of Economics, Arizona State University

SVEN W. ARNDT
Professor of Economics, University of California, Santa Cruz

MALCOLM D. BALE
Economist, World Bank, Professorial Lecturer, School of Advanced International Studies, Johns Hopkins University

JOHN T. CUDDINGTON
Professor of Economics, Stanford University

ALAN V. DEARDORFF
Associate Professor of Economics, Associate Chairman, Department of Economics, University of Michigan

JOEL B. DIRLAM
Professor of Economics, University of Michigan

ROGER D. HANSEN
Jacob Blaustein Professor of International Organization, School of Advanced International Studies, Johns Hopkins University

H. ROBERT HELLER
Vice President for International Economics, Bank of America

D. GALE JOHNSON
Provost, Eliakim Hastings Moore Distinguished Service Professor, Department of Economics, University of Chicago

ROBERT O. KEOHANE
Professor of Political Science, Stanford University

MICHAEL W. KERAN
Vice President, Director of Research, Federal Reserve Bank of San Francisco

RACHEL McCULLOCH
Associate Professor of Economics, Harvard University

RONALD I. McKINNON
Professor of Economics, Stanford University

GORDON W. SMITH
Associate Professor of Economics, Rice University

ROBERT M. STERN
Professor of Economics, University of Michigan

RICHARD JAMES SWEENEY
Associate Professor of Economics, Claremont Men's College

ROBERT D. TOLLISON
Professor of Economics, Virginia Polytechnic Institute and State University

THOMAS D. WILLETT
Horton Professor of Economics, Claremont Graduate School and Claremont Men's College

PREFACE

Since World War II, rising global prosperity has been encouraged by an international economic system committed to increasing free exchange of goods and services across national boundaries. Following the disastrous tariff wars which aggravated the Great Depression, the commitment to reduce trade barriers has been implemented largely through a series of multilateral agreements negotiated under the General Agreement on Tariffs and Trade (GATT).

In the 1970s the international economy has become increasingly unstable. The international monetary system, established at Bretton Woods in 1944 and built on fixed exchange rates, collapsed in 1971 and a new system, built on floating rates, has emerged. The system was severely shaken in 1973–1974 when the OPEC cartel quadrupled oil prices. In recent years the value of the dollar has fallen precipitously against other major currencies, notably the Japanese yen, the German mark, and the Swiss franc. The dollar's decline in the fall of 1978 reached panic proportions, forcing what may be the beginning of a major change in U.S. policy toward its rising inflation.

The 1970s have also seen a marked rise in protectionist sentiment in the United States and abroad. The success of the OPEC cartel has encouraged other Third World nations to create similar cartels, and although these have not been notably successful, negotiations are underway to create commodity agreements which some observers fear will serve the same purpose. Increasing concern about foreign imports has also been expressed in relation to the Japanese and German trade surpluses—especially regarding steel, automobiles, and electronics—and to rising imports of manufactured goods from Third World countries.

Mounting instability creates pressures for insulation from instability, and that often means protection from trade. The situation became so serious in the fall of 1978 that for a time it appeared that the Tokyo Round of GATT negotiations might collapse. The threat of tariff wars was real. It was a threat to the very basis of the postwar global economy.

With such issues at stake, the Institute asked Richard James Sweeney, an international trade and finance specialist at Claremont Men's College, to help assemble a national group of economists to examine current issues of the international economy—especially the issues of free trade and protectionism—and to consider proposals for reform. In particular, we were interested in reexamination of traditional arguments for free trade in light of current circumstances, in consideration of the ways in which U.S. domestic economic policies influence the international economy, and in suggested methods of dealing with the growing political forces which influence the shape of trade policy.

It is clear that a great deal is at stake for all nations which engage in trade—not only for the advanced industrial nations, but for the developing countries which depend on outlets for their growing export industries. Moreover, the stakes are not solely economic; they are also political. How policymakers respond could well determine the future of the entire international economic system and the global prosperity it has made possible.

This is the first institute book dealing exclusively with international economic problems. Economic problems related to the Third World, and to U.S.–Third World relations, are dealt with in more detail in *The Third World: Premises of U.S. Policy,* published in the fall of 1978.

H. Monroe Browne
President,
Institute for Contemporary Studies

San Francisco, California
February 1979

I

Introduction

1

JOHN T. CUDDINGTON
RONALD I. McKINNON

Free Trade versus Protectionism: A Perspective

The positive theory of free trade. Protectionism, the monopoly tariff, and international retaliation. Noneconomic arguments in favor of tariffs. Historical movements in trade policy: Great Britain, the United States. Trade restrictions during the 1929–1933 economic collapse. Tariffs, devaluation, and unemployment. U.S. commercial policy and the 1962 Trade Expansion Act.

Since the second Great War, trade among the industrialized countries has expanded to an unprecedented extent—much faster than the rise in national output in Europe, the United States, and Japan. For example, imports into the United States rose to about 9.5 percent of gross national product (GNP) in 1978, compared to only 4.5 percent in the early 1950s. This doubling of the importance of imports—with a commensurate increase on the export side—is largely associated with a surge of trade in manufactures: automobiles, aircraft, computers and other electronic products, consumer durables, chemicals, and so forth. For individual European countries at the present time, imports now constitute about 25 percent of total national expenditures.

This massive increase in trade has been fostered by substantial reductions in tariff barriers on industrial products, in spite of considerable political tension and opposition. An extraordinarily protectionist piece of legislation—the Burke-Hartke bill—that would have effectively halved American imports, was (unsuccessfully) introduced into the U.S. Congress in the recession of 1970–1971. In the United States at the present time, a tariff war is threatened by an American law requiring the president to impose countervailing duties on foreign products containing export subsidies. Currently, European and Japanese farmers have succeeded in obtaining highly protected domestic markets—for which the yen or mark prices of some agricultural products may be several times those prevailing on world markets.

With the exception of agriculture, how, then, has this political tension been resolved largely in favor of more—rather than less—international trade? How do circumstances in the postwar period, and the weight of arguments which economists use, differ from those of earlier periods when protectionism prevailed?

In light of the widely disparate views of economists on most public policy issues, their virtually unanimous espousal of free trade for the past century and a half has been remarkable. Since Adam Smith, economists in the mainstream have advocated the free operation of the market mechanism, both domestically and internationally, to obtain the most efficient use of economic resources. Smith argued that labor productivity, which ultimately determines society's overall standard of living, depends directly on the extent of the division or specialization of labor—which in turn is limited by the market for the goods labor produces. Minimizing restrictions on international trade hence will maximize the market for domestic goods and opportunities for the division of labor—with consequent enhancement of both national output and domestic well-being.

In addition to the favorable effect on productivity resulting from greater division of labor, free trade increases national output by encouraging production of goods which the economy can provide at relatively low cost compared to other nations. As classical economists Torrens and Ricardo pointed out, a country need not have an absolute advantage in the production of any good. It can, nevertheless, unambiguously increase the value of its output by greater specialization in products in which it has the least disadvantage. That is, allocating domestic resources on the basis of *comparative* (not necessarily absolute) advantage benefits both domestic residents and the world as a whole. With few exceptions, therefore, classical international trade theory indicated that to maximize societal well-being, man-made impediments to international exchange should be kept to a minimum.

THE "MONOPOLY" TARIFF AND OTHER ARGUMENTS FOR PROTECTION

The strong endorsement of free trade by the classical economists remains firmly entrenched in modern writings on foreign-trade policy. The major qualification to the doctrine from a single country's point of view involves the case where a country is large enough to influence its terms of trade—

i.e., the price of its exports in terms of imports. In such a case, the country can enrich itself at the expense of foreigners by exploiting its monopoly power in the market for its exports and/or monopsony power in the market for its imported goods. In the theoretical literature, this tariff, whereby a country unilaterally exploits its international monopoly power to the fullest extent, has been called the "optimum tariff." We shall refer to it as a "monopoly tariff," to avoid misunderstanding about the meaning of "optimum." Although an individual nation can gain by levying a monopoly tariff to increase the relative price of its exports, the world as a whole necessarily loses because of the resulting misallocation of resources.

An important consideration for countries contemplating a monopoly tariff is that its trading partners may not accept it passively. To limit their losses and to encourage the trade-restricting country to reconsider, other countries may erect retaliatory tariff barriers of their own. Successive retaliations ultimately harm all countries by reducing world trade, and with it, international specialization.

Although a nation large enough to affect world prices may not find it advantageous to reduce tariffs unilaterally when faced by monopoly tariffs from abroad, multilateral tariff reductions should be mutually beneficial. On the other hand, small countries which cannot affect world prices can unambiguously gain by reducing their import duties—even unilaterally. Such a move, however, also benefits foreigners; this fact presumably tempts domestic policymakers into bearing (temporarily?) the resource misallocation costs of their tariffs in the hope of extracting foreign concessions in exchange for trade liberalization. It is possible but unlikely that countries may use tariffs to alter favorably the terms of trade without retaliation; otherwise, the general presumption in favor of free trade to maximize domestic and world welfare remains intact.[1]

Given the strong theoretical justification for free trade, except in the case of a monopoly tariff, it is surprising to find that high tariffs and other restrictive trade policies have been predominant in both developed and underdeveloped countries over the last hundred and fifty years. Free trade has been the exception rather than the rule in international commercial relations (see Figures 1 and 2, summarizing the tariff histories of the United States, Great Britain, and Canada). While there have been ebbs and flows since the early 1800s, average tariff levels have generally been high. In practice, the policy recommendation of free trade has often been disregarded. While the monopoly tariff argument and possible retaliation may explain tariffs in particular situations, such as the OPEC (Organization of Petroleum Exporting Countries) oil cartel, it can hardly provide a complete explanation for existing restrictions on wide classes of both manufactured and agricultural products—particularly in less-developed countries.

Tariffs often reflect noneconomic arguments for protection, such as national defense or the promotion of industries which increase national prestige (e.g., steel mills). Tariffs are often "second-best" policies used to correct domestic economic distortions, such as unduly high or rigid industrial wages, or to protect "infant" industries. By a second-best policy, economists mean the best viable policy given certain political, economic, or other constraints which prevent authorities from choosing the optimum, or "first-best," policy prescription. Such real-world constraints on policymakers may prevent free trade from ever being universally adopted.

Although high tariffs and other trade restrictions have characterized the histories of both European and American commercial policy, there have been two concerted moves towards free trade. The first was the British liberalization of the early 1800s, highlighted by the repeal of the Corn Laws in 1846. Britain maintained this free-trade policy until the McKenna duties of 1916 and remained relatively liberal even longer, until it succumbed in 1931 to a worldwide rash of protectionism brought on by the collapse of the world economy and international monetary system based on the sterling/gold exchange standard.

Figure 1
Average Import Duties, United States, 1792–1974

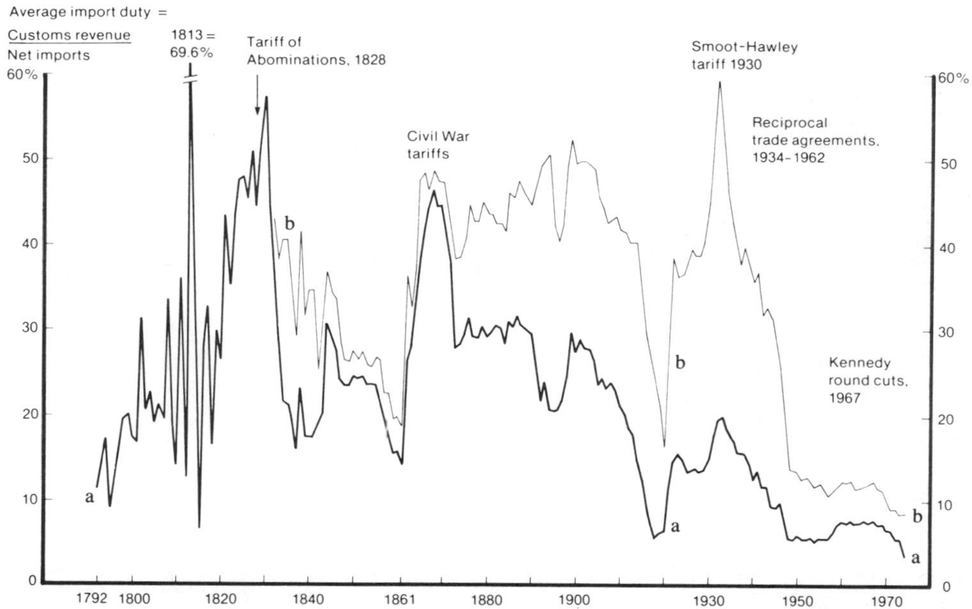

Source: U.S. Census 1976: series U193, U1211, U212, Y353; idem 1975; table 1370. See Kindleberger and Lindert (1978:221-22).

[a]Duties as a percentage of all net imports.
[b]Duties as a percentage of dutiable imports only.

Figure 2
Average Import Duties, United Kingdom, 1796–1972, and Canada, 1868–1972
(selected years)

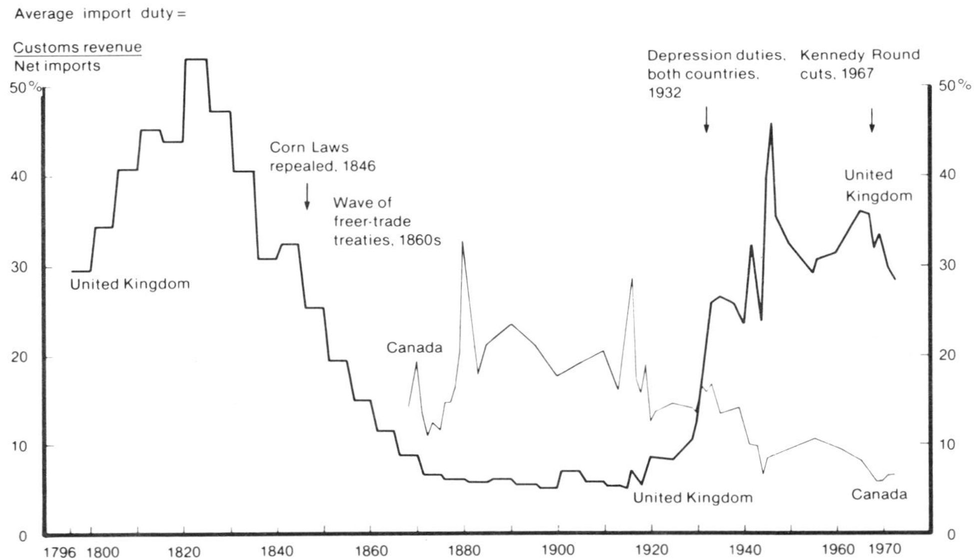

Source: United Kingdom: Imlah 1958:121, 160; Mitchell and Deane 1965:284, 394, 395; Mitchell and Jones 1971:130, 159; Great Britain 1974:263, 328. Canada: Urquhart and Buckley 1965:173, 197, 198; Canada, various years. See Kindleberger and Lindert (1978:221-22).

*Duties as a percentage of all net imports.

Note: Some of the ratios compare fiscal-year customs revenues with calendar-year imports.

The second prolonged movement towards freer trade was initiated by the U.S. delegation to the 1933 World Economic Conference of the League of Nations. In 1934 the evolving U.S. free-trade policy was embodied in the Reciprocal Trade Agreements Act. The act authorized the president to negotiate bilateral reductions in the prohibitive Smoot-Hawley tariffs, which had resulted from the congressional debacle of legislative logrolling at the beginning of the world depression in 1930. Except for a pause during the war, the U.S. drive towards trade liberalization was sustained into the late 1960s by successive renewals and modifications of the 1934 act. After the war, world efforts to foster freer trade were made under the auspices of the General Agreement on Trade and Tariffs (GATT).

Much can be learned about the relationship between modern commercial policy and classical arguments for free trade by contrasting the early British free-trade movement with the worldwide liberalization efforts initiated by the United States after World War II.

THE BRITISH POLICY OF UNILATERAL FREE TRADE IN THE 19th CENTURY

Prior to the nineteenth century, Britain had not always been the leading advocate of noninterventionist policies. As Mathias (1969:83) points out:

> From the sixteenth to the mid-eighteenth century a general assumption prevailed that government had a necessary role in attempting to ease the problems afflicting the economy by interfering with natural market mechanisms. . . . The greatest stimulus to legislation was "an attempted defence against the vagaries of economic dislocation." . . . Underlying much of the legislation was a great fear of unemployment, particularly in the textile districts, with its attendant political problems.

By the 1820s, however, British imperialism began to take on a new free-trade orientation, with *laissez-faire* ideals of Smith and Ricardo being seen as an alternative to the mercantilist policy of comprehensive restrictions on international exchange.

While rapid industrialization brought prosperity to Britain, it also created a need for new markets and cheap raw materials. Smith and others recognized the potential of large foreign markets in both regards. Trade liberalization would allow cheap material inputs to be imported by manufacturers. Also, foreign demand for British products would be increased by providing resource-abundant less-developed countries with higher export earnings.

As the principal agent in many of the markets in which it traded, Britain found that the gains of free trade could be secured largely by unilateral trade liberalization. Although other industrializing nations were influenced by Britain's posture of pure free trade, for the most part they provided tariff protection for their infant manufacturing industries. U.S. protective legislation can be traced back to 1813, when tariff rates were increased to levels averaging well over 50 percent. Despite changes under different administrations, they remained highly protective until the Reciprocal Trade Agreements Act of 1934. Canada maintained high tariff barriers after confederation in 1867 in order to limit foreign competition, particularly from the United States, and thereby promote rapid industrialization.

Although Britain's unilateral adoption of free trade increased the efficiency of resource allocation and the growth in industrial output, the policy was not without opponents. As Smith, and especially Ricardo, had emphasized, groups with vested interests in import-competing industries would be harmed by free trade. Any policy change would have domestic income distribution effects which could not be ignored. Such effects were widely recognized in debates over the repeal of the British Corn Laws, which protected British agricultural interests from cheap imports of corn. Ricardo predicted that landlords would suffer reduced rents on their property—a fate which he treated lightly, given his belief that landlords contributed little to national productivity. On the other hand, manufacturers and, to a lesser extent, industrial laborers would benefit from free trade because of the resulting decline in raw material and food prices.

For this reason, Manchester manufacturing interests were among the most vociferous advocates of trade liberalization. Together with sympathetic intellectuals and academicians, they formed the Anti–Corn Law League, an organization which did much to popularize Smith's conviction that free trade ultimately benefited all groups by increasing national income and productivity. They emphasized that free trade was in the "general interest," and downplayed the associated income redistribution. But, as McCord (1970:10–11) points out,

> the activities of the Anti–Corn Law League cannot, however, be seen simply as an academic argument about the economic benefits of agricultural protection, for political and social factors also entered largely into the conflict. The campaign against the Corn Laws was entered into partly to provide a rallying-point for radical energies, and a focus which could bring together all the varied interests that for one reason or another disliked the social and political predominance of the landed interest in Britain.

With the British economy operating at high rates of capacity utilization during the mid-nineteenth century, free trade could only increase productivity by reallocating resources towards high-growth sectors in which the economy had comparative advantage. Flexibility of Britain's economic structure, and the gradual increase in labor mobility which accompanied industrialization, facilitated the required adjustment. Inevitably, however, vested interests in import-competing sectors were adversely affected.

Neoclassical economists, particularly Kaldor, Hicks, and Scitovsky, have argued convincingly that the efficiency gains from free trade are always sufficient to enable the gainers to compensate the losers from trade liberalization. Thus, with an appropriate (costless) mechanism for redistributing domestic income, free trade could make everyone better off.

In the real world, of course, a politically acceptable distribution of the gains from free trade is seldom guaranteed.

Consequently, whether or not a free-trade policy prevails depends on the relative political power of disparate interests. Kindleberger (1973:236–37) attributes the success of the free-trade movements in Britain and later in the United States primarily to the role of special interest groups:

> The fundamental cause for the change in commercial policy was in each case a change in the structure of the economy, and the rise to political dominance of the group which benefited from lower tariffs: manufacturers in Britain, and mass production [interests] in the United States.

Britain maintained its free-trade policy through the prosperous mid-1800s and into the twentieth century, in spite of difficulties experienced in the 1870s and 1890s partly due to increased foreign competition. It was not until the depths of the Great Depression that Britain finally turned to trade restrictions, after repeated but unsuccessful attempts to stem the rise in world protectionism and to prevent collapse in the international monetary system.

THE GREAT DEPRESSION AND THE COLLAPSE OF WORLD TRADE

Commercial policy in the United States from 1861 to 1934 differed greatly from the British policy. Salvatore Schiavo-Campo (1978:173–74) explains:

> The fall of the Democrats from power, and the Civil War, sparked the beginning of a gradual but steady increase in protectionism. U.S. commercial policies were to remain highly restrictive for the following 70 years, with the exception of a brief interlude at about the time of World War I. . . . After the war, the pleadings for protection by the new industries that had been built up during the war years combined with the return of the Republican party to the Presidency to produce in 1922 a resumption of restrictive commercial policies.

The trend towards greater tariff protection for domestic industries in the United States was accompanied by similar movements in other industrializing nations. Even in Britain there was growing protectionist sentiment as reflected in the McKenna duties of 1916 and in the Safeguarding of Industries Act of 1921.[2] Several international efforts to stem the growing restrictionist trend were initiated primarily by Britain. In 1928 the World Economic Conference of the League of Nations attempted to negotiate a tariff truce among its European members. Meanwhile, in the United States, however, the Republican Party was building an election platform advocating increased protection for depressed American agriculture. The league's tariff-truce agreement therefore dwindled from lack of U.S. interest and protectionist pressure in Europe. In the end, only Britain, Belgium, Switzerland, and the Scandinavian countries ratified the agreement.

By the end of 1929, when the American stock market collapsed foreshadowing the world economic collapse, many nations had instituted at least moderate trade restrictions. These restrictions were rapidly increased as the world depression deepened, and as countries acted unilaterally to stimulate their economies and to prevent further increases in unemployment. In the United States, the new Republican administration imposed high protective tariffs under the Smoot-Hawley Act of 1930. Although the initial intention had been only to protect agriculture, an orgy of political logrolling and lobbying power dramatically increased protection for many other products. The passing of the bill brought a wave of foreign retaliation and competitive devaluations in a vain attempt to prevent further national output declines. Finally, in September 1931, Britain could no longer maintain the value of the pound in terms of gold, and was forced to allow the currency to depreciate. By the end of the year, tariffs were also increased in a further attempt to improve the balance of payments and the unemployment situation. The British free-trade era had come to an end.[3]

From the standpoint of classical international trade and welfare theory, the competitive devaluations of the early 1930s could only be explained by the monopoly-tariff argument *cum* retaliation. Such an explanation seems inadequate, however, in light of the across-the-board and extraordinary high tariffs that prevailed. Countries suffered a severe drop in income, much more than just the loss in gains from trade. Why, then, did countries not perceive it to be in their interest to unilaterally reduce trade barriers in the many cases where they presumably had no power to influence the terms of trade? Were the rationalizations for tariffs noneconomic or, alternatively, reflections of the power of certain special-interest groups to gain at the expense of others in the domestic economy? Was trade restriction a second-best policy, given the depressed state of the world economy?

To answer these questions, we must reexamine the classical theory, which presumes that the price incentives resulting from supply and demand ensure full utilization of resources. In the depressed economic environment of the 1930s, market mechanisms guaranteeing the efficient allocation of all resources were obviously inadequate. In the face of severe unemployment, therefore, arguments for free trade which relied on classical theory became suspect.

The Great Depression presented a situation where some resources were not simply misallocated. They were not allocated at all. In this predicament, policymakers could increase national output by operating on two fronts. The first involved attempts to improve the allocation of resources which were already employed, but inefficiently. The second approach—and obviously the more fruitful one in the 1930s—focused on increasing the employment of idle resources. Nowadays, monetary and fiscal policies are generally used to meet this second objective—not always successfully.

In the 1930s the economics of aggregate demand management was not well developed. Furthermore, the use of monetary policy for stimulating domestic output was limited by the authorities' preoccupation with balance-of-payments and exchange-rate considerations. Given constraints on the use of monetary and fiscal policies which prevented authorities from maintaining full employment, the latter turned to tariffs to limit foreign competition and to raise domestic output and employment. Unfortunately, the resulting stimulant to domestic output was small relative to the tremendous decline in foreign demand that resulted from the world economic collapse, and was exacerbated by beggar-thy-neighbor tariff policies.

It is interesting to note that two well-known economists, W. Arthur Lewis and J. M. Keynes, advocated the use of tariffs to divert domestic spending from imports towards home production in the early 1930s. Keynes, however, considered tariffs to be a second-best alternative to exchange-rate devaluation as a cure for Britain's balance-of-payments problems. Given the preoccupation of the monetary authorities with the value of the British pound in terms of gold, Keynes saw tariffs as a possible means of stimulating aggregate demand. In addition to inducing a substitution towards domestically produced goods, he considered increased tariffs to be the least contradictory means of raising much-needed revenue to finance expansionary increases in government expenditure. Thus, the tariff's revenue-raising and protective aspects were both considered important.

It is clear, however, that Keynes advocated tariffs only as a second-best solution. Once the Bank of England finally gave in to downward pressure on the pound and devalued in September 1931, Keynes contended that tariffs were no longer necessary. Nonetheless, British authorities followed the devaluation by a substantial increase in tariffs before the end of 1931.

The experience from 1930 to 1933 shows that countries sometimes perceive tariff increases as a means of raising domestic employment, particularly when aggregate demand management policies are constrained by other policy objectives. Whether one considers this a second-best policy is a matter of interpretation and perspective. It is unquestionably true, however, that imposing tariffs to increase demand for domestic goods will reduce imports from abroad correspondingly. Thus, increasing barriers to imports is a beggar-thy-neighbor policy that often provokes retaliatory measures which ultimately harm all nations.

Given that tariffs may in some cases allow a country to increase employment, albeit at foreigners' expense, it is important to determine how different domestic interests will react to commercial policy changes. In contrast to full-employment situations—in which expansion in one sector necessarily involves withdrawal of resources from less-profitable sectors—with high unemployment, increased tariffs are likely to produce less disagreement among different sectors in the economy. With high unemployment, much greater emphasis will be placed on policies that increase the overall level of national output. It is unclear, however, whether greater protectionism or trade liberalization will emerge. Output-expanding policies usually benefit all domestic groups, at least to some degree, thereby masking adverse changes in relative income shares. Because the success of tariffs in stimulating domestic output depends critically on how other nations respond, however, policy effects on the *international* distribution of income and employment will be a primary consideration. That is, domestic policymakers will carefully assess the foreign income and employment effects of their policy in light of any anticipated sympathetic or retaliatory action by other nations.

THE U.S. RECIPROCAL TRADE AGREEMENTS ACT OF 1934

By 1933 it was clear that unilateral attempts to stimulate domestic output by erecting high tariff barriers only encouraged retaliation by other nations and further depressed the world economy. The combination of high tariff barriers and weak international demand meant that individual countries had little hope of gaining through unilateral action to reduce trade barriers. The industrialized nations realized that reciprocal trade reductions, coupled with expansionary monetary and fiscal policies, had the greatest potential for providing mutual increases in output and employment. Each country's expansionary policies would reenforce similar policies taken by its trading partners.

As a first step toward coordinated action, the U.S. delegation to the 1933 World Economic Conference recommended an immediate tariff truce and removal of exchange-rate restrictions which had mushroomed from 1929 to 1932. This measure was to be followed up by gradual elimination of tariff walls and coordinated expansion in monetary and fiscal policies to increase world demand for output.

In 1934 the U.S. Congress passed the Reciprocal Trade Agreements Act, giving the president wide authority to negotiate bilateral tariff reductions. The authority was subject to renewal every three years, but in the intervening period the administration would have a free hand in tariff negotiations. Senate ratification of every tariff treaty was no longer required. The act emphasized that trade liberalization was to be reciprocal in nature, a tacit recognition that a U.S. move toward freer trade would affect foreign as well as domestic residents. As Kreinin (1975:315–16) points out, the Trade Agreements Act of 1934 was

> an antidepression measure designed to open up new export markets for American products. The offer of reciprocal tariff concessions was not an end in itself; it was meant to induce foreign countries to open their markets to American products. . . . The economic end of attaining higher efficiency is usually given some lip service, but it is not held in high regard.

The role played by special-interest groups in shaping the 1934 act was limited, relative to its importance in early British as well as U.S. legislation. In fact, the Reciprocal Trade Agreements Act marks a significant change in the power of special-interest groups, according to recent work by Steven Brenner (1977). He argues that lobbying pressure for tariff legislation was substantially reduced with the act's transfer of tariff-negotiating authority from Congress to the president. Brenner (1977:1–2) notes that:

> Before 1934 protection-seeking economic interests had been very successful in influencing congressional tariff-making. . . . The structure of information costs made the direct benefits of protection more visible than the costs. The structure of preferences and the institutions of voting by representatives implied intransitive aggregated social preferences which manifested themselves as logrolling deals which increased protection. . . .
>
> The Trade Agreement Program moved trade policy-making to the bureaucrats of the executive branch. The new decision-makers had different objectives than did elected representatives; they wanted the program of tariff-bargaining to succeed.

It thus appears that our conjecture that high unemployment should make conflicts among special-interest groups less important is consistent with the evidence that the political influence of protectionists was not a major force in shaping the Reciprocal Trade Agreements Act. The consequences of trade promotion on the *redistribution* of domestic income was not a primary consideration. It was the expected effects on *total* output and employment that were at issue.

While the different pressure-group interests tend to be less in conflict when unemployment is widespread, one might expect that questions of income redistribution would reemerge as economic conditions improved. If tariffs are redundantly high, as with Smoot-Hawley, they can be cut initially with impunity. As the economy approaches full capacity, the reserve of idle resources shrinks. Further moves toward free trade will eventually require that already employed factors of production be reallocated toward industries in which the country has comparative advantage. This, of course, is detrimental to the interests of immobile factors in import-competing industries, which will take action to limit the dislocative effects resulting from freer trade.

This is, in fact, what happened in the United States as the economy recovered from the Great Depression and returned to more prosperous times. Successive renewals of the president's tariff-negotiating authority under the Reciprocal Trade Agreements Act placed increased emphasis on limiting the losses from policy-induced shifts in demand. Kreinin (1975:315) remarks that

> most extensions of the law have embodied a ''no-injury'' philosophy—trade liberalization was to be accomplished with minimum injury to domestic industry. This philosophy found expression in the escape clause, peril point, and national security provisions of the act.

U.S. commercial policy has had two main thrusts since 1934. On the one hand, a concerted effort has been mounted to liberalize import restrictions through reciprocal bilateral agreements on a commodity-by-commodity basis. The extent of trade liberalization has been limited, however, by the stipulation that it cause no injury to domestic industries. While such a precondition could be overridden in 1934 because virtually every industry was in bad straits, it has become a binding constraint on trade liberalization efforts as the economy moved closer to full capacity. For economies near full employment, such protective no-injury clauses are clearly inconsistent with the dictates of comparative advantage. They reflect the ability of particular domestic groups to benefit at the expense of others. As mentioned above, this problem was anticipated even in early classical writings on the gains from trade. More recent work has placed greater emphasis on the role of income-distribution effects, and has demonstrated the possibility of conflicts between a group's short-run and long-run interests due to short-run factor immobility.

Policymakers have not neglected the short-run adjustment costs arising from the reallocation of resources towards sectors exhibiting comparative advantage. Wages in many industries have become more inflexible with the growth of trade unions. Greater specialization and division of labor have reduced interindustry mobility, making it increasingly difficult to reabsorb workers who become unemployed because of increased import competition.

Recognizing the conflict between comparative advantage and the no-injury clause, the 1962 Trade Expansion Act changed the focal point of American trade legislation. It placed much greater emphasis on adjustment assistance to workers, firms, and industries adversely affected by trade liberalization. Rather than to provide permanent protection against more efficient foreign producers, the new measures encouraged movement of resources into the industries in which the United States was competitive. Through temporary adjustment assistance, the legislation hoped to reduce the potential conflict among different domestic interests concerning future movements towards freer international trade.

CONCLUSION

In comparing the free-trade movements of Britain in the mid-nineteenth century and the U.S. efforts in the twentieth, the most noteworthy difference is that Britain's free-trade policy was adopted and maintained unilaterally.[4] In contrast, the 1934 U.S. Reciprocal Trade Agreements Act allowed the president to permit freer foreign access to American markets only when equivalent concessions were granted by foreign governments. Reciprocity has remained the cornerstone of U.S. trade legislation in the postwar period. Furthermore, under the auspices of the GATT, it has become the fundamental principle in multilateral negotiations to reduce both tariffs and nontariff barriers on a worldwide basis.[5]

Comparing these two cases sheds considerable light on the many issues which trade negotiators and policymakers must consider. We have seen that when trade is unrestricted, increased markets and greater specialization in production increase world income. Unfortunately, allocating resources according to the dictates of comparative advantage may harm some individuals or industries who face increased foreign competition. Government policies may be required to redistribute equitably among domestic residents the higher total income guaranteed by free trade. During the transition to free trade, adjustment assistance may also be justified on equity grounds.

Modern writings on "the political economy of tariffs" emphasize the importance of domestic pressure groups anxious to increase their well-being at the expense of others. When unemployment is widespread, however, policy-induced changes in income *shares* become less important than their effects on the *total level* of income. All groups typically benefit at least to some extent from any policy that raises domestic output. Thus, changes in tariff policy may meet less resistance when resources are underemployed, as long as increased employment is expected. Underemployment may create a political environment in which policymakers attempt to stimulate domestic production by shutting out foreign competition. On the other hand, moving to freer trade may be seen as increasing output, leading to international efforts to foster reciprocal increases in export demand. Whether the reduced pressure-group conflict that results from high unemployment leads to increased or decreased protectionism is, to some degree, a historical accident. In the case of the Great Depression, it was only after beggar-thy-neighbor tariff policies were seen to be blatantly unsuccessful that nations turned to multilateral negotiations to expand trade. It does seem clear, however, that unemployment makes *unilateral* tariff reductions unlikely.

When the economy is near full employment, in contrast, unilateral trade liberalization may be undertaken. It depends on the political power of domestic interests which would gain relative to those which would lose from such a policy change. At full employment, income redistribution effects become more significant in policy discussions than incremental effects on total income.

With a sharp recession in the United States in 1975–1976 and prolongation of this recession in Europe and Japan into 1978–1979, coordinated measures to expand trade remain very important. No major industrial country is likely to have the political staying power to maintain free trade unilaterally—as Britain did in the later nineteenth century. Hence, quarreling over export subsidies on industrial products, or over undue protectionism in agriculture, must be resolved in multilateral forums such as the General Agreement on Tariffs and Trade. Uninhibited nationalism in economic policymaking has the potential to destroy the basis for the remarkable postwar economic prosperity industrial nations have enjoyed—and to which many less-developed countries aspire.

2

RACHEL McCULLOCH

Determinants and Implications of U.S. Trade Performance

Exchange rates and the U.S. trade deficit. The role of comparative advantage. Measures of trade performance. The merchandise trade balance and the current account balance. The United States, Japan, and OPEC. Income elasticities of import and export demand. International competitiveness of U.S. industries. Inflation and cost competitiveness. Industry interactions. Adjustment assistance. The oil-trade deficit.

U.S. trade performance reached a turning point in 1965, when the merchandise trade balance fell for the first time since World War II. The first merchandise trade deficit of the century was recorded in 1971. That was also the year of the "Nixon shocks," devaluation of the dollar, and the short-lived Smithsonian agreement to salvage the Bretton Woods system of fixed exchange rates. However, exchange rate realignments in 1971 and subsequent years provided at best a partial answer to U.S. trade problems. While the merchandise trade balance moved to a near-record surplus of $9 billion for 1975, it subsequently plummeted to an unprecedented $31 billion deficit in 1977.

Just as the events of the late 1960s and early 1970s called into question and eventually undermined the Bretton Woods system, so has recent experience raised doubts about the successor system of floating exchange rates. In particular, the prolonged decline of the dollar relative to the German mark and the Japanese yen, along with the failure of dollar depreciation to restore balance in the trade account, has aroused skepticism concerning market-determined exchange rates. Furthermore, dramatic growth rates for some categories of U.S. imports, particularly from Japan and the less-developed countries (LDCs), have posed a politically troublesome problem of internal adjustment for the United States and have stimulated renewed debate on the virtues of a liberal trade policy.

Newspaper headlines today report American workers displaced by exports from Japan and from such LDCs as Korea, Taiwan, and Brazil, along with record U.S. payments for imported oil, burgeoning trade deficits, the sinking dollar, and the soaring yen. Faced with a trade deficit that won't go away, U.S. policymakers now search for structural explanations. Slow recovery abroad from the sharp recession of the mid-1970s is invoked to explain the lagging U.S. export growth. Accordingly, Japan and West Germany are called upon to raise their own growth rates and thereby to import more U.S. goods. U.S. negotiations with the Japanese focus upon the huge bilateral trade balance, and seek new ways to slow Japanese encroachment into U.S. domestic markets while opening up the highly protected Japanese market to U.S. goods, particularly to agricultural products. Other critics of recent U.S. trade performance focus instead on the nation's failure to curtail oil imports. Still others blame current trends in U.S. manufacturing, citing the lack of export orientation of most U.S. producers, inadequate capital investment and research and development (R&D) expenditures, and ever-increasing safety and environmental regulation.

This chapter analyzes recent U.S. trade performance overall and within particular sectors. The major determinants of U.S. trade performance are identified, along with their implications for alternative policy choices.

THE ROLE OF COMPARATIVE ADVANTAGE

U.S. trade performance reflects the nation's comparative advantage, at least when market forces are allowed to determine trading patterns. The principle of comparative advantage states that mutual benefits from trade can be achieved when each country exports those goods in which it has a *relative* cost advantage—even if one trading partner has an *absolute* cost advantage in every industry. Comparative advantage is thus relevant mainly for the composition of trade, i.e., differences in competitiveness across industries, rather than the nation's overall trade performance.[1]

The principle of comparative advantage rests upon *potential* differences in relative costs and prices between countries. Countries export those goods which would be relatively cheap in the absence of trade and import those which would be relatively expensive. The comparison is not of actual costs, but of those (hypothetical) costs which would be observed in the absence of trade.[2] Trade along lines of comparative advantage tends to reduce cost differences actually observed. In a world in which transport costs, trade barriers, and lack of complete information together played a small role in determining trade flows, trade could virtually eliminate cost differences. This would not mean that comparative advantage was failing to operate, but rather that it was operating very well.

Most trade is that of goods or services for money, instead of direct barter transactions of goods for other goods. Actual trading decisions are determined by money prices, not by relative prices. Comparative advantage therefore can operate only when there is an appropriate exchange rate between currencies. For trade to occur, the pretrade dollar cost of some foreign goods—as calculated using the exchange rate between dollars and francs or marks or pounds—must be lower than the prices of some competing domestic goods, while the opposite is true for other goods. However, because exchange rates are determined not only by the flow of goods and services, but also by transfers and by capital transactions, an equilibrium exchange rate will not necessarily yield balanced trade. A merchandise trade deficit or surplus, by itself, provides no evidence of exchange-rate disequilibrium, nor of the failure of comparative advantage.

The international competitiveness of particular industries depends upon comparative advantage as reflected in the underlying structure of the economy, but it also depends on government policies influencing the allocation of resources and on exchange rates between currencies. New government policies or exchange rates can immediately affect an industry's international competitiveness, even though the underlying structure of productive capacity changes only gradually.

HOW SHOULD U.S. TRADE PERFORMANCE BE MEASURED?

U.S. government agencies regularly publish a number of summary measures of U.S. foreign trade performance. The most frequently cited of these are the *merchandise trade bal-*

ance and the *current account balance*. The "trade balance," as reported in newspaper headlines, is usually the merchandise trade balance—the difference between the total value of exports and imports in a given time period. Only trade in *goods* is included—not services—and one reason is the relative ease of data collection. However, many users of balance-of-payments statistics still believe that trade in goods (or just manufactures) better reflects the "true" current state of the producing economy, even though services have come to dominate the nation's gross national product (GNP).

Exports embody the current services of domestic labor and capital, while imports in a sense substitute their foreign counterparts. In contrast, a major part of services transactions is generated by *past* foreign investments and agreements covering the use of technology, trademarks, and the like. These transactions are less directly linked to current employment and capacity utilization at home and abroad.[3] Other services transactions, however, such as travel, transportation, and insurance, are currently produced by capital and labor, and are thus quite similar to merchandise trade. The analysis here focuses mainly on merchandise trade, although most of it applies to the other types of services.

The trade balance indicates the net extent to which U.S. demand for current production falls upon foreign suppliers, or foreign demand upon U.S. suppliers. A deficit shows that some U.S. demand is being met from foreign sources. In a Keynesian framework focusing upon total aggregate demand as a key determinant of output and employment, a merchandise trade deficit may be interpreted as a "leakage" from aggregate demand, exerting a downward pull on the level of economic activity. This Keynesian analysis leads some critics to say that U.S. jobs are being lost to foreigners, or "exported." However, such an interpretation is valid only in special circumstances.[4]

The current account balance is the sum of the merchandise trade balance, the balance on services (including investment income, royalties, travel and shipping, insurance, etc.), and net transfers (including official and private foreign aid, gifts, pension payments, etc.). All international transactions *other than* the sale or purchase of assets appear in the current account.

The current account balance indicates the change in the net asset position of the United States with respect to the rest of the world. When an individual spends more for goods, services, interest payments on past loans, gifts, and the like, than he receives through corresponding transactions, the difference must be made up by reducing his net asset holdings. He may thus draw down cash holdings or a bank account, sell stocks or bonds, or borrow from others. Likewise, a U.S. current account deficit means that the United States has decreased its net asset position internationally; i.e., foreigners must add to their net holdings of U.S. assets. In the balance-of-payments accounts, this is reflected by a U.S. capital account surplus exactly equal to the current account deficit.[5]

Looking at this relationship in another way, in any period when foreigners want to invest more, on net, in U.S. assets than Americans want to invest in foreign assets, the U.S. current account *must* be in deficit, for that is the only way in which the desired changes in international asset positions can be realized. In other words, Americans must accept a positive net flow of goods, services, and transfers in order to reduce their international asset position. This does not imply that the capital account "drives" the current account, or the reverse. Rather, the two are simultaneously determined through interactions with prices, interest rates, exchange rates, and income levels. However, the capital account and the current account are linked in many ways, and it is misleading to assume that each has a separate life.

Table 1 reviews the composition of the U.S. current account in recent years. The merchandise trade balance peaked in 1964 and recorded its first deficit in 1971. Since then, its performance has been characterized by dramatic swings. Military transactions, a major negative item at the height of the Vietnam war, now play a much smaller role. Transfers, which include foreign aid, have been another consistently negative current account item, but their real value (adjusted for inflation) today is much smaller than in the immediate post–World War II period. The only consistently positive and growing entries are net investment income and "other services," which include fees and royalties generated by foreign direct investment. That is why some critics argue that the United States is becoming a *rentier* economy, living off wealth accumulated in the past.

INTERRELATIONSHIPS WITH THE SUMMARY STATISTICS

The overall merchandise trade balance or the current account balance can be disaggregated by regions or by broad commodity class (Tables 2 through 5 do this for the trade balance). A breakdown by regions of the record 1977 deficit (Table 2) reveals two large negative components, the bilateral trade deficit with Japan, and the deficit on trade with members of the Organization of Petroleum Exporting Countries (OPEC)—a reflection of the nation's huge expenditures for imported oil. Together these are approximately equal to the overall merchandise trade deficit, making it plausible to conclude that these two items "caused" the deficit. However, this emphasis upon bilateral balances would make sense only if each international transaction occurred in a vacuum. In fact, all transactions are interrelated, so a policy that reduced the Japanese and OPEC trade deficits would be likely also to reduce surpluses on trade with other regions.

In a world of multilateral trade and payments, Japanese foreign exchange earnings generated by that country's surplus on trade with the United States are used to buy the primary products which constitute the lion's share of Japanese imports. Lower sales to Japan by the suppliers of these materials mean smaller purchases of machinery and other goods from

Table 1

U.S. Current Account Account Balance, 1960–1977 (billions of dollars)[a]

	1960	1965	1970	1971	1972	1973	1974	1975	1976	1977
Merchandise trade balance	4.9	5.0	2.6	−2.3	−6.4	0.9	−5.3	9.0	−9.4	−31.1
Military transactions, net	−2.8	−2.1	−3.4	−2.9	−3.6	−2.3	−2.1	−0.9	0.3	1.3
Investment income, net[b]	3.4	5.4	6.2	7.3	8.2	12.0	15.5	12.8	15.9	17.5
Travel and transportation, net	−1.0	−1.3	−2.0	−2.3	−3.0	−3.1	−3.1	−2.5	−2.2	−3.0
Other services, net[b]	0.6	1.4	2.2	2.5	2.8	3.2	4.0	4.6	4.7	4.7
Goods and services balance	5.1	8.3	5.7	2.3	−2.1	10.8	8.9	23.1	9.4	−10.6
Transfers	−2.3	−2.9	−3.3	−3.7	−3.9	−3.9	−7.2	−4.6	−5.0	−4.7
Current account balance	2.8	5.4	2.4	−1.4	−6.0	6.9	1.7	18.4	4.3	−15.3

Sources: Council of Economic Advisors 1978:36; U.S. Department of Commerce 1978*b*: Part 2, pp. 16-17.

[a]Details may not sum to totals because of rounding.

[b]Fees and royalties from U.S. direct investments abroad and foreign direct investment in the United States are excluded from investment income and included in other services.

Table 2

U.S. Merchandise Trade Balance by Principal Areas, 1960–1977 (billions of U.S. dollars)

	1970	1971	1972	1973	1974	1975	1976	1977
Worldwide[a]	2.7	−2.0	−6.4	1.3	−2.3	11.0	−5.9	−26.7
Developed countries:	0.4	−3.7	−6.7	−1.5	3.2	8.8	3.6	−4.4
Canada	−2.0	−2.3	−2.5	−2.6	−2.0	0.0	−2.1	−3.6
Western Europe	3.1	1.2	−0.3	−1.9	5.0	9.2	9.6	6.3
Japan	−1.2	−3.2	−4.1	−1.4	−1.7	−1.7	−5.4	−8.1
Australia, New Zealand, and South Africa	0.6	0.6	0.2	0.6	1.8	1.3	1.5	1.0
Communist areas in Europe and Asia	0.1	0.2	0.5	1.9	1.2	2.2	2.6	1.6
Less-developed countries:	2.2	1.6	−0.1	0.3	−7.2	−0.5	−12.4	−24.3
Oil-exporting LDCs	0.1	−0.2	−0.4	−1.7	−12.2	−8.7	−14.6	−21.9
Other LDCs	2.4	2.0	0.6	2.4	5.5	8.7	2.4	−2.3

Source: U.S. Department of Commerce 1976:5; idem 1978*c*:5.

[a]The worldwide merchandise balances reported here differ from the corresponding values in other tables because of differences in treatment of shipping costs, insurance, etc., and of military transactions. Details do not sum to area and worldwide totals because of rounding and exclusion of some military shipments from totals.

the United States. Furthermore, to the extent that the United States did succeed in shifting American and Japanese demand away from Japanese goods and toward competing U.S. goods, this would tend to produce excess capacity in Japanese traded-goods industries while creating inflationary pressure in corresponding U.S. industries. The result would be to improve the competitiveness of Japanese suppliers relative to their American rivals in the markets of the other industrialized nations and the LDCs. Both responses would tend to produce lower surpluses for the United States on other trade. This does not mean that the United States should abandon its attempts to penetrate the protected Japanese market. Lower Japanese trade barriers for goods in which the United States has a comparative advantage are in the long-term interests of both nations. However, U.S. gains in achieving overall trade balance through direct reduction in the bilateral deficit with Japan would nevertheless be offset to some extent by lower surpluses elsewhere. Increased restrictions on U.S. imports from Japan could also help the United States to achieve overall trade balance, but in this case there would be no long-term benefits for either nation. Such measures delay the process of adjustment to changes in international comparative advantage and, paradoxically, actually undermine U.S. export growth in its areas of greatest competitiveness.[6]

In the case of OPEC, the story is slightly different, since respending of surplus dollars occurs in large part through OPEC lending to other nations. If the United States reduces its spending for imported oil, total OPEC foreign earnings would decline. This may lower somewhat OPEC's imports from the United States, but at the margin it will affect the United States mainly through reduced demand by borrowers relying upon unspent oil revenues recycled in world capital markets. The U.S.–OPEC deficit would therefore fall by somewhat less than the reduction in the value of U.S. oil purchases. U.S. surpluses with some other regions, however, could be substantially reduced.

A breakdown of the merchandise trade balance along product lines shows how U.S. comparative advantage has evolved in recent years. Table 3 indicates significant differences in trade performance and trends across sectors, although every category deteriorated between 1975 and 1977. A large and, until 1975, growing surplus on trade in foods, feeds, and beverages reflects the recent strength of U.S. agriculture. The rapidly increasing deficit on industrial supplies and materials has been dominated by oil imports; the United States is a major producer of many primary products, and has exported more than enough in recent years to cover the cost of required non-oil imports in this category. Capital goods are a continuing source of strength for U.S. trade performance, although net trade in this area has fallen off somewhat since 1975. The automobile industry, a major manufacturing sector in the United States, has experienced a steady decline in its trade balance since 1960. This trend is likely to accelerate with the entry of LDC automobile exporters in the next few years. Consumer goods also show a declining trend, in part reflecting the rapid growth of U.S. imports from Japan and the LDCs.

Disaggregating trade performance within manufacturing also reveals a marked divergence of trends, with some sectors moving into deeper deficit while others have increasing surpluses. Table 4 shows the trade performances of selected products that have experienced persistent growth or decline in their trade positions since 1960. The products with growing trade balances are from industries with relatively high expenditures for R&D. Except for automobiles, the declining trend products are from low-R&D industries. Table 5 shows the overall trade positions of the five industries identified by the U.S. Department of Commerce as R&D-intensive.[7] Here again, rising trends are evident. In contrast, the trade performance of the remainder of the manufacturing sector shows an increasing deficit. These statistics suggest that U.S. comparative advantage in manufacturing lies in the production of R&D-intensive goods.

Table 3

U.S. Merchandise Trade Balance by Major Product Grouping, 1960–1977 (billions of U.S. dollars)

	1960	1965	1970	1971	1972	1973	1974	1975	1976	1977
Foods, feeds, and beverages	−0.1	0.9	−0.3	−0.3	0.2	6.1	8.1	9.6	8.2	5.7
Industrial supplies and materials	0.0	−2.1	−1.6	−4.5	−7.0	−7.4	−24.4	−19.3	−32.3	−42.1
Petroleum and products	−1.1	−1.6	−2.4	−3.2	−4.3	−7.8	−25.7	−26.0	−33.5	−43.6
Capital goods, except automotive	4.9	6.6	10.4	10.9	10.8	13.5	20.8	26.3	26.6	25.6
Machinery, except consumer type	3.7	5.4	7.8	7.5	7.7	9.6	15.3	20.2	20.0	20.1
Civilian aircraft, engines, parts	1.0	1.0	2.5	3.1	2.6	3.4	5.0	5.4	5.8	5.1
Automotive vehicles, engines, parts	0.6	1.0	−1.7	−2.7	−3.3	−3.4	−3.4	−1.2	−4.3	−5.8
Consumer goods (nonfood), except automotive	−0.5	−1.5	−4.6	−5.5	−7.6	−8.1	−8.0	−6.7	−9.2	−12.9
Total merchandise trade[a]	4.9	5.0	2.6	−2.3	−6.4	0.9	−5.3	9.0	−9.4	−31.1

Source: U.S. Department of Commerce 1970: Table 4; idem 1978*b*: Part 2, Table 3; USIER 1976: Table 78.

[a]Also includes military transactions and other trade not classified by product group.

Table 4

U.S. Trade Balance for Selected Manufactures (billions of dollars)

	1960	1965	1970	1971	1972	1973	1974	1975	1976	1977
Aircraft and parts[a]	1.0	1.0	2.4	3.0	2.5	3.6	5.3	5.6	4.5	5.3
Computers and parts	0.0	0.2	1.2	1.1	1.2	1.6	2.1	2.1	1.9	3.7
Other nonelectric machinery[b]	2.6	0.8	4.4	4.2	4.3	5.7	8.8	12.5	10.7	12.3
Basic chemicals and compounds	0.1	0.6	0.9	0.8	0.7	1.0	1.4	1.6	1.4	1.7
Motor vehicles and parts[a]	0.6	0.9	−1.8	−2.9	−3.5	−3.7	−3.0	−0.6	−2.5	−5.0
Steel products	0.2	−0.5	−0.8	−1.9	−1.9	−1.5	−2.3	−1.7	−1.5	−3.7
Textiles, clothing, and footwear	−0.4	−0.8	−2.2	−2.8	−3.3	−3.3	−2.9	−3.0	−3.7	−5.2
Consumer electronics	−0.1	−0.3	−1.1	−1.3	−1.7	−2.0	−1.9	−1.6	−2.6	−2.7

Source: USIER 1977: Table 27; U.S. Department of Commerce 1978*a*: Tables 5–8 (1977).

[a]Excludes engines.

[b]Excludes aircraft and auto engines and parts, and office machinery.

Table 5

U.S. Trade Balance in R&D-Intensive and Non–R&D-Intensive Manufacturing Industries 1960–1977 (billions of dollars)[a]

	1960	1965	1970	1971	1972	1973	1974	1975	1976	1977
Chemicals[b]	1.0	1.6	2.4	2.2	2.1	3.3	4.8	5.0	5.2	5.4
Nonelectrical machinery[c]	3.0	4.1	5.6	5.3	5.3	6.9	10.8	14.6	14.8	13.6
Electrical machinery[d]	0.8	1.0	0.7	0.5	0.3	0.5	1.7	2.7	1.8	1.8
Aircraft[e]	1.0	1.0	2.4	3.0	2.6	3.6	5.2	5.6	5.7	5.2
Professional and scientific instruments[f]	0.2	0.4	0.7	0.7	0.7	0.8	1.3	1.5	1.4	1.5
All R&D-intensive manufacturing[g]	5.9	8.1	11.7	11.7	11.0	15.1	23.9	29.3	29.0	27.6
All non–R&D-intensive manufacturing	−0.2	−2.0	−8.3	−11.7	−15.0	−15.4	−15.6	−9.5	−16.5	−24.4

Source: National Science Board 1976: Table 1-24 (for 1960–1976); U.S. Department of Commerce 1978*a*: Tables 5, 6 (for 1977).

[a]Details may not add to totals because of rounding.
[b]Includes drugs and related products.
[c]Includes aircraft and auto engines.
[d]Includes communication equipment.
[e]Except engines.
[f]Includes optical goods and photographic equipment and supplies.
[g]All product groups included above.

DETERMINANTS OF THE TRADE BALANCE

The merchandise trade balance reports the net extent to which foreign demand falls upon domestic suppliers. This reflects the overall levels of demand at home and abroad, and the relative attractiveness of alternative supply sources. As national incomes grow over time, so does the total demand for goods and services, whether for current consumption, intermediate inputs, or investment. However, not only the overall level of economic activity, but also its composition will affect the trade balance. For example, investment activity abroad is especially important for U.S. export performance, since the United States is a major world supplier of capital equipment. How total demand is allocated between domestic and foreign suppliers depends on tastes and on the overall competitiveness of alternative sources. Tastes, broadly defined, include both individual preferences and such demand-side influences as the age composition of the population, labor force participation, and family size. Competitiveness depends upon the relative cost of similar goods from alternative sources as well as upon distinguishing characteristics of products or their suppliers.

Analyses of recent U.S. trade performance have focused on the trade balance implications of national growth rates and of their deviations from trend. The income elasticity of a nation's demand for imports is a statistical measure of the "pure" effect of long-term domestic income growth when overall competitiveness of imported goods relative to their domestic substitutes remains the same. Similarly, the income elasticity of export demand measures the effect of long-term income growth rates abroad on a nation's exports. Since estimated income elasticities reflect both national tastes and existing barriers to trade, the values will be affected by major trade policy changes.

A much-quoted empirical study of world trade patterns, based on data for the period 1951–1966, uncovered important differences in income elasticities of import and export demand across the country (Houthakker and Magee 1969:111–25). While the U.S. income elasticity of demand for finished manufactured goods was found to be exceptionally high, the overall U.S. income elasticity of import demand was about average for the group of industrialized nations studied. On the export side, however, the income elasticity of foreign demand for U.S. goods was extremely low. Thus, even with no deterioration in U.S. international competitiveness, the U.S. trade balance should fall over time unless incomes abroad grow much more rapidly than those in the United States. In contrast, the calculated income elasticity of Japanese import demand was somewhat lower than that for the United States, while its export elasticity was much greater than that of any other nation studied—thus furnishing one possible explanation for a persistent tendency to surplus (see Chapter 13 by Keran).

Much of the debate triggered by the drastic decline in the U.S. merchandise trade balance from a surplus of $9 billion in 1975 to a deficit of $31 billion in 1977 concerns the role played by national business cycles—deviations of growth rates from their trends—rather than by long-term growth trends themselves. The large 1975 surplus was in part the result of a depressed economy in the United States which kept import demand unusually low, and a more vigorous economic performance abroad with attendant U.S. export growth. In 1977 the situation was reversed, with economic growth lower than usual for the major U.S. trading partners and near-boom conditions in the United States. According to one analysis, U.S. exports in 1977 would have been $10 billion higher in 1977 if cyclical recovery in the rest of the world had matched that in the United States (Lawrence 1978:159–85).

INTERNATIONAL COMPETITIVENESS*

The ability of a U.S. firm to sell abroad or to compete successfully against imports depends on a number of economic considerations: (1) dollar costs of labor, capital, and intermediate inputs; (2) productivity of factors, as determined by technology, factor proportions, and factor quality; (3) exchange rate of the dollar; (4) terms of delivery, insurance, and credit; (5) product characteristics, both objective and subjective, as perceived by the buyer; (6) seller reputation and service facilities.

The first four items together determine the *cost competitiveness* of the U.S. firm's product relative to its foreign rivals. The four considerations are not, however, independent. More productive factors command higher market prices. Conversely, high factor costs provide an incentive to reduce costs through research and development or reorganization of production. High dollar costs resulting from more rapid inflation at home than elsewhere contribute to depreciation of the dollar relative to other currencies. A government reluctant to allow its currency to depreciate may instead subsidize credit for foreign purchasers, help exporters to find customers abroad, or assist domestic producers in modernizing their plant and equipment.

Delivered cost is one dimension of competitiveness. The fifth and sixth considerations listed are sources of *differentiation* of the product or its supplier from potential competitors—features such as superior performance or reliability which may compensate for a relatively high delivered cost. Of course, even for a unique product, delivered cost has an important influence on export performance through its effect on total world demand.

*Some material in this and subsequent sections is adapted from McCulloch (1978).

Cost Competitiveness

Analyses of cost competitiveness tend to focus primarily on differences in labor costs across countries. Although other influences may be important, the cost of labor is the largest single component—on average, about one-half of total value added in manufacturing. Furthermore, because capital is highly mobile internationally, the cost of capital to a particular industry is likely to be similar in all advanced countries; likewise, trade in intermediate inputs tends to equalize their prices. Since labor mobility is more restricted, substantial wage differentials between the United States and its trading partners can persist over time.

The United States has been a high-wage economy for many years. However, wages in the other industrialized nations have risen rapidly in the recent past, and average labor costs in Sweden, Canada, and West Germany now exceed those in the United States. Across industries, U.S. wages show greater dispersion than abroad. In 1976 the United States had the highest hourly wages of any industrial nation in primary metals and motor vehicles—high-wage industries in all countries—but was below Canada, Sweden, and West Germany in average pay of workers in textiles, apparel, and footwear, industries with below-average earnings in all countries (USIER 1977:99–101).

Cross-country hourly wage comparisons may be misleading, since the relevant measure in determining international cost competitiveness is not labor cost per hour, but labor cost per unit of output. Since 1960 labor productivity (output per hour) has risen more slowly in the United States than in other industrialized countries, in part reflecting the initial high level already attained by the United States. However, because wages have also risen more slowly in the United States than elsewhere on average, unit labor costs have grown less rapidly in the United States than in Canada, Europe, or Japan.

Two trends often cited in connection with reduced U.S. cost competitiveness are recent declines in R&D, and capital spending by U.S. manufacturing firms. As long as productivity gains are not fully reflected in higher wages, the cost competitiveness of a given industry can be increased through additional research and development and capital expenditures, or through improved management. However, it is important to recognize that the very success of these strategies in any one industry is likely to *reduce* cost competitiveness of other industries through higher input costs, exchange-rate appreciation, or other channels.

The cost disadvantage of some U.S. industries producing standardized goods is probably too great to be overcome through foreseeable improvements in productivity. Low-skill, labor-intensive industries such as textiles, footwear, and apparel pay relatively low wages in all the industrialized countries—low, even when adjusted for measures of labor "quality" such as education and experience. However, labor costs are far lower still in LDCs like Taiwan, Hong Kong, and Brazil, which have gained a rapidly increasing share of the world market for these products despite formidable barriers to trade. In some other industries, including steel and automobiles—both labor-intensive relative to U.S. manufacturing as a whole—wages which are high even by U.S. standards (again, adjusting for labor quality) have impaired international cost competitiveness.

Product Competitiveness

Some U.S. products, usually new products and often from the high-technology industries, have no close competitors in world markets. The United States, with its giant research establishment and abundant supply of skilled labor, scientists, and engineers, has enjoyed a temporary world monopoly position for many unique products. In most cases, however, that advantage is eroded sooner or later through imitation or through international diffusion of the required technology.

Until the 1950s it was widely accepted that the United States, clearly a capital-abundant economy, had its comparative advantage in the production and export of capital-intensive goods. However, empirical investigations revealed just the reverse: that U.S. imports are actually more capital-intensive than its exports.[8] This finding stimulated a new wave of research into the determinants of U.S. trading patterns. Subsequent studies highlighted the roles played by skills or "human capital" on the one hand, and R&D on the other; in empirical investigations the two are difficult to separate, since industries with high R&D also employ a high proportion of skilled workers. The results confirmed that U.S. export performance has been strongest in the high-technology industries. One recent study, for instance, concluded that differences in R&D intensity alone could explain up to three-fourths of total variation in export performance across manufacturing industries (Lowinger 1975:221–36).

The notion that U.S. comparative advantage lies in "new" goods has been elaborated in the product-cycle theory, which interprets much of U.S. trade as reflecting stages in adjustment to successful innovation. According to this theory, new products change their characteristics over time, becoming increasingly standardized and thus amenable to production by relatively less-skilled workers. In the early stages of product development, rapid interaction between market and producer is advantageous as alternative product characteristics are explored. Also, since reliability may be low, convenient access to service facilities can be crucial to market success. The initial innovation and production process thus requires considerable inputs of skilled labor. As standardization proceeds and the market expands in response to the falling price, however, the need for skilled labor is greatly reduced and cost competitiveness begins to exert a decisive influence on location decision—particularly when an innovation has been emulated successfully by other producers. This product-cycle scenario has been documented for a number of new products, including pharmaceuticals, consumer electronics, and office machinery.

Because the innovating country—typically, but not always, the United States—gradually loses its competitiveness for a given product as the cycle proceeds, some attention has been given to policy measures which would slow down the cycle, delaying the shift of production to lower-cost locations. Among measures suggested are legal restraints on the rights of innovating firms to exploit their unique technology through direct foreign investment or licensing of foreign production. Such suggestions tend to overlook the dynamic nature of the product cycle. Although it might be possible to delay the shift abroad of production of particular goods, such restraints lower the profits from innovation. This in turn could discourage future R&D investments, diminishing the flow of new products with which the cycle begins, and retarding export growth. Measures which stimulate innovation, rather than retarding diffusion, may therefore yield greater long-run benefits.

EXCHANGE RATES, PRICES, AND TRADE

International cost competitiveness of U.S. goods and services depends on both exchange rates and relative inflation rates. If the dollar depreciates 6 percent in relation to the German mark and the United States experiences 10 percent inflation, with 4 percent in West Germany, the relative cost competitiveness of U.S. and West German goods will be unchanged. Exchange-rate movements alone, therefore, will not explain changes in trade performance. Differences in national inflation rates must also be brought into the analysis.[9]

Much has been made of the failure of dollar depreciation to bring U.S. merchandise trade flows or the current account back into balance. U.S. inflation, however, has wiped out a large part of the cost-competitiveness gain which would have otherwise resulted from recent exchange-rate movements. Furthermore, while the dollar has depreciated rather spectacularly relative to some currencies, it has appreciated in relation to others. In particular, the dollar has strengthened relative to the Canadian dollar and the pound sterling—the currencies of the two largest U.S. trading partners. Dollar depreciation has helped U.S. competitiveness in these markets against goods supplied by Japan, West Germany, and a few other countries with appreciating currencies, but not in relation to these nations' own domestic suppliers. Similarly, many LDCs have pegged their currencies to the dollar or have depreciated relative to the dollar.[10] Finally, as noted earlier, the exchange rate is determined by capital account as well as by current account considerations. A merchandise trade deficit or current account deficit in itself therefore provides no evidence as to whether the exchange markets are operating properly.

While it is widely agreed that crucial links exist between exchange rates and prices on the one hand, and between exchange rates and trade on the other, there is far less agreement at present about the speed of these effects, and sometimes even about the direction. Ironically, consensus among economists concerning the adjustment process in a flexible exchange-rate system was much greater before the float began. Prior to recent experience with the operation of a flexible rate system, it was generally agreed that a trade deficit would lead, other things equal, to exchange-rate depreciation, thereby tending to restore trade balance. It was also agreed that rapid inflation—or, more precisely, inflation more rapid than abroad—would cause exchange-rate depreciation both indirectly, through the effect of cost competitiveness on the trade balance, and directly, through capital-market responses. Exchange-rate depreciation would then help to restore equilibrium in international transactions.

Less well anticipated before the float was the slow, and sometimes actually perverse, effect of exchange rates on the trade balance and the further inflationary pressures accompanying exchange-rate depreciation. The "J" curve hypothesis, based on post–1971 experience, predicts that—for at least some period of time—dollar depreciation can worsen the trade balance rather than improve it. The reason is that most transactions involve a lag between placing of orders and actual payment for goods received. Orders calling for foreign currency payment will require increased dollar outlays at the new exchange rate. Thus, the dollar size of the trade deficit will rise to the extent that prearranged payments are fixed in terms of foreign currency rather than in dollars. The country will "round the J" only when export and import volumes have had time to adjust to the new relative cost configurations. But that adjustment may be delayed indefinitely if resulting higher prices of imported raw materials and intermediate inputs along with higher wage demands fuel a new round of domestic inflation.[11]

INDUSTRY COMPETITIVENESS IN GENERAL EQUILIBRIUM

The foregoing discussion of international competitiveness suggests a menu of policy measures which could be used to improve the relative performance of U.S. industries. Besides the most obvious—tariff or quota restrictions—such measures include investment or R&D incentives, subsidized export financing or insurance, and U.S. tax changes favoring domestic over foreign investment. These measures and many others have been used or proposed at various times as cures for ailing trade performance in specific U.S. industries, or even as preventive medicine for relatively buoyant sectors.

Policies such as these can indeed bolster the trade position of some industries. It is far less certain, however, that such policies can improve the nation's *overall* competitiveness in the sense of increasing the overall trade balance. The reason is that each industry's performance is linked to the rest of the economy. Whether incentives are industry-specific or merely induce a higher degree of response in some industries than in others, the increased competitiveness of some sectors will reduce, directly or indirectly, the competitiveness of other sectors.

The first source of interaction is an interconnected market for productive factors, raw materials, and intermediate inputs—a market that is tapped by all U.S. industries. As some industries increase their market shares domestically and abroad, their expansion will draw capital and labor from other parts of the economy, possibly also leading to expansion of overall employment and capacity utilization. Factors drawn into the expanding industries will tend to receive higher financial rewards. Similarly, the prices of primary inputs and intermediate goods will be bid up. This process means higher costs for the slower-growing industries. The inflationary pressures of growth in other sectors of the economy will be greatest, of course, when there is little overall slack or where supply bottlenecks are important. The pull of resources into expanding industries creates a natural and desirable incentive for stagnant sectors to contract, but it may also cause dislocations, as declining industries become increasingly unable to compete in international markets. Older industries with slower growth rates are especially likely to suffer from the exit of capital, entrepreneurial talent, and younger and more skilled workers.

A second way in which the success of some industries may be linked to the declining competitiveness of other sectors is through the balance of trade. With flexible exchange rates, the improved trade positions of some sectors will induce the exchange rate to appreciate, at least relative to what the rate would have otherwise been. This makes other sectors of the economy less cost competitive, even if they have been unaffected by input market spillovers and by unfavorable tax-expenditure developments. Improved trade performance in some sectors may also influence overall commercial policy by weakening the case for protectionist or mercantilistic options. Thus, vigorous trade performance of some industries may encourage a more liberal trade stance.[12] While this is desirable for the economy as a whole, it may exacerbate the adjustment problems of specific stagnant industries (see Chapter 9 by Bale for a discussion of adjustment assistance).

A third link between one industry's competitive position and that of the rest of the economy comes through foreign demand. The ability of U.S. firms to sell their products abroad depends in large part on the ability of foreign firms to sell in the United States. When the United States uses quota arrangements such as "orderly marketing agreements" to slow the penetration of domestic markets by foreign sellers, it reduces the purchasing power available abroad to buy U.S.–produced goods and services. Furthermore, by preventing LDCs from expanding their industrial base along lines dictated by comparative advantage, the United States and other industrialized nations pursuing similar policies retard the growth of these economies and thus forego an important future source of export demand.

One rationale for restricting imports is to ease the adjustment problem for declining U.S. industries by reducing the rate at which they are forced to adjust. Sometimes the restrictions allow already uncompetitive industries to maintain a constant share of the domestic market—to *grow* at the same rate as domestic demand. This so-called "fair" division of markets between domestic and foreign suppliers means no adjustment at all. More important, such "adjustment" measures can actually exacerbate adjustment problems by reducing the pull of resources into what would otherwise be rapidly growing export industries.

A final problem is that, except for tariffs, most policies designed to enhance the competitiveness of particular sectors use up actual or potential tax revenues. The rest of the economy thus winds up with higher taxes, lower government services, or both.[13] Even when incentives are not sector specific, the result is similar. One important example is the U.S. trade adjustment assistance (TAA) program for trade-impacted industries. By subsidizing the unemployment benefits of workers laid off by trade-impacted industries, the TAA program has actually discouraged those workers from seeking new jobs elsewhere. Many postpone job search, hoping to be recalled by their former employers when and if output levels rise.[14] Trade-impacted firms are eligible for technical advice, subsidized loans, and the like, to assist these firms in modernizing their operations—again, to persist in their current business lines of activity. Because these benefits are confined to trade-impacted industries, the TAA program subsidizes and encourages the nondisappearance, or sometimes even expansion, of firms and whole industries which have lost their international comparative advantage—at the direct cost of other, more competitive industries.[15]

OIL IMPORTS AND THE TRADE DEFICIT[16]

Net U.S. imports of crude petroleum and products in 1960 were at a rate of about 600,000 barrels per day, generating a modest deficit item of about $1 billion in the trade account. Although U.S. dependence upon imported oil was already viewed as a risk to national security during the 1960s,[17] domestic consumption and imports increased steadily, and net imports reached an average rate of 1.5 million barrels per day by 1970. Growth of the oil-trade deficit began to accelerate in 1973, fed by continuing increases in net import volume as well as by large increases in the dollar price of oil set by OPEC. Net average import volume by 1977 was almost 9 million barrels per day, producing a net petroleum trade deficit of a staggering $43.6 billion, larger than the *total* record merchandise trade deficit for the year.[18]

Given the overwhelming size of the oil-trade deficit, it is tempting to conclude that oil is to blame for poor overall U.S. trade performance, and is the major factor underlying persistent depreciation of the dollar relative to the Japanese yen and the German mark. Many analysts have yielded to the temptation, and there is some truth in their view. Nevertheless, emphasis upon the role played by oil imports can be misleading, and at least some policy proposals intended to improve overall trade performance through a reduction in the oil deficit could well have perverse consequences.

While growth of the oil-trade deficit was clearly one factor in the deterioration of the U.S. trade balance between 1975 and 1977, it was surely not the only factor. The net U.S. position declined in every broad industrial sector (see Table 2) and for every trading region (Table 3). Even the trade balances of the high-technology industries showed sharply lower growth rates (Table 5). Thus, even without a higher oil bill, the U.S. position would have worsened. It is also noteworthy in this connection that both West Germany and Japan have relatively larger net expenditures for imported oil than has the United States, yet their trade accounts are in surplus and both have experienced persistent currency appreciation.

In the simplest terms, a given deficit on oil trade indicates the surplus which must be generated by net sales of other goods and services and of capital assets in order to achieve overall balance and to avoid downward pressure on the international value of the dollar from this source. However, huge U.S. payments for imported oil result in large—although not equally huge—expenditures for U.S.-produced goods and services, both by OPEC members and by those nations benefiting indirectly from recycled oil revenues. Furthermore, some OPEC revenues are used to buy U.S. assets, another source of countervailing pressure on the dollar.[19] The remaining gap, however large, leaves the United States with three basic options: to take measures which directly reduce imports of oil, to allow exchange-rate movements to promote adjustment through trade in other goods and services, or to use export incentives and/or import restrictions to increase the size of the trade surplus on non-oil trade.

Much attention at home and abroad has been focused upon the need for a U.S. energy policy—i.e., a package of policy measures to reduce overall energy use or induce the substitution of other energy sources for those based on imported petroleum. Oil differs from other trade in that even a large depreciation of the dollar is likely to have little effect on oil imports. Since oil prices continue to be set in dollars, currency devaluation has no direct effect on the cost of U.S. imports, although dollar depreciation indirectly influences the size of future OPEC price increases.[20] Price-based measures to reduce imports or total consumption through tariffs or taxes are politically unattractive and probably relatively ineffective. The short-term price elasticity of demand for petroleum products is very low. The longer-term elasticity is considerably higher. Coal, however, the most obvious medium-term alternative in power generation, has major drawbacks of its own because of air pollution problems and the environmental consequences of strip-mining. And whatever their motive, higher energy costs mean yet another source of inflationary pressure for the U.S. economy.

Recent emphasis has been upon measures to curtail consumption without a drastic price increase. These include nonprice measures such as the 55-mile per hour speed limit and automobile fuel-economy standards, as well as proposals to tax or prohibit the sale of appliances or machinery with relatively high energy demands. It should be stressed that measures relying upon means other than higher prices for petroleum products nevertheless raise costs of affected goods and services, thus exerting inflationary pressures of their own.

CONCLUSIONS

An understanding of what is actually happening to U.S. trade, and why, is an obvious precondition for intelligent policy choices. This chapter has analyzed recent U.S. trade performance—overall, by industrial sector, and with particular nations and groups of nations—and has linked trends in trade performance to income growth in the United States and abroad and to changes in U.S. international competitiveness. Because of their important implications for U.S. policy, several conclusions should be underscored:

- Comparative advantage influences relative trade performance across industries rather than overall national trade performance. Trade guided by comparative advantage—i.e., by relative costs—insures the greatest mutual benefits to trading nations, but does not rule out the decline of particular industries and associated costs of adjustment. When comparative advantage is shifting over time, some sectors will necessarily experience declining production or employment, at least relative to the rest of the economy, and sometimes absolutely. This provides no evidence that comparative advantage doesn't work, or that the exchange-rate system is not functioning appropriately.

•Overall trade performance is determined by income growth in the United States and abroad, and by U.S. international competitiveness, i.e., cost relative to foreign counterparts, and distinguishing characteristics of goods and their suppliers. U.S. competitiveness is currently strongest for new and unique products, and weakest for standardized products in which high labor costs outweigh the U.S. factor-productivity advantage. R&D-intensive industries have shown steady improvements in their trade balances since 1960, while non–R&D-intensive industries have shown increasing deficits.

•Between 1975 and 1977, U.S. overall trade performance worsened dramatically. Declines or sharply reduced growth rates were evident for every industrial sector and in trade with every world region. Although the large increases in the bilateral trade deficit with Japan and the deficit on trade with OPEC nations dominated the figures, the U.S. trade balance would have fallen significantly even without these developments. Other factors which played a role in the 1975–1977 trade-balance deterioration were business cycles in the United States and abroad, and exchange-rate movements.

•The effects of dollar depreciation on U.S. competitiveness must be viewed in tandem with the rate of inflation, since inflation at home erodes (and foreign inflation increases) U.S. cost competitiveness gained through exchange-rate realignments. There is reason to believe that depreciation in itself exerts pressures for further inflation. Thus, the United States, a deficit country with unsatisfactory price performance, may be caught in a vicious cycle of inflation and dollar depreciation unless policymakers succeed in resisting inflationary pressures arising through the international adjustment process.

• The competitiveness of a given industry cannot be viewed in isolation. Better performance in one industry tends to be associated with reduced competitiveness of other sectors through a variety of interindustry linkages. Even when industries respond to general incentives intended to spur capital investment or R&D, the costs and competitiveness of other industries will be affected. When import restrictions or adjustment assistance enable a trade-impacted industry to sustain a higher production level than would otherwise be possible, this retards the growth of U.S. export industries and can actually exacerbate trade-adjustment problems for the economy.

• The nation's large oil deficit can be met head-on, through an energy policy to limit imports, or indirectly, by adjustments in exchange rates or commercial policy to produce a larger surplus on other international transactions. Either method, however, will mean additional inflationary pressures for the U.S. economy.

3

RYAN C. AMACHER
ROBERT D. TOLLISON
THOMAS D. WILLETT

The Divergence between Theory and Practice

The recent increase in trade barriers. Pressure groups and international trade. The free-rider problem. Consumer lobbies. The cost of protectionism. The conflict between producer and consumer interests. Political logrolling. Economic nationalism and special interest groups. GATT and the Kennedy Round. The trend toward a liberal world economy.

During the postwar period, the industrial countries made enormous progress toward reducing tariff levels and other government restrictions which stifle and distort world trade.

This progress slowed noticeably, however, in later years. In fact, recent trade policy in both the United States and Europe has been to increase, rather than reduce, trade barriers. Shoes, steel, textiles, and television sets have all been subjected to increased U.S. government import restrictions.

Such trade restrictions are usually harmful to most citizens of a country. Why, then, are they so prevalent? Why has the balance of forces been reversed, so that those pressing for increased trade barriers now have become stronger than those seeking to reduce them? Some people argue that the answer lies in weaknesses in the case for liberal trade policies and that, whatever relevance that case may once have had, it has become increasingly less relevant to the modern world economy. The AFL-CIO has so argued in attempting to explain its switch to advocacy of protectionism.[1]

A few legitimate exceptions to the general case for free trade do exist, and a strong case can be made for government policies to reduce hardships involved in adjusting to changing world economic conditions. Such considerations, however, explain only a small portion of actual trade barriers.

One must look elsewhere for the major explanations of why the theory of international trade is so often violated in practice. The heart of the answer is that trade barriers are determined politically. In political decision-making, when issues are complex, individuals and groups often have poor information about their interests. And even when they do have such information, the power to influence policy outcomes is unequal.

In recent years a subbranch of economics and political science called "public choice theory" has emerged to study imperfections in the political process, just as economists have studied imperfections in the price system.[2] This approach has helped explain why governments often adopt policies favoring small but well-organized and politically influential groups at the expense of most of the general public as consumers and taxpayers. One example of this political "bias" may be found in the widespread use of barriers to international trade.[3] The resurgence of protectionism is the combined result of increased competition from abroad and the decline of foreign policy considerations which encouraged trade liberalization during most of the postwar period.

THE POLITICAL DETERMINANTS OF TRADE POLICIES

Producers

The government can be a potential resource or threat to every industry. Because of government's wide range of powers, producers can use favorable legislation as an alternative to more efficient production to enhance their income and wealth. Few of the state's powers are more promising in this regard than its ability to protect industries from foreign competition.

The amount of lobbying effort by producers for state protection from competition will be influenced by a number of factors, especially by the size of the group seeking protection. Individual producers will often look to others to bear the costs of protectionist lobbying, since the benefits of regulation accrue to all firms in the industry, while the costs of lobbying accrue individually. With many producers in an industry, each will tend to go along for a "free ride"—that is, will enjoy the benefits of other producers' efforts, but not make an effort themselves. This free-rider problem, as economists call it, occurs when each individual or firm will gain from the group's overall efforts, but not much extra from its own efforts.

With few producers, the lobbying effort of each in relation to the whole is important enough that individual gains from one's own lobbying exceed the costs. If a small group of firms can get protection with large potential benefits, it will make economic sense for each firm to lobby for it. Since small groups can minimize the free-rider problem, they will often be successful in seeking protection from international competition. The recent successes of the highly concentrated steel industry in securing increased trade barriers in steel may be a good example.

Not all industries which are effective in lobbying are concentrated, however. Some, such as the textile industry with its many members, are innovative enough in organizational design to overcome free-rider problems, and are able to protect their interests through trade barriers.

Consumers

The free-rider problem also applies to the role of consumers in the formation of international economic policy. While consumers may be the prime beneficiaries of more liberal trade and investment policies, they are a large and widely dispersed group who face exceedingly high costs of organizing to resist restrictions on domestic and international competition. Individually, consumers gain small direct benefits from trade liberalization, and the efforts of any one of them to reduce trade barriers will generate benefits primarily for others. Thus, it would not pay the typical consumer to oppose trade restrictions actively. Each consumer would have great incentives to free ride, hoping that other consumers would bear the costs of pressing the case for free trade.

Consumer complacency, of course, is not unlimited with respect to the costs of protection. The bigger the coalition favoring protection and the broader the range of protection, the more consumers in general will actively oppose it. And the growth of activist consumer interest groups helps to reduce this inequality. To date, however, consumer lobby groups have not been as politically effective in opposing trade barriers as producer groups have been in supporting them. Yet it should be noted that firms making heavy use of imported products do often lobby against trade restrictions, as do export firms which might suffer from foreign retaliation.

For the same reasons that it does not pay consumers to lobby against trade restrictions, they tend to be poorly informed about the benefits of competition. Thus, polls show that consumers often favor protection and regulatory interference in the economy—against their own interests.

The issue of trade barriers is usually put to the public in terms of saving jobs. No one wants to see people thrown out of work, but few people see the longer-term costs of protectionism—including higher prices and reduced productivity, as the incentives decline to adapt to changing economic conditions. It is easy for voters to identify with those in distress and to see job losses without seeing where new jobs will come from. They therefore often support trade restrictions for individual commodities and products without appreciating how such restrictions impose costs on the economy and reduce their own welfare (for further discussion of this job loss issue, see Luttrell [1978]).

Politicians

In a democracy, politicians must continue to win votes to stay in office. Though elected officials may sometimes vote on principle, often they will be influenced by whether a position on an issue is expected to win or lose votes. On visible issues, therefore, politicians have an incentive to follow public opinion polls. And on less visible issues, they are encouraged to increase their campaign contributions by supporting the interests of organized groups. Since domestic interest groups often have greater incentives to lobby for protection than do those favoring free trade, the typical congressman will tend to face incentives which are biased toward protection.

The legislative bias toward protection is strengthened where representative democracy is geographically based. Under geographic representation, a legislator's prospects for reelection usually depend on his ability to represent local interests. Representatives who are successful at obtaining public expenditures which benefit their districts are more likely to be returned to office. With seniority, their ability to route programs and policies in favor of their districts will increase (for evidence, see Plott [1968], and Crain and Tollison [1977]).

A similar argument holds with respect to reducing competition against important local producers. One of the major concerns common to individuals in a community is their interest in the vitality of the community's economic base. In many instances, a high proportion of the district's members may directly or indirectly receive their incomes from a single firm or industry, as in company towns with geographically concentrated industries like steel, automobiles, textiles, or lumber. When economic activity is geographically concentrated, it is possible for representatives to win political support by serving as spokesmen for the economic interests in their home districts. It is therefore not surprising that tariffs often are decided on the basis of their economic impact on certain regions.

It should be noted that the conflict between producer and consumer interests stressed here is quite different from the conflicts between workers and capitalists posited in Marxist literature. The conflict is rather a coincidence of interests of workers and businessmen in each particular industry to restrict competition at the expense of all consumers, including workers and businessmen in other industries.

Attempts to redistribute income toward certain regions through the legislative process are not always successful, of course. Since any one tariff typically benefits only a small minority and hurts everyone through higher prices, a single tariff may have difficulty passing a geographically based legislature; a broader bill favoring more geographically concentrated industries might have a better chance.[4] Such a bill could be in the self-interests of many legislators, even though it would be likely to leave society worse off on balance by distorting world prices and relinquishing some of the gains from trade.

The legislative process promotes inefficient social pork-barrel legislation, such as unnecessary public works and trade barriers, because each member of Congress has incentives to get benefits for his home district "financed" primarily by taxpayers or consumers who live in other districts and states. Thus, the tendency for producers to be more effectively represented than consumers is magnified in cases where the benefits are perceived to accrue largely to local producers, but a high proportion of the costs are borne by consumers living in other congressional districts. Yet if all politicians arrange such legislative transactions for their constituents, most people will be made worse off. Each politician sees most of the costs of local projects as falling on members of other jurisdictions; but in order to get his pet project passed, he must vote for the pet projects of his colleagues. Such geographically oriented vote trading or log-rolling leads to an inefficient result for society as a whole. Yet this sort of behavior continues, because each district and representative cannot afford to withdraw unilaterally from the political competition.[5]

This tendency toward protectionism is strengthened by the U.S. legislature committee system, in which disproportionate weight on particular issues accrues to members, and particularly to chairmen of committees and subcommittees dealing with these issues. Since both political parties have tended to appoint local members to committees dealing with strong local interests, the resulting importance of a small number of legislators on particular issues permits effective and concentrated lobbying efforts by producers.

These considerations help explain why the U.S. Congress has traditionally been much more protectionist than the executive branch.[6] Indeed, the executive branch in the United States has played an important role in advancing the cause of liberal trade and investment in the post–World War II period. Whereas legislators have strong incentives to respond to local pressures for protection from competition, decision-makers in the executive branch tend to respond to broader considerations.

Despite the importance of political pressures from special interests, such pressures are not the only cause of protectionism. Some short-term protectionist measures reflect widespread public sympathy for economic groups injured by foreign competition. Moreover, in some cases there may be widespread support for local ownership of particular industries, or for the employment of a certain percentage of native citizens in the work force, as independent social objectives (see, for example, Breton [1964] and Johnson [1965]). Also, a country may derive prestige from certain kinds of industrial production, independently of its economic value. These types of satisfaction, broadly viewed as pride in the local economy, may also contribute to pressures for protectionism.

Such arguments must be examined with care, however. Virtually every special-interest group desiring protection from foreign trade attempts to cloak its arguments in terms of broad social objectives, and one must be on guard to separate a valid case for economic nationalism from arguments advanced by special interests. There are no easy answers to these types of problems. Protection desired as a *broad* social goal ought to have *broad* social support. We should be aware of how special interests in all types of governmental structures may gain disproportionate power to influence trade policy. In other words, while not all protectionist measures represent the triumph of special interests over the general interest, all too often this is the case.

THE CAUSES OF INCREASED PROTECTIONISM

Why has the power of protectionist forces increased in recent years? To answer this question, we must briefly review some history. In designing the international economic system after World War II, leaders vividly remembered the economic chaos of the 1930s, during which the spread of protectionism and economic nationalism severely disrupted world trade and generated serious international political conflicts. With the gigantic costs of unbridled protectionism being so clearly apparent, it is not surprising that considerable effort was spent towards fostering international economic cooperation.

The perceived importance of establishing and maintaining liberal trade policies was further enhanced by the emergence of the cold war. Liberal trade policies by the United States were perceived by a series of American presidents as important for strengthening the economies of our Western trading partners, and this in turn was viewed as an important step in fostering political stability and combating communism.

For many years such concepts were an important complement to the traditional economic arguments for free trade policies, and helped to generate a remarkable series of programs of trade liberalization. During most of the postwar period the U.S. executive branch was able to orchestrate America's trade policy and to foster multilateral trade liberalization without interference from Congress and domestic producer groups. The executive branch used trade policy during this period as an instrument of foreign policy, and was able to enjoy bipartisan congressional support. Its success in pushing for freer trade illustrates both the role of national leadership in a representative democracy, and the fact that political forces pushing for protectionism do not always carry the day in the trade arena.

The easing of cold war pressure and the restoration of economic prosperity in Europe reduced the power of arguments within the United States that overriding national security concerns required liberal trade policies. Many U.S. observers became increasingly critical of the nation's failures to exert perceived economic interests more strongly in negotiations with Europe. Complaints about defense-burden sharing, trade, and exchange-rate policies became more prevalent. This increased dissatisfaction was an important factor underlying the international portions of the August 1971 New Economic Policy, and of Treasury Secretary Connally's "strong arm" tactics with the Europeans which attempted to link trade, monetary, and national security issues in order to improve the overall U.S. bargaining positions.

As foreign policy constraints on protectionist pressures have weakened, other factors have contributed to the resurgence of protectionist pressures. First, there was a gradual erosion of the most-favored nation principle (Article I of the General Agreement on Tariffs and Trade [GATT]), which stated that all trading partners were to be treated on the basis of nondiscrimination—that is, no country could give preferential treatment to any other country. The most-favored nation principle and the policy of separating trade issues from other international issues worked well until the mid-1960s. From the U.S. perspective, major causes of the erosion of the most-favored nation principle lay in the establishment of a common agricultural policy and preferential trading agreements by the European Economic Community.

The protectionists jumped on the loss of momentum toward further liberalization at the end of the Kennedy Round of tariff reductions. Increased competition from foreign producers had particularly affected many of the traditional manufacturing industries in which the U.S. comparative advantage had long been eroding. These industries are heavily unionized, many by unions affiliated with the politically potent AFL-CIO, and the AFL-CIO's subsequent abandonment of its traditional trade position and its new support for restrictive legislation provided substantial endorsement of the protectionist cause. At the same time, agricultural sector support for freer trade declined, largely in response to increased agricultural protection in Europe which limited U.S. exports.

A further problem has been that GATT, our main international framework for trade matters, deals primarily with import tariffs. Although remarkable success has been achieved in reducing import tariffs even in the face of the new wave of protectionism, and although tariff increases have been relatively minor, recent trade restrictions have taken the form of export restraints, international investment restrictions, and nontariff barriers—which are not covered effectively by

GATT. In recent years the most common response to protectionist pressure has been to impose formal or informal quotas through executive agreements, rather than legislatively mandated tariff increases.

The proliferation of protectionist agreements has not been primarily the result of the executive branch turning more protectionist than Congress, but rather of a decline in the president's ability to control Congress on these issues. Most recent protectionist measures taken by U.S. presidents have been motivated to hold off even stronger protectionist measures that they feared would otherwise be enacted by Congress.

In industrial countries, this new protectionism, this wave of mercantilism, differs from the old mercantilism in that it is not primarily engineered by a national elite to secure power rather than plenty. Instead, it reflects the increase in the influence of domestic pressure groups in securing policies which have important international repercussions (see Malmgren [1970–1971]). In many of the under-developed countries, on the other hand, restrictionist forces are more like the old mercantilism, in that they seem mainly directed to national power and to the welfare of the ruling elites in these countries. In industrial countries, the new mercantilism is less concerned with trade surpluses and more concerned with the particular adjustment problems and the economic positions of powerful pressure groups. It is motivated more by the aggregation of a number of special interests seeking political protection than by the general feeling that national prosperity and prestige require trade surpluses.

THE OUTLOOK FOR THE FUTURE

Although the future can never be predicted with certainty, current political and economic trends suggest that protectionism is likely to continue to rise slowly in the foreseeable future. Despite frequent predictions, general economic warfare is not likely to break out as it did in the 1930s. The lessons of that complete breakdown in international economic cooperation are still sufficiently remembered by national leaders to strongly limit the possibilities of a recurrence. Rather, the danger is of a "cooperative" movement toward greater protectionism in all of the major industrial countries (see Willett [1979]).

The current prevalence of trade barriers is explained by the operation of the political process. The basic case for liberal trade policies has not weakened. The problem is that special interests have become increasingly effective in securing policies which damage the general interest.[7]

A continuation of the recent trend is not inevitable, however. There are some optimistic signs. The loosening of the seniority system in Congress may reduce the disproportionate influence enjoyed by special interests. And there are signs that the public, encouraged by public-interest consumer advocates, is becoming increasingly aware of how government restrictions can harm consumer interests. There has been substantial movement toward deregulation of the transportation industries. This momentum, and the general concern with the contribution of government policies to inflation, could well spill over into substantially increased public opposition to protectionist trade policies.

The pressures for increased protectionism pose a serious threat both to the effective operation of the U.S. economy and to the leadership of the United States in promoting a liberal rather than restriction-ridden world economy. While the relative power of the United States has declined during the postwar period, the remaining importance of U.S. influence should not be underestimated. Determined efforts in the United States to avoid giving in to protectionist pressures will not go unnoticed abroad. The place to begin opposing the rising tide of world protectionism is right here at home.

4

SVEN W. ARNDT

Macroeconomic Policy and Trade Problems

The old international monetary order and the NIEO. Fixed and floating exchange rates. International specialization and market linkages. The interdependence of national economies. Interest rates, and speculative investment. The transmission of inflation between nations. The need for flexibility.

In the postwar era, international monetary arrangements were based on fixed but adjustable exchange rates. During the same period, the thrust of international commercial relations pointed toward free trade and open competition. In the early 1970s the international monetary order collapsed as the major trading nations switched to floating exchange rates, and the system of free trade and specialization fell under the mounting threat of a rapidly rising protectionist sentiment and of increasingly open anticompetitive intervention by governments and international institutions. All this has, of course, been accompanied by talk of an emerging new international economic order (NIEO).

The old order, during which world trade and product grew at unprecedented rates, appears to have lost its appeal; it is as yet not clear where the search for a new order shall take the international community. What is clear, however, is that perceptions and attitudes have changed dramatically. The old order was animated by a sense of interdependence and common purpose; by the belief that the diverse and not always reconcilable aims and aspirations of nations would be best—though not perfectly—served by international cooperation in an environment of free trade and open competition. The new spirit, on the other hand, is inward looking and chauvinistic, afraid of economic change and opposed to competition, uncooperative, impatient, and bent on denying the relevance of experience.

A fixed exchange-rate regime is viable only so long as member nations play by the rules, and conduct compatible macroeconomic policies. A free-trade regime is viable only so long as members play by its rules, and assign to competitive forces a dominant role in the allocation of world resources. Membership in any system imposes responsibilities and constraints along with the benefits it bestows. When nations come to feel that the costs of membership exceed the rewards, it becomes rational policy for them to seek more fruitful alternatives. That is, to some extent, what happened to the postwar exchange regime, as countries increasingly refused to accept the restraints it imposed on their freedom to conduct independent macroeconomic policies. And it is also the active ingredient impelling nations toward the new protectionism; in this case it is unwillingness to face the competition from more productive and efficient foreign producers.

Having found the old order wanting, members are embarked on an effort to build a better one. That is as it should be, if it were not for a dark and dangerous undercurrent giving impetus to the dissolution of the old order. There surely has occurred a loss of common purpose, but is there not also more—a willful denial of the positive and nurturing role of international community? A belief that "dropping out," and withdrawal behind floating rates and protectionist barriers, bring costless liberation from irksome international obligations? Consider the new protectionism, which proceeds against all accumulated experience on the assumption that it can serve the special interests without inflicting serious harm to the public interest and without tearing the delicate web of international civility. And consider the expansionist binges upon which a number of nations embarked in the belief that floating rates had made them free. The euphoria over this liberation from responsibility was fleeting, indeed, as reckless domestic policies led to rampant inflation and runaway currency depreciation. The bittersweet aftertaste has found expression in the swelling call for a return to the "discipline" of fixed exchange rates.

There is nothing inherent in fixed exchange rates that would make them a better system. Nor do they provide inherently more discipline. Unless certain conditions are satisfied, they will not work at all. These conditions include, as we shall see, coordination of the macroeconomic policies of member countries.

THE CHANNELS OF TRANSMISSION

Countries depend upon each other because their citizens are specialized. Specialization necessitates trade, and trade takes place in markets. Markets, in turn, are interconnected, because to a greater or lesser extent every commodity, asset, and factor of production in the world is related to others as a substitute or complement. Anything which disturbs the market for one of these generates repercussions in all the others, the strength of each repercussion depending on the degree of substitutability or complementarity.

As countries have pursued the rewards of international specialization and trade, they have established a complex network of market linkages. These arrangements facilitate mutually beneficial exchange, but they also increase a country's exposure to shocks and disturbances originating abroad. Rational economic policy will hence not push linkages beyond the point at which costs and benefits are in rough balance, for at that point the gains from specialization and trade will have been fully exploited.

Monetary Policy: Transmission of a Disturbance

In an interdependent world, economic disturbances are broadcast beyond the borders of the country of origin. Like ripples on a pond, price, income, and wealth effects are spread around the globe. They are felt most strongly in countries and markets with the closest links to the point of origin. Let us examine the transmission process by considering the repercussions of a monetary expansion in the United States.

When the Federal Reserve increases the money supply, the immediate effect is a decline in interest rates and in the cost of credit. Lower interest rates, however, reduce the relative attractiveness of dollar-denominated assets, and encourage investors to shift the composition of their portfolios toward foreign assets. A capital outflow materializes. Whether this attempted stock-shift succeeds depends, as we shall see below, on the nature of the exchange regime. To the extent that it succeeds, the flow of funds must ease credit conditions and thus lower interest rates abroad. Hence, the liquidity-raising, interest rate–reducing effect of the domestic monetary expansion has been transmitted to the rest of the world via linkages among financial markets. The strength of the transmission rises with the size of the domestic financial sector and the openness of the foreign sector.

These portfolio adjustments tend to take place comparatively swiftly in response to changes in relative rates of return. Then, as the expansionary policy raises output, incomes, and prices at home, a new round of adjustments is set in motion. An increase in income increases saving, which in turn increases wealth. Normally, a rise in wealth increases the demand for all assets, including those denominated in foreign currencies. To the earlier stock demand for foreign assets we must now add the wealth-induced flow demand. In combination, and in the absence of offsetting forces, these demand changes exert upward pressure on foreign asset prices and downward pressure on foreign interest rates. Along the financial channel, therefore, transmission takes place by means of the adjustments triggered by relative price and income-wealth changes.

A second transmission channel operates through linkages among commodity markets, and is manifest in variations in the balance of trade. When the monetary expansion increases income and employment, the demand for imports rises, the proportion of the income increment which is devoted to imports being determined by the marginal propensity to import. When Americans spend more on foreign goods, they boost foreign production and employment, provided that excess capacity exists abroad. Otherwise, the demand expansion raises prices abroad. This explains why countries suffering from unemployment will welcome the American stimulus, while those with little spare capacity will deplore it for its inflationary consequences.

From the American point of view, a successful monetary expansion is one which boosts employment and output while maintaining a stable price level. In that event, the spillover into imports is determined exclusively by income effect. If, on the other hand, the domestic price level does rise, the spillover includes a relative-price effect which encourages domestic and foreign users to switch from American to foreign products. Again, where foreign activity is stagnant, the spillover will be welcome; where it is not, the United States will be accused of exporting inflation.

A third channel of transmission, but one which we shall not consider in detail, operates through linkages among labor markets. A rise in relative wages and salaries in one country creates incentives for the international migration of labor. As a result, the supply of labor declines in low-wage countries and rises in high-wage countries, and the divergence among wage rates is reduced. On the whole, countries have installed elaborate and effective constraints on the movement of workers, although the migrations of Mexican workers to the United States and of southern European workers to the north represent important exceptions.

In each case, the transmission tends to reduce divergences among countries' economic conditions. The more extensive are a country's connections to its trading partners and the linkages of its markets to those abroad, the greater will be the influence of external events on interest rates, prices, and wages, and on output and employment at home. If the influences emanating from abroad are consistent with domestic objectives, they will be welcome; if they are not, the country will seek to insulate the home economy. As we shall see, flexible exchange rates offer a partial means of insulation.

To illustrate the importance of transmission, consider a dispute which arose in the early days of the Carter administration. Using the analogy of a locomotive pulling a train, American officials urged Germany and Japan to stimulate their economies in order not only to improve their own output/employment picture, but, through the spillover effects described above, to help pull the Western world out of a general economic slump. American officials felt that spare capacity was ample in the two countries, implying that expansionary policies would lead mainly to output and employment increases and not to inflation. The Germans and Japanese disagreed strongly, arguing that their economies were operating much closer to full capacity than American officials realized.

In their view, the suggested policy initiatives would lead primarily to inflation at home. Confronted with the choice between boosting employment and incomes abroad and maintaining price stability at home, both governments elected the latter.

The Role of Exchange Rates

We have seen how changes in relative prices and incomes in one country are telegraphed around the world. In tracing the effects of a monetary expansion, however, we have ignored exchange rates. Inasmuch as variations in exchange rates may enhance or destroy the attractiveness of foreign assets and commodities, they play a critical role in the transmission of disturbances.

Whether a foreign asset represents a worthy investment depends on its relative yield, as we have seen. But since it is the yield expressed in the investor's home currency which matters, the cost of moving into and out of foreign exchange must enter into the profit calculation. If the exchange rate on the day the investment is repatriated is identical to today's rate, the yield is given by the foreign rate of interest. If it is higher, the yield is greater than the foreign rate of interest. Since, however, the future exchange rate is not known to the investor at the time he makes his decision, he must form an expectation about the future movement of exchange rates. If he *expects* the exchange rate to rise, the appeal of the foreign asset is enhanced: the *expected* depreciation of the home currency raises the *expected* yield of the foreign asset.

Since these expectations are formed in an uncertain world, the yield which is ultimately realized may be quite different. By establishing an *open* position in foreign exchange, the *speculator* takes a deliberate risk. Not every investor, however, is prepared to accept the exposure of an open position; many will seek to protect themselves by using the hedging opportunities provided through the forward exchange market. In that market, in which currencies are traded for future delivery, the investor promises to deliver the proceeds of his foreign investment at a specified future date for a specified price. That price is the *forward* rate of exchange which, being known to him now, enables him to calculate the foreign yield exactly. The investor has *covered* himself by selling foreign exchange forward. The advantage of *covered interest arbitrage* over the uncovered arbitrage undertaken by the speculator is, of course, that it eliminates the risk inherent in unanticipated movements in exchange rates.

The rate of return on the foreign asset thus depends on the foreign interest rate, and on the difference between *spot* and *forward* exchange rates. If the two exchange rates are identical, a simple comparison of home and foreign interest rates will suffice. Otherwise, the rate of return, expressed in the investor's home currency, rises as the forward rate rises relative to the spot rate. Hence it is possible for a foreign asset carrying a lower rate of interest to represent the preferred investment, provided that the excess (in percent) of the forward over the spot rate more than offsets the excess of the home over the foreign interest rate.

When exchange markets are efficient and participants—especially banks and foreign-exchange brokers—are alert to profit opportunities, they will arbitrage funds among countries until interest rates and spot and forward exchange rates have reached levels equalizing returns on assets. In practical terms, any differences which remain will then be due to differences in the inherent riskiness of assets, with the more risky asset having to pay a higher rate of return. During the arbitrage process, interest rates and exchange rates will be changing, until all opportunities for the profitable transfer of funds have disappeared and a condition known as interest rate parity obtains.

Thus, when the monetary expansion reduces interest rates in the United States, it creates incentives for outward interest arbitrage. As investors move to shift funds into foreign assets, they bid up the spot prices of foreign currencies and, through their covering operations, they bid up the forward price of the dollar. The dollar depreciates spot and appreciates forward and, together with appropriate adjustments in interest rates, the system reestablishes interest parity. When exchange rates are flexible and exchange markets are sensitive to changes in demand and supply, exchange rates will be quick to adjust, and thereby to eliminate incentives for further arbitrage. When exchange rates are fixed, interest parity can be established only by changes in the two rates of interest, with the home rate rising and the foreign rate falling. To the extent that a system of fixed exchange rates places a greater burden on adjustments in the foreign rate of interest, to that extent will the credit-easing effects of the American monetary policy be transmitted more fully to other economies.

Floating rates thus tend to mute the force of transmission along the financial channel. They also mute transmission along the commodity channel, for when the expansionary monetary policy raises the demand for imports, it raises the demand for foreign exchange. In the absence of countervailing pressures, this tends to push up the price of foreign exchange and thereby to reduce the attractiveness of imports. Thus, the spillover created by the domestic expansion is turned back by depreciation of the home currency. The depreciating currency bottles up the expansionary pressures, and as a result their impact on domestic income and employment is enhanced, but so is the inflationary potential of an inappropriate or excessively expansionary policy. This has been a lesson which several countries have had to learn the hard way since the introduction of floating exchange rates in 1973.

Fixed Exchange Rates

The governments or central banks of two countries may fix the exchange rate between their monies by promising to buy and sell them at the agreed rate of exchange. So long as private demand and supply in the foreign exchange markets are in balance at this rate, no actual intervention is required. On the other hand, when an excess demand or supply threatens to push the exchange rate away from its targeted level, central bank sales of the currency in excess supply will have to take place.

When the expansionary monetary policy creates an excess demand for foreign exchange, the central bank must supply the extra exchange demanded in order to prevent the domestic currency from depreciating. In supplying foreign exchange, however, it withdraws domestic money from private circulation. Thus, while the monetary expansion itself increases the domestic money supply, the exchange-market intervention reduces it. Consequently, the private sector's excess demand for foreign exchange (and excess supply of the domestic currency) will vanish when the central bank, through its exchange-market intervention, has withdrawn enough domestic money from private hands to reestablish a proper balance between actual and desired cash balances.

The phenomenon just described implies that imbalances in the foreign exchange market created by monetary disturbances are temporary and self-correcting, *provided* that the central bank refrains from neutralizing these automatic adjustments by continually issuing new money.

Exchange-market intervention by the central bank withdraws dollars from private circulation, but it also injects foreign monies into private circulation. Thus, under fixed exchange rates, monetary expansion in one country leads through the exchange rate–fixing intervention of the central banks to money creation in partner countries. Money creation is thus transmitted, and unless partner countries are able to neutralize these tendencies, they will lose effective control over their own money supplies.

Loss of control over monetary policy was one of the issues which led to the demise of the postwar fixed exchange–rate regime. Deficit countries found that money balances were draining away through the mechanism of the central banks' exchange-market intervention, thus depriving them of effective control over the domestic money supply. Surplus countries, on their part, found themselves forced to accept money supply growth rates which were incompatible with domestic macroeconomic stability. And neither side was willing to undertake timely adjustments in the targeted levels of their exchange rates in order to eliminate imbalances in exchange markets.

In other words, countries insisted on fixing their exchange rates, but then refused to conduct domestic policies which were compatible with those rates. The disagreement stemmed from differences in national economic objectives and in inflation tolerances. In order to maintain established exchange rates, surplus countries would have to accept higher inflation rates, or deficit countries to reduce theirs. In the absence of a convergence of inflation tolerances and of effective coordination of macroeconomic policies, exchange rates could not for long be kept at their targeted levels. The switch to floating rates in early 1973 was undertaken in an effort to regain control over national money supplies and inflation rates. It was an inevitable event in a world in which the economic goals and objectives of member nations had become incompatible.

Real Disturbances

Flexibility in exchange rates thus shelters a country from external monetary disturbances by mitigating the force of transmission. The country is freed from the need to defend a given exchange rate, and consequently enjoys greater policy autonomy. There is in general, however, neither automatic nor complete insulation against foreign disturbances; only the availability of an additional policy instrument, namely monetary policy, with which domestic objectives may be pursued.

Critics of floating rates sometimes complain that the system is ineffective as an insulator against real disturbances. But that is exactly as it should be. If the world's scarce resources are to be allocated efficiently, if the benefits of specialization and trade are to be exploited to the fullest, and if economic development is to come to the world's poorer nations, real changes must be allowed to occur and their effects transmitted.

To be sure, real phenomena such as shifts in comparative advantage and changes in competitiveness are bound to impose economic hardships on the industries and individuals affected. In a just and compassionate society, efforts will be forthcoming to spread the burden of adjustment and to ease its cost. Enlightened public policy will be sensitive to the special interests without losing sight of the public interest. The essential flaw in anticompetitive manipulation of exchange rates and in protectionism is that they are inimical to the public interest.

CONCLUSION

A floating exchange rate keeps domestic monetary disturbances in and foreign ones out. Whether floating rates are desirable is hence to some extent a question of whether destabilizing monetary shocks originate mainly at home or abroad. Floating rates will be preferred by countries whose domestic economies are more stable than the world around them, because floating rates provide protection against destabilizing monetary influences from abroad. Countries with low inflation tolerances will defend themselves against having to import the higher inflation of their inflation-prone neighbors by adopting flexible exchange rates.

Since a floating rate forces a country to swallow whole the instability it creates, closing off all avenues for the exportation of domestic instability, a country which is unable to conduct steady macroeconomic policies may prefer to fix its exchange rate, thus maintaining a safety valve for releasing excessively inflationary or deflationary pressures. Such a policy represents a means of importing the relative stability of the surrounding world. To derive maximum benefit from this policy, however, the country cannot be too large in relation to the rest of the world. A very large country so dominates the world that domestic instability generates global instability.

In a world in which countries generate different inflation rates, the high-inflation country's currency must depreciate and the low-inflation country's currency appreciate. These exchange-rate adjustments are necessary to compensate for inflation-created divergences in national price levels. Unless countries are able to agree on common inflation rates and to maintain macroeconomic policies consistent with those rates, exchange rates will need to be continually adjusted. Under such conditions, flexibility in exchange rates is absolutely essential. Countries wishing to fix their exchange rates must first find ways to coordinate their macroeconomic policies. In today's world that is a most difficult task.

The basic problem lies with control over the money supply and interest rates. In many countries, governments have been unable to reconcile conflicting domestic claims and objectives. In choosing flexible rates, countries hoped to gain greater autonomy in matters relating to monetary and fiscal policies. Many, however, confused autonomy with freedom to do anything they pleased. They created money faster than their economies could use it. The result was rampant inflation which a depreciating exchange rate prevented them from exporting. Though governments tried to blame the inflation on the depreciating exchange rate, the major cause of both was excessive monetary expansion. Countries had become the victims of their own reckless policies.

A well-functioning exchange-rate regime should permit the transmission of real phenomena, for only then can nations exploit fully the gains from specialization and exchange. Anticompetitive intervention designed to extract special benefits for one country constitutes beggar-my-neighbor acts. It is as inimical to the public and international interest as are the more conventional forms of protectionism.

The essential lesson is clear: neither system of exchange rates is superior in any fundamental sense. Flexible and fixed rates both bring benefits and impose costs. Each is right for the right circumstances. Neither insulates a country from the effects of changing real conditions. In a world in which countries are united in their macroeconomic objectives, have overlapping unemployment/inflation preferences, and possess the political will to harmonize monetary and fiscal policies, fixed rates will be appropriate. In a world such as the one in which we live these conditions are not met. Flexibility of exchange rates is therefore the only viable option. While flexibility provides a measure of autonomy in matters of monetary policy, recent events have shown that reckless macroeconomic policies lead to volatile exchange rates and financial crisis.

II

Institutions and Problems

5

H. ROBERT HELLER

The Changing International Monetary System

The structure and flexibility of the new international monetary system. Bretton Woods. The International Monetary Fund and Special Drawing Rights. Monetary supplies and inflation. Currency pegging in 1978. Private capital markets. Eurocurrency, and the instability of the dollar.

Recent events have brought about a significant change in the international monetary system. The process of change was instituted in August 1971, when the United States severed the link between gold and the U.S. dollar; since then most major currencies have floated in international currency markets. The abrupt decline of the value of the dollar in late 1978 forced a significant change in U.S. foreign exchange policy. While these measures have temporarily arrested the decline of the dollar, its position as the centerpiece of the international monetary system has been severely eroded, and the extent of its further erosion hangs on the wisdom of Washington's policymakers.

The international monetary system, by adapting to a changing world environment during the last decade, showed its resilience and capacity for change without provoking a major crisis that might have seriously disrupted international trade and finance. Its movement has been evolutionary rather than revolutionary, and one can expect that the process of adapting the system to the requirements of a changing world economy will continue in the future. One of the hallmarks of the new international monetary system is that it provides for greater flexibility and scope for further change than the Bretton Woods system which it replaces. At the same time, the role of the International Monetary Fund has been broadened so as to enable this central institution to perform its duties within the more pliable reformed system.

The international monetary system encompasses all rules and conventions that govern financial interactions among nations. It consists of the legal structure governing the conduct of international monetary relations, such as the Articles of Agreement of the International Monetary Fund, and the operational framework within which international monetary transactions are conducted.

Understanding the main features of the Bretton Woods system of par values for currencies will clarify recent changes in the international monetary system. These changes were incorporated in the Second Amendment to the Articles of Agreement of the International Monetary Fund that became effective on 1 April 1978. The most important changes in those amendments are those affecting the exchange rate system and those affecting control over international liquidity.

We will also analyze how these changes have affected national monetary policies, especially the control or containment of inflation.

THE BRETTON WOODS SYSTEM

Towards the end of World War II the Bretton Woods conference laid the groundwork for a liberalized postwar international monetary system. This Bretton Woods system, as it came to be called, was designed to avoid the economic chaos and instability of the period between the two world wars, a period which had witnessed serious inflationary episodes, massive underemployment, and disruption of world trade due to protectionism. These problems were accompanied by great international currency market upheavals, which in themselves became a major source of world economic instability. The Bretton Woods system of fixed but adjustable par values was designed to overcome the problem of competitive currency depreciation for domestic reasons, for this problem was a particularly troublesome feature of the interwar period.

The Bretton Woods system provided for a dual anchor to currency values: gold and the dollar. These two important international reserve assets were linked at the fixed rate of $35 per troy ounce of fine gold. The dollar was to be freely convertible into gold—and vice versa—at that price. All other currency values were to be expressed in terms of either numerical. By this means, a complete currency grid was established which defined the value of all currencies in terms of a common *numéraire,* and thereby also provided for consistent cross-rates of exchange among the various currencies.

Exchange rates were to be adjusted only in cases of fundamental disequilibrium. What constituted a fundamental rather than a temporary disequilibrium was left undefined, an omission which played an important role in the eventual demise of the entire system.

Another important feature of the Bretton Woods system was the way in which it provided for international liquidity. International liquidity is composed of the reserve assets that are unconditionally available to any country's monetary authorities for balance-of-payments intervention purposes. The traditional international reserves of central banks were gold and convertible foreign currencies—of which U.S. dollars and pounds sterling accounted for the bulk of all currencies held.

The Bretton Woods system supplemented these traditional international reserve assets with the resources of the newly established International Monetary Fund (IMF). Together with the Special Drawing Rights (SDRs) created through the 1968 First Amendment to the Articles of Agreement, the IMF reserve position, gold, and convertible currencies are the generally recognized components of international reserves.

In providing international liquidity to its member countries, the IMF assigns a *quota* to each country when it becomes a member. The size of the quota is determined by the country's relative position in the world economy. That country then pays to the IMF an initial *subscription payment* equivalent to its quota, and the fund in turn makes credit facilities available to the member. A member normally pays 25 percent of its subscription in assets other than its own currency, such as dollars or SDRs. Those amounts establish a positive *reserve position* which may be utilized by the member automatically if the country needs the funds for balance-of-payments purposes. Additional drawings are made in four so-called *credit tranches,* each one of which is equal to 25 percent of a country's quota. The IMF will approve drawings in the first credit tranche if the country is making reasonable efforts to overcome its payments difficulties. Each subsequent tranche drawing requires greater justification. The increasing difficulty of drawing higher credit tranches is important to IMF purposes, because it assures the implementation of measures designed to reduce members' balance-of-payments deficits.

These general credit facilities have been supplemented in recent years by various special credit facilities that are available to IMF members under specified circumstances. Among these special facilities are the Compensatory Financing Facility, the Buffer Stock Facility, the various oil facilities, the Extended Facility, and the Supplementary Financing Facility. The cumulative possible currency purchases that can be made under all facilities combined amount to over 450 percent of quota, although it is unlikely that any one country would be able to qualify for all facilities simultaneously.

The IMF has also created its own reserve asset, the Special Drawing Right (SDR), which can be transferred among member countries and certain eligible international organizations. The SDR is a genuine supplement to the volume of international reserves. Special Drawing Rights were distributed in 1970, 1971, and 1972 to member countries of the IMF opting for participation in this scheme. These initial allocations amounted to $9.5 billion, and obligated countries to hold on average (measured over a five-year period) at least 30 percent of their SDR allocations and to accept up to three times their allocation in payment. Further allocations of SDR 12 billion (equal to about $14 billion) will be made in the 1979–1981 period. SDR drawings are not conditional upon the implementation of a balance-of-payments adjustment program, but constitute resources freely available to member countries.

The Bretton Woods par-value system had profound implications for the conduct of international trade and finance. By providing for stable exchange rates, it reduced uncertainty for firms engaged in international commerce and finance. At the same time, trade barriers such as quotas and tariffs were often reduced or eliminated, and international capital movements were encouraged through the introduction of free convertibility for most of the world's major currencies. Consequently, world trade and capital flows expanded rapidly, helping to increase living standards around the world.

Another important feature of the Bretton Woods system, as for any fixed exchange-rate system, was that it transmitted inflationary (or deflationary) pressures between countries. This particular feature played an important role in the system's eventual collapse. Under fixed exchange rates, if, in a country maintaining fixed exchange rates, the monetary authorities expand the money supply at a rate faster than the increase in the demand for money, two outcomes are possible: prices may increase, or the excessive domestic money stock will be used to purchase foreign goods and assets and therefore will be acquired by foreigners. The first possibility is unlikely in an integrated international economy with fixed exchange rates, since competition will force prices to remain uniform all over the world. Instead, residents will spend more money on imported goods and foreign assets, thereby transferring their excessive money balances to foreigners. Foreigners then have a choice: they may willingly hold those balances or, more likely, convert them through their country's central bank into their own currency. The end result is an increase in the foreign money supply, which in turn will increase inflationary tendencies abroad. Hence, an excessive monetary expansion in one country will be transmitted to other countries, and inflationary pressures will be spread around the world.

It has been argued that an excessive monetary expansion by the United States in the late 1960s and early 1970s sharply increased the volume of dollars held abroad. It has also been suggested that foreigners reduced their demand for dollar balances during the same period, converting the dollars they already held into local currency. Under either scenario, an excess supply of dollars found its way into international reserve holdings and led to an increase in the rate of monetary expansion around the world. Since the early 1970s the expansion of the world money supply has consistently been in excess of 10 percent, and so has been the world rate of inflation since 1974.

Many countries were unwilling to tolerate such high rates of imported inflation. But the only way they could influence U.S. policy was to exchange their dollars for gold. In August 1971, U.S. gold reserves amounted to $10 billion, while the country's liquid liabilities to foreign monetary authorities had mushroomed to over $40 billion from $33 billion in the previous month. Since the United States could no longer honor its gold pledge, it suspended the gold conversion privilege of central banks, and by thus cutting the link between the dollar and gold, it abolished a parity for the dollar, allowing it to float. In turn, many countries reciprocated and allowed their currencies to float in terms of the dollar.

In December 1971 a last-ditch effort was made in the Smithsonian Agreement to piece together a system of viable cross-exchange rates. But in view of the differences between various countries' inflation rates, the system was bound to break down. In early 1973 most of the major currencies were again allowed to float, and many have been floating ever since.

It is ironic, in retrospect, that a shortage of international reserves was seen to be the major problem confronting the international monetary system in the late 1960s, and that in response to this need the IMF created the Special Drawing Rights. In fact, it turned out that SDR supplements to international reserves were made in precisely the years of high reserve growth—1970, 1971, and 1972. Since then, it has been suggested by Mr. Witteveen, the former Managing Director of the IMF, that SDRs be used in conjunction with mandatory reserve requirements to *control* the growth of world liquidity, rather than in their original role as a supplement to international reserves.* In this fashion the SDR might well become the central reserve asset in the international monetary system that would again limit the aggregate expansionary potential of the world financial system.

*See his Frankfurt speech to the Conference Board, reprinted in *IMF Survey* (28 October 1975).

REFORMING THE INTERNATIONAL MONETARY SYSTEM

After the collapse of Bretton Woods, a major effort was launched to reform the international monetary system, with the International Monetary Fund playing the central role in the process. In July 1972 a Committee on the Reform of the International Monetary System was established and held a series of meetings over the next two years. However, the oil crisis of 1973–1974 and the ensuing world economic slowdown made it impossible to agree on specific reforms, and the committee adopted an evolutionary approach instead. The current international monetary framework was established by the Second Amendment to the Articles of Agreement of the IMF, which became effective on 1 April 1978.

The key feature of the new system is the freedom for countries to choose exchange arrangements that suit their own needs. Article IV of the new set of articles sets forth members' obligations as well as the role of the IMF (relevant sections are reproduced in Appendix A to this chapter).

In essence, member countries are no longer compelled to observe specific par values for their currencies, but are obligated to pursue domestic economic policies that are conducive to stability, and to refrain from actions such as competitive depreciations which would harm other countries.

In reality, IMF member countries observe widely different exchange arrangements. According to the fund's 1978 *Annual Report,* in mid-1978 ninety-five countries pegged their currencies, sixty-three of them pegged to a single currency, fifteen to the SDR, and seventeen to another currency basket. In addition, six countries participated in the European joint float—the snake; five had crawling pegs, and twenty-seven had other exchange arrangements, including free floating. While the Bretton Woods system relied on fixed exchange rates to encourage—if not to force—countries to pursue sensible domestic policies, the new system views stable international economic conditions as the *result* rather than the cause of stable domestic conditions. Obligations of countries are expressed negatively—to refrain from harming others. Countries have no positive obligation, as they had under the Bretton Woods system, to intervene in international currency markets.

This important change in emphasis resulted from the experience gained under the Bretton Woods system. To many observers, it was precisely the obligation to intervene in international currency markets under the Bretton Woods system that led to worldwide domestic instability. By making domestic stability the beginning rather than the end of the process, an important change was effected.

Of course, it is difficult to achieve satisfactory economic policies in over 130 different countries and to ensure against abuse. Section 3 of Article IV thus allows the IMF to exercise surveillance over member countries' exchange-rate policies (excerpts are reprinted in Appendix B). It is important to note that the fund's specific surveillance powers concern only exchange-rate policies. Each member has the right to adopt an exchange-rate system of its own choice. The IMF's power of surveillance is therefore restricted to a country's specific policies pursued within its freely chosen system. The precise nature of surveillance will have to be developed on a case-by-case basis, since it is unclear how much power the fund can actually exercise. While it already has significant power over countries applying for credit, its power over surplus countries is largely limited to exhortation.

It also remains to be seen whether the IMF will publicly criticize policies of important member countries. It is one thing to chastise the Seychelles; it is quite another to take on the United States or Germany. The IMF depends on the cooperation of its largest member countries, and little would be gained by purposely alienating them. In that connection, it is significant to note that the U.S. policy measures announced on 1 November 1978 were not taken within the framework of IMF surveillance—in spite of the fact that the fund contributed $5 billion to the resources marshaled in that policy package.

In the sphere of international liquidity, the increased access of countries to private capital markets has brought about a fundamental change. Under the Bretton Woods system, the supply of international reserve assets was fairly inflexible; but those assets are now available to countries in almost any quantity. This is true both for individual countries and for all countries taken together. A fundamental change has occurred in the supply of foreign-exchange reserve assets. Under the Bretton Woods system, the U.S. balance-of-payments deficit reflected more or less the increase in foreign reserve holdings of foreign central banks. The current international monetary system provides an almost unlimited supply of reserve currencies through the interaction of central banks and unregulated commercial banks in the off-shore currency markets. On the one hand, this increased flexibility makes it possible to finance much larger international imbalances—such as that caused by the OPEC (Organization of Petroleum Exporting Countries) price increase. The *Eurocurrency markets* played a major role in this recycling process by expediting the direct flow of funds from surplus to deficit countries. In bypassing *national money markets,* these intergovernment funds could be moved from country to country without disturbing domestic monetary policy unnecessarily. It also contributes to an efficient international allocation of savings and investment funds. It has been estimated that about one-third of net (inter-commercial bank) Euromarket lending is to central banks. Undoubtedly, these financial markets contribute significantly to the efficient use of global resources.

On the other hand, the existence of these international capital markets eliminated the last vestiges of the global constraint on reserve creation that existed under Bretton Woods. The lack of control over international reserves has important implications for the control of worldwide inflation. No global restraint exists any longer on inflation. Each country now must do its best to control its own inflation—as encouraged by the new Article IV. Control of inflation rests entirely with individual countries. Thus, the present system, which diversifies responsibility for inflation control, may result in more inflation than the older system, which provided a global constraint.

The exclusive dominant position of the U.S. dollar on the international financial scene has been severely shattered by the inability of the United States to bring excessive monetary expansion—and therefore inflation—under control. This policy failure led first to the breakup of the Bretton Woods system. Now it is likely to lead also to the erosion of the stature of the dollar as the leading international financial asset. Efforts are under way to establish a European Monetary System that will provide a zone of monetary stability for Europe. If successful, this system will present a powerful challenge to the hegemony of the U.S. dollar in international financial markets.

It is incumbent upon the United States to respond to this challenge in a positive fashion by restoring monetary order at home and in international currency markets. The first steps toward such a positive policy were taken by President Carter on 1 November 1978. But it will take great persistence and determination to persevere in the struggle against the inflationary erosion of the purchasing power of the dollar and its central role in the international monetary system.

6

WALTER ADAMS
JOEL B. DIRLAM

Unfair Competition in International Trade

International safeguards against unfair competition. The steel industry and its fight for protection. VRA, quotas, unilateral and bilateral agreements. The trigger price system in the steel market; its effect on inflation, competition, and industry modernization.

A free enterprise economy is built on the proposition that free competition should be the rule of trade. In the United States, public policy has been designed not only to promote free competition, but also fair competition. The antitrust laws—aimed at protecting the integrity of the competitive free enterprise system—prohibit collusion and monopolization, along with those predatory types of behavior which tend to undermine that system. The intent of these statutes is not to protect competitors, but to protect competition in domestic commerce.

In international trade, there are parallel safeguards in the United States against unfair competition. These include the Antidumping Act of 1921, and Sections 303 and 337 of the Tariff Act of 1930, respectively directed against subsidized imports and unfair import practices. The broad purpose of the Antidumping Act is to prevent foreign monopolies from abusing their power to discriminate in price by sales in this country at prices that would result in net receipts below those on sales in the home country. All major trading nations agree that dumping constitutes an unfair competitive practice when it injures a domestic industry. The General Agreement on Trade and Tariffs (GATT) specifically provides for antidumping laws and regulations. In adopting a more general provision against unfair import practices, the United States has gone beyond the GATT. This provision, hitherto rarely invoked (except in cases of patent infringement), could be used to prevent importers from employing tactics that either extend monopoly power, or exercise it to exploit U.S. customers. The countervailing duty statute, like the Antidumping Act, is designed to protect domestic producers against unfair competition from abroad. The unfairness in this case consists in a foreign government's granting subsidies, bonuses, or bounties that are designed to aid exports. Again, the GATT specifically allows for its members to apply countervailing duties, following a finding that a domestic industry has been injured. The present U.S. statute goes somewhat further, permitting a tariff increase without a finding of injury.

Unfortunately, it is difficult to draw a clear distinction between free competition and fair competition—especially because firms and industries subject to competitive pressure tend to regard *any* competition as *unfair* competition. Such confusion is particularly pronounced when competition comes from abroad. This, of course, is a fairly typical reaction of any industry (such as textiles, television receivers, or shoes) which is losing its comparative advantage to other countries.[1] The steel industry is a prime example of this problem. The industry's tenacious battle against import competition illustrates the difficulty of protecting the competitive process against protectionist demands of powerful special interests.

THE POLITICAL ECONOMY OF PROTECTIONISM IN STEEL

For decades, the steel industry in the United States has been afflicted by the typical maladies of a secure oligopoly. Entry has been at a minimum, or nonexistent; innovation has been slow; price policy has been uniform and inflexible, except in an upward direction; and, while leadership has rotated among the top firms, prices have been anything but market-determined. Moreover, until 1959 the industry had little to fear from foreign competition, so that its members felt it was safe to follow tacitly collusive and consciously parallel price and product policies. From time to time mavericks disturbed this pattern, but eventually they decided to become part of it.

This pattern lasted until 1959, when the domestic steel strike allowed a rising tide of imports to sweep into the United States. Once the domestic industry understood that these imports were not temporary, and that they were undermining the foundations of their oligopoly, U.S. steelmakers organized their response. They began to modernize their plants, substituting the oxygen converter for outmoded open-hearth furnaces, introducing vacuum degassing, and making a (belated) start on continuous casting. They also tried to block imports by administrative action under existing trade legislation.

Initial attempts at administrative action were unsuccessful, because the standards of the Trade Expansion Act of 1962 and the Antidumping Act of 1921 were too stringent to permit a finding of import-caused injury. Given the rigid price structure prevailing in the United States, it was impossible to prove that any injury which the steel industry sustained was other than self-inflicted.

Following administrative defeats, the industry lobbied for amendment of the Trade Expansion Act to obtain quota protection. And as early as 1967, bills began to surface in Congress providing for statutory limits on steel imports; other industries (shoes, textiles, electronics, etc.) facing intense foreign competition joined forces with steel. These protectionist efforts peaked when Representative Burke (Massachusetts) and Senator Hartke (Indiana) submitted an omnibus bill providing for mandatory import quotas on a number of products. By 1968 the forces supporting legislative quotas had begun to jolt the State Department. To undercut support for congressional quotas, the department (with administration blessing) persuaded the major steel-exporting countries—Japan and the members of the European Community (EEC)—to enter into a Voluntary Restraint Agreement.

STEEL IMPORT QUOTAS

Under the Voluntary Restraint Agreement (VRA), scheduled to go into effect on 1 January 1969, Japan's steel imports were limited to 5.8 million tons and EEC imports to 5.8 million tons annually, compared with their then current levels of 7.5 million and 7.3 million tons, respectively—with provision for annual growth of 5 percent in allowable quotas.

Within three years, the domestic industry found the VRA unsatisfactory. Quotas had not been established for specific products, nor for individual exporting countries other than Japan. Moreover, both the Japanese and the Europeans claimed that fabricated structural steel and cold-finished bars were not included in the VRA limitations. Because the VRA quota was expressed in tonnage terms, they rapidly expanded their shipments of stainless steel and other high-value products to the U.S. market—despite their promise to "try to maintain approximately the same product mix and pattern of distribution" as before the accord was signed. The effect of this upgrading in imports was that the total *value* of steel imports was as high in 1970 as in 1968, despite a 25 percent decline in the *volume* of imports during the same period.

As a result, the three-year extension of the agreement—announced by the White House on 6 May 1972—contained specific tonnage limitations on three categories of specialty steels (stainless, tool, and other alloys), and set the quotas at less than the 1971 import level. Fabricated structural steel and cold-finished bars were specifically included in the agreement; the participants agreed to maintain their product mix and their customary geographic distribution pattern; and a 2.5 percent (instead of the former 5 percent) annual increase in tonnage of allowable imports was applied to Japan and the EEC.

The extended VRA was monitored by the Treasury and the Customs Service. The exporting countries not only had to agree among themselves to observe the VRA, but also to set up machinery so that foreign producers could arrive at mutually satisfactory export quotas to the U.S. market. In other words, under U.S. pressure, Japanese and European steel producers were obliged to set up cartels to arrange for their share of the U.S. market, and to engage in activity that was suspect, if not illegal, under the Treaty of Paris which created the European Economic Community. More important, however, the connivance between the domestic industry, the State Department, and foreign steel producers to limit imports triggered an antitrust suit by Consumers Union, which charged that the VRA constituted a *prima facie* conspiracy under the Sherman Act. While the Supreme Court eventually upheld the State Department's authority to insulate the agreement from the antitrust laws, it left little doubt that the foreign signatories to the pact could be held accountable for participation in any trade restraints. In any event, the decision was clear enough to persuade all concerned that the VRA should not be renewed when it expired in May 1975.

The steel industry now supported a new measure that did not risk trust violations. And, in December 1974, Congress enacted the Trade Reform Act which directed the International Trade Commission (ITC) to provide relief (including quotas) for industries injured by rising imports, and allowed the Treasury to impose countervailing duties to offset export assistance. The initial complaint, filed by U.S. steel and other producers, was dismissed by the Treasury on technical grounds. But a second action by the specialty steel producers succeeded when the ITC ruled that the domestic firms were indeed injured by rising imports, and recommended that the president impose quotas on four categories of specialty steel products.

Stating that quotas were inflexible and relatively undesirable, the president gave Japan, the EEC, and Sweden ninety days to enter into voluntary "orderly marketing agreements" before approving the commission's recommendation. The Japanese gave in under the threat, but the other countries resisted. Quotas were imposed, as a result, with the Japanese benefiting and the EEC losing, as compared to the original commission recommendation (see Table 1).

Under EEC pressure, President Carter requested the ITC to reopen the case, and at hearings held in September 1977 the U.S. specialty steel firms were shown to be operating profitably, with prices up and output expanded. If the industry was suffering, it was because of the persistent low levels of expenditure on durable goods, not the availability of imports. Nevertheless, a majority of the ITC found that existing quotas were justified. And the administration responded to political pressure and threw in the sponge. Although he had ultimate authority, the president refused to modify the quotas.

It is revealing that steel producers have admitted they would prefer an "orderly marketing agreement," including foreign producers, to regulate world trade in steel in place of unilaterally imposed quotas. That is, in the words of the *Wall*

Table 1

**Stainless and Specialty Steel Import Quotas (tons)
United States**

Exporter	Recommended by ITC 1976–77	Quotas Imposed by the President			Imports 1975	Average Imports 1970–74
		1976–77	1977–78	1978–79		
Total	146,000	147,000	151,500	155,900	153,700	152,000
EEC	34,000	32,000	33,000	33,900	28,700	29,000
Japan	63,500	66,400	68,400	70,000	78,000	66,000
Sweden	23,500	24,000	24,700	25,500	22,800	–

Street Journal, they would prefer an international cartel to what they have now.

THE ECONOMIC EFFECTS OF STEEL QUOTAS

The steel industry's maneuverings on behalf of import quotas probably had pernicious economic consequences. They must have had a chilling effect on the intensity of import competition, and import sales were probably reduced during the period when remedies were being considered. The success of the specialty steel producers in securing quota relief, for example, may have had inevitable side effects on the importation of carbon steels.

There is hard evidence that the VRA increased steel prices and raised costs to American industry and consumers. Between January 1960 and December 1968, a period when imports were surging, the composite steel price index rose 4.1 points—or 0.45 points per year—compared to an increase of 26.7 points, or 6.67 points per year, in the four years between January 1969 and December 1972, while the VRA was in effect. Steel prices increased at an annual rate fourteen times greater after the import quotas went into effect than in the previous nine years (Comptroller General 1974:23). Products subjected to particularly strong import pressure prior to the VRA evidenced greater price increases than other steel products after the VRA became effective, again highlighting the anticompetitive effects of the quotas. One estimate is that steel quotas imposed a burden of about $386 million annually on the United States (Magee 1972). Other, less conservative, estimates put the annual cost burden of VRA in the $500 million to $1 billion range (Comptroller General 1974:23).

The application and threat of stringent steel quotas has profound implications for the battle against inflation. While it may be difficult to specify the quantitative importance of steel in the wholesale price index, there can be little doubt that steel price increases trigger and "justify" concomitant price increases for a host of other products, particularly where oligopoly is pervasive. Public policy, therefore, would be remiss in artificially insulating steel prices from the competitive import pressures.

Quotas are also contagious, especially in times of weak demand, and are reminiscent of the "beggar-thy-neighbor" policies of the industrial nations during the Great Depression. Thus, the Europeans forced Japan to accept a "voluntary restraint" agreement on steel shipments into the EEC at the same time that the United States imposed specialty steel quotas on the major exporting countries. The commitment by Japan restraining exports to the EEC represented, in effect, a 23.8 percent reduction from the previous level.

Bilateral agreements, such as Japan's with the EEC, reinforced by the mandatory quotas unilaterally imposed by the United States, are significant because they help lay the groundwork for comprehensive, multinational agreements controlling world trade in steel. These agreements, of course, are the dream of influential members of the world steel community.[2] While it remains problematical whether a worldwide steel cartel will come into being, the American steel industry will certainly continue its efforts to restrict imports. Thus far, its major efforts have been directed not at tariff protection, but at quotas and "orderly marketing agreements" which set an absolute maximum to allowable competition.

THE TRIGGER PRICE SYSTEM FOR STEEL

The latest step in steel's march toward protectionism was the trigger price system, administered by the U.S. Treasury.[3] Promulgated 6 December 1977, this scheme in effect puts a floor under the price of imported steel, and thus allows the domestic industry to increase prices without fear of competition. The industry wasted little time. On 7 December it announced a 5.5 percent hike across the board, followed by a 1.1 percent rise in April 1978. By year's end "list" prices had gone up 9.5 percent, while "transaction" prices had increased nearly 15 percent (*Wall Street Journal,* 26 September 1978).

These increases have been variously estimated to cost the economy from $1 billion to $6 billion annually, and they were only the beginning. On 8 May 1978 the Treasury announced that trigger prices would be *increased*—5.5 percent on sheet, plate, wire, and cold-finished bars; 13.9 percent on angles; 14 percent on reinforcing bars; and 14.5 percent on flat bars. And in July 1978 the Treasury increased them by roughly 4.86 percent (*Wall Street Journal,* 26 September 1978). Altogether, for the calendar year 1978, the Treasury raised trigger prices by 10.63 percent. In short, while ceremonially wringing its hands about inflation, the government itself was promoting inflationary price increases by a pivotal industry.

While the Treasury claims that trigger prices are not minimum prices, it does admit that "most foreign producers have raised their prices to the trigger price level to avoid an anti-dumping investigation." Treasury considers this a "voluntary decision," and finds it "understandable" and "reasonable" (U.S. Treasury 1978:30). In other words, Treasury concedes that, irrespective of an exporter's legal rights to sell at lower prices, as a matter of practical reality trigger prices are in fact minimum prices.

Since the trigger prices were set at a level close to domestic list prices, two inevitable consequences resulted: (1) importers could now raise prices that formerly reflected world market conditions to the higher level dictated by trigger prices, and (2) domestic producers could and did raise actual prices to at least the list price, thus wiping out the discounts from list which market conditions formerly compelled them to grant. Furthermore, domestic producers, protected by the minimum prices established under the trigger price system, were now free to raise list prices—so that they would be higher than import prices—to at least the extent of the accustomed differential between domestic and foreign prices.

Various estimates have been made of the inflationary impact of the trigger price system. The Federal Trade Commission (FTC) arrived at a direct increase in the cost of steel to consumers of $1 billion (FTC 1977:559). An administration official estimated the direct price effect to be roughly in the range of $800 million to $1.2 billion. Kurt Orban, an international expert intimately familiar with steel markets, places the estimated cost increase at $4 billion. If the domestic steel industry is to be believed in its claim that imports have caused transaction prices to be $60 below list, then estimates could range up to $6 billion. Our own more conservative estimate would place the immediate cost of inflation to the American economy at roughly $3 billion.

The consequences of trigger prices for the economy do not disappear at the boundaries of the steel industry. The billions of dollars of cost increases will spread to steel users, who will raise their prices as steel prices go up. Also, with the onset of the trigger price mechanism, the steel industry is removed from the category of industries susceptible to the strategic anti-inflationary influence of imports.

Especially ominous are the long-run implications of trigger pricing. The publication and elaborate enforcement of minimum prices, as all students of industrial economics know, provide efficient techniques for insuring concerted action among producers conscious of their interdependence. The trigger pricing system carries this process one step further. It provides wholly reliable, government-certified, minimum price lists, subject to adjustment on a quarterly basis. Every domestic producer of wire rod, for example, will at all times know the minimum price at which this product can be imported and made available at every major port in the United States. Importers will be privy to the same information. To allow—or, in this case, to compel—foreign steel producers to observe price floors on every major steel product carries *ad extremis* conduct which the Justice Department now finds in contravention of the antitrust laws.[4] Through the intercession of government, producers can easily pursue a policy of coordinated price escalation and still remain within the structures of the antitrust laws.

Most cartels break down—fortunately—because their members have a proclivity and incentive for cheating. A maverick cuts prices, expands his market share, and destroys the mutual trust on which the cartel is based. The trigger pricing system, especially when it is linked with a similar system enforced by the European Economic Community, achieves cartel goals without assigning market shares to its participants. By requiring minimum import prices, it forecloses price competition as a means of winning new customers. Market shares will tend to change little, if at all. Most important, the bargaining and negotiations that in the past kept import prices flexible, and that forced the domestic firms to quote varying discounts below their list prices, will have been effectively subverted. In short, with the trigger price mechanism, who needs a cartel?

CONCLUSION

The tribulations of the U.S. steel industry are largely self-inflicted. Throughout the post–World War II period, the industry has persistently chosen to charge high and inflexible prices, and has refused to meet competition in the marketplace. It has been in the forefront of every postwar inflation with the exception of that following the Arab oil embargo. As the *Wall Street Journal* reported on 14 July 1977, "the base price of hot rolled sheet steel has climbed about 63% to the present [1977] $283.50 per ton from its $173.50 a ton level when government wage and price controls ended in April 1974." It has climbed an additional 15 percent since the trigger price system was instituted in 1978 (*Wall Street Journal,* 26 September 1978).

At the same time, the industry's postwar performance has been hampered by an almost endemic technological backwardness. Thus, according to the International Iron & Steel Institute, 81 percent of Japan's crude steel in 1976 was produced in efficient basic oxygen furnaces compared with only 63 percent of U.S. output. By contrast, higher-cost open-hearth furnaces accounted for 18 percent of U.S. crude steel production, but for only 0.5 percent in Japan. Moreover, 35 percent of Japanese steel was produced by the labor-saving continuous casting method, more than triple the 11 percent in the United States. Also, the Japanese appear to benefit from economies of scale by using giant blast furnaces to an extent unparalleled in the American steel industry (*Wall Street Journal,* 3 August 1977).

The record simply does not bear out the claim that the domestic industry's problems can be blamed on unfair competition from abroad. While there undoubtedly has been sporadic dumping of some steel products by some countries at some times, there has been no persistent predatory dumping of substantial proportions. Nor can the U.S. industry legitimately claim that exporters of steel to the United States are beneficiaries of massive subsidies, which give them an unfair advantage over their American rivals. The Federal Trade Commission found that subsidies were, in fact, for practical purposes, nonexistent: the Japanese industry has benefited from a subsidy of one-fifth of one percent of U.S. sales revenue, the French by about three-fifths of one percent, the German and Belgian steelmakers not at all (FTC 1977:367-69).

In short, there seems to be little justification for granting the U.S. steel industry's protectionist demands. To do so can only exacerbate inflation, restrict competition, and insulate the industry from market pressures to modernize its aging and outworn facilities.

7

ROBERT D. TOLLISON
THOMAS D. WILLETT

Foreign Investment and the Multinational Corporation

Internationalization of economic activity since World War II. Opposition to multinational corporations. Technology transfer. Double taxation. Income distribution. National security, special interests, and investment restrictions. The case for liberalization.

The resurgence of foreign investment and the rise of the multinational corporation have been dominant developments in the postwar world economy. They have been accompanied by greater recognition in the United States of international economic interdependence. Developments in the early and mid-1970s—the devaluation of the dollar—clearly showed Americans that theirs was not a completely closed economy.

Scholars and officials as well as business and labor leaders took note of the trend toward the internationalization of economic activity well before the 1970s.[1] The growth of international trade in most countries was even more rapid during the postwar era than their usually high growth rate of domestic economy. Facilitated by liberalized trade barriers and improved transportation and communications, most industrial countries recorded strong increases in the proportions of their gross national product (GNP) made up of exports and imports.

By the 1960s, however, exports and imports were no longer the most important source of increased international economic activity. In the last two decades, activities of multinational firms have been growing even more rapidly than international trade.[2] The proportion of foreign earnings in the total profits of American corporations has grown from 8.6 percent in 1957 to 12.1 percent in 1970 to 26.9 percent in 1974. Annual sales of U.S.-related firms abroad are substantially greater than export sales from the United States; in fact, they are greater than the entire GNPs of all but a few countries.[3]

According to the Department of Commerce, the sales of majority-owned U.S. affiliates of U.S. multinationals have risen from a little under $100 billion in 1966 to almost $300 billion by 1973. By comparison, exports by American multinationals in 1973 were $70 billion.

The phenomenal postwar growth of the multinationals has become a controversial issue worldwide. One side sees multinationals as the best hope for stimulating economic development and reducing poverty in less-developed countries. Many Third World leaders, on the other hand, see multinationals as generators of obscene capitalist profits and exploitation, political manipulation, and cultural dependence. Nor have the multinationals been free from opposition in the industrial countries.

Not long ago, many writers viewed the resurgence of the multinationals as the death knell for the nation-state.[4] They argued that the economic interdependence fostered by the multinationals was growing much more rapidly than political interdependence, and that political integration would inevitably follow in the wake of increased economic integration. This scenario looks less likely today, in part because opponents of the multinationals have proven to be more politically potent in both the less-developed and industrial countries than the "interdependence" school theorists envisioned. The predictions of this school have fallen victim to the resurgence of protectionist pressures in the industrial countries and to increased economic militancy in developing countries, exemplified by demands for a New International Economic Order (NIEO). False analogies with the oil "cartel" have led many Third World leaders to exaggerate their own community power. In some cases this has improved the balance of bargaining power between multinationals and developing countries, but in others it has led to nationalizations without adequate compensation, as well as to prohibitions on new foreign investment. While these have brought short-term political benefits to Third World leaders, they have done so only at considerable economic cost.

Higher-income countries also face pressures to limit foreign investment in their economies. During the 1960s, concern grew in Europe about the so-called technology gap, which created strong pressures to limit expansion of American high-technology firms; there was also pressure to protect indigenous firms in industries such as aircraft and computers, whether they were economically efficient or not. Foreign governments have not only restricted investment in sensitive areas of the economy; they have also become increasingly involved in bargaining over technology inflows and direct foreign investment—using government's monopoly power to extract favorable arrangements.

The U.S. government encouraged foreign investment during the postwar period. While this position may have reflected in part the influence of business interests, it was also based on a broadly supported liberal economic philosophy, and on beliefs that the United States should contribute to economic development abroad for both humanitarian reasons and national security. Foreign investment was viewed as being mutually beneficial to home and host countries. The view of foreign investment as a partial substitute for foreign aid justified explicit government policies to encourage foreign investment, such as favorable tax treatment and investment guarantees.

Today this philosophy is under attack within the United States. The same factors which have increased protectionist pressures (Amacher, Tollison, and Willett 1979) and reduced support for foreign aid (Willett 1979*b*) have increased pressures to limit foreign investment. In particular, the decreased salience of the cold war—and with it, the belief that liberal economic policies were important to combat communism—have enhanced the influence of special interests seeking investment restraints.

Foreign action to limit investment inflows bolster these arguments. Why should the United States follow liberal economic principles when they are consistently being violated abroad?

It is important to note that arguments for liberal policies are not identical with arguments for policies which encourage foreign investment. Government policies which subsidize foreign investment must be examined to determine whether they support general or only special interests. In this regard, recent legislation which has limited tax breaks on foreign investment can be justified as a move toward liberal policies, rather than away from them. On the other hand, proposals to remove credit for taxes paid abroad would amount to double taxation of foreign investment, and therefore be illiberal. Thus, moves to decrease or increase taxation of foreign investment cannot always be equated with moves toward or away from liberal policy.

THE ARGUMENTS *FOR* RESTRICTING FOREIGN INVESTMENT

The opposition to freedom of international flows of direct investment comes from many sources. Arguments based on national security and balance-of-payments reasons will not be considered here. The former go beyond the scope of economics (although economic considerations are relevant), and the latter are thought by most economists to be a distinctly inferior alternative to removing balance-of-payments disequilibrium through an appropriate combination of macroeconomic and exchange-rate policies (see Chapter 4 by Arndt).[5] This section concentrates on the types of arguments concerned with employment, income distribution, and national economic advantage.

In the United States, much of the opposition to direct foreign investment and multinational corporations comes from organized labor. The AFL-CIO shift toward protectionist trade policies has been accompanied by opposition to foreign investment. Indeed, the AFL-CIO has used the expansion of foreign investment to argue that traditional international trade theory is no longer relevant.[6] Despite its appeal, this argument is invalid. The relationships between trade, labor, and capital movements have been the subject of considerable investigation by economists.[7] The basic case for liberal trade policies and for liberal investment policies is the same. Within this framework, let us now consider the major arguments raised for restricting foreign investment.

"Bigness Is Bad" Arguments

A major criticism of multinational enterprises and direct foreign investment might be termed the "bigness is bad" view. In Barnett and Muller (1974) such views are quite popular with Marxist critics of capitalism. This view perceives bigness as synonymous with monopoly, which causes economic exploitation, political corruption, and international financial instability.

Advocates of such arguments frequently overlook elementary economics. Size cannot always be equated with the degree of competition. Vertical integration, as practiced by many domestic and multinational corporations, is not necessarily anticompetitive (Weston and Peltzman 1969). Many large firms face a very competitive environment, while some small firms enjoy monopolies. That multinationals are sometimes larger than the governments they deal with does not automatically imply that they hold all the cards. The balance of bargaining power depends, rather, on particular market situations. Nor is the pursuit of special interests through government actions limited to large firms.

Claims that multinationals disrupt the international financial system are also highly exaggerated. For example, one highly publicized finding is that U.S. multinationals have more international short-term assets than the central banks of all major industrial countries put together. It is often implied that multinationals jeopardize international financial stability. This view ignores the fact that capital flows by multinationals have generally been stabilizing rather than destabilizing, having moved exchange rates toward equilibrium rather than away from it. Even when multinational actions are destabilizing, central banks have greater effective power to offset capital shifts than simplified statistical comparisons might suggest.[8]

Although it would be naïve to assert that multinationals can do no wrong, blanket condemnations of them are based on faulty analysis and generalization. The appropriate response to abuses by multinationals are specific remedies, not across-the-board restrictions.

National Advantage Arguments

Proposals for restricting foreign investment often rest on arguments that national economic welfare will be increased as a result. These arguments fall into two major categories: terms-of-trade and tax arguments.[9] International trade theory is quite helpful in considering both of these.

Terms-of-trade effects and technology transfer. By transferring technology abroad, American firms increase the likelihood of foreign competition in the future. While firms face incentives to consider this when setting prices at which technology is transferred, each firm will evaluate the future effects on themselves, not on the rest of the economy. Therefore, in strictly nationalist terms, private firms will have a tendency to set the price of technology too low and to transfer too much technology abroad (Baranson 1976; Gilpin 1975). Where several U.S. firms have similar technology which does not exist abroad, their competition will tend to lower the price of technology transfers. The United States could prevent this by reducing competition and by establishing monopoly prices through control of such transfers.

There is, in fact, a long history of government attempts to limit the export of technology and trade secrets. A prime example is England during the industrial revolution. There are serious disadvantages in limiting technology transfers, however. Such limitations require an extensive bureaucratic apparatus, which is often not successful. And while levels of restriction that are optimal on nationalist grounds can be determined in theoretical models, there is little reason to be confident that government policies will approach such optima in practice.

But the strongest argument against investment and technology controls is the same as the argument for liberal trade policies in general. Many kinds of economic restrictions can be used to bring gains to some at the expense of others. But almost everyone is likely to end up worse off if they all succeed. This holds just as true for nations within the world economy as for individuals and groups within a national economy. The basic case for liberal policies is not that they always maximize short-run gains, but that they serve enlightened and longer-run interests in avoiding a world riddled with restrictions.

Taxation. Another prominent argument for restricting investments abroad arises from their tax consequences. Investments abroad generate tax revenues for foreign governments, whereas taxes on domestic investment remain at home.

Under the prevailing tax arrangements, foreign subsidiaries of U.S. corporations are allowed to count tax payments to the host country as a credit against their tax liabilities in the United States.[10] However, it is only the after-tax income on foreign investments which contributes to domestic GNP. Private investors, therefore, will only care about their total taxes, not whether they are paid at home or abroad, whereas the United States will benefit only from taxes collected at home. The national benefits from domestic investment, *vis-à-vis* foreign investment, will thus be greater than the private benefits, and there will tend to be excessive foreign investment from a strictly nationalist viewpoint.

Economists who have studied the question are agreed that, in the absence of retaliation, the maximization of short-run national advantage would call for taxing foreign investment at a substantially higher rate than domestic investment (Kindleberger 1968; Krause and Dam 1964; Musgrave 1969; Hufbauer et al. 1975). Although the tax advantage provides a rationale for restricting direct investment and technology transfers abroad, there are reasons—which have been stressed by some of the writers cited above—for not pursuing such policies. Existing tax credit arrangements were originally devised to avoid double taxation of international investment, and thereby to minimize the extent to which domestic tax arrangements distorted the global allocation of investment. While some nations individually might gain from double taxation, global economic efficiency would suffer as the costs of investing in other countries would be artificially increased. Since the host country provides public services consumed by the foreign investor, it seemed most reasonable to assign primary taxing rights to the host rather than the home country.

For countries with relatively balanced inflows and outflows of capital, this assignment would make little difference. The assignment does tend to favor net capital importers relative to traditional net capital exporters like the United States, since the amounts of tax payments are usually not fully offset by increased government costs. Thus, there is some justification to the arguments that current tax arrangements do not give us maximum advantage. However, even though double taxation of foreign investment might serve America's short-term advantage, it would be both good economics and good foreign relations to overlook the opportunity, since temporary benefits could probably be obtained only at the expense of increased impediments to international exchange—a development which would serve no country's long-run interests.

Effects on Jobs and on Labor's Income

Although advocates of restricted foreign investment and technology transfers usually state their case in terms of securing national advantages, their actual motivation is often to improve the economic position of one group at the expense of the rest of the population.

Groups seeking protection cannot merely claim their right to increased incomes. They are more likely to win public support for a restriction by arguing for preservation of jobs. Thus, much of the attack on foreign investment is in terms of an alleged export of jobs.

The AFL-CIO argues that foreign investment and technology transfers have had a large negative impact on employment. Business has countered with studies showing that the companies with the greatest overseas expansion have increased domestic employment at rates well above average. These findings, however, cannot determine whether the expansion of domestic employment would have been even more rapid if plants had not been set up in other countries. Despite empirical research, we do not have conclusive evidence on the net impacts of foreign investment on U.S. jobs, except that they are likely to vary considerably from one instance to another (Bergsten, Horst, and Moran 1978: Chapter 4).

The primary problem with the employment impact debate is that the disputants talk almost exclusively about job creation and destruction in the short run and ignore the long run. In a dynamic economy, however, changes are always occurring. Demand rises in some areas and falls in others, causing employment opportunities to expand in some industries and decline in others. The job creation and destruction associated with international trade and investment should not be viewed in isolation, but rather as part of a perpetual reallocation of resources, responding to domestic as well as to international developments. Although these adjustments may sometimes be costly in both human and economic terms, the solution does not lie in abolishing change. Public concern with the dislocative effects of foreign investment should be met with adjustment assistance or temporary income-support measures, not with permanent limitations on capital exports. The Trade Act of 1974 expanded the government's adjustment assistance programs to include short-term unemployment resulting from capital exports as well as increased imports (see Chapter 9 for a more complete discussion of adjustment assistance).

The case for permanent restrictions is that they would alter the distribution of income. The possibility of moving production overseas reduces the ability of workers to secure high wage demands, just as the possibility of workers changing jobs limits the scope of employers to set wages below competitive levels. Similarly, in a capital-intensive country such as the United States, limitations on capital exports will alter the effective relative abundance of domestic factors of production in the same way as would limitations on imports.[11] In both cases the relatively scarce factor, labor, would become even scarcer compared to the abundant factor, capital, shifting the distribution of income away from capital toward labor.

There is considerable disagreement among researchers about the size of such potential redistribution effects. Some studies have suggested they could be quite large, while others suggest they would be relatively small. In any event, despite the rapid expansion of foreign investment activities, labor's share of the distribution of income has actually increased slightly over the postwar period (Bergsten, Horst, and Moran 1978: Chapter 4).

Though the redistributive effects of limiting capital exports explains the hostility of the AFL-CIO toward capital mobility, they should not persuade consumers and the general public. Where the general distribution of income is the problem, the solution should be found in federal tax and expenditure policies. Attempts to alter and redistribute income through trade and investment restrictions should be seen as the special-interest measures that they are.

RESPONDING TO ILLIBERAL POLICIES ABROAD: A SUGGESTED STRATEGY

A number of foreign governments discourage free exchange of advanced technology and high-technology products between the United States and themselves. Some industrial countries encourage domestic production of high-technology goods which were previously imported as part of their development strategies. Others use import controls to play U.S. producers off against each other (see, for example, Bergsten [1974]).

The United States cannot expect completely liberal trade investment policies overseas. National security goals or special-interest pressures may render *laissez-faire* unfeasible in some countries. However, retaliatory responses may sometimes be necessary when countries are not pursuing legitimate objectives in limiting investment and technology flows. This poses a dilemma to free-trade advocates: how should a liberal country respond to illiberal actions by others?

One alternative is to not retaliate at all. Such a passive response would reduce the risks of pursuing illiberal policies abroad, however. This could lead to more frequent adoption of such policies, with results that could ultimately prove quite damaging to the U.S. economy. Furthermore, a passive policy would almost inevitably cause Congress to pass its own measures. While the United States should not take monopolistic advantage of others, it cannot remain indifferent to other countries' predatory policies.

On the other hand, it would not be feasible nor desirable for the U.S. government to try to exert countervailing power in every transaction involving potential government monopoly power abroad. Such a strategy would end up with the government attempting to control the majority of international transactions. In most instances, the amount of monopoly power which national governments can exert over the terms of international transactions is relatively small. For many types of products, in all but a few nations, each represents individually only a very small share of the world market. Restrictions cannot significantly damage U.S. interests in such instances unless many countries follow such policies in concert.

When the potential economic damage to the United States appears to be large, retaliatory policies may be the only appropriate response. But retaliatory actions should not be undertaken hastily, and should be limited to cases where there is a good chance that foreign governments will reduce investment barriers as a result. A country must have a viable ultimate threat of retaliation, but attempts to negotiate barrier reductions should always come first.

One of the major difficulties in this area is that many investment restrictions may be motivated by legitimate national concerns. But what are the bounds for legitimate restrictions, and how do we decide when these bounds have been overstepped?

Although an international consensus on what constitutes legitimate investment barriers would be desirable, it is unlikely in light of current differences in attitudes between countries (Keohane and Ooms 1975). It is important to begin searching for general principles in this area, however.

One attractive principle would be for foreign investment restrictions to be as nondiscretionary as possible. An example of this is the U.S. policy which allows only a limited percentage of foreign ownership in certain designated industries related to national security (e.g., communications). Other examples might be requirements that an industry employ *X* percent of indigenous labor, or that *Y* percent of basic industries be locally owned. Such nondiscretionary rules would not be seen as seeking specific terms-of-trade advantages, and could be treated as substantively different in nature from cases involving foreign-investment review boards. Thus, so long as there were no special concessions offered to particular trading partners, nor a case-by-case setting of the rules, the presumption would be that such policies were not designed primarily with beggar-thy-neighbor motivations and would not be the subject of retaliation.[12]

CONCLUSION

The arguments for restricting the export of American capital and technology are not, on balance, convincing. Across-the-board adoption of such policies would be undesirable. Although some restrictions might bring at least short-term economic gains to groups within the United States, they would be at the expense of long-term costs through reduced economic efficiency, increased bureaucratization of economic activity, and increased international political frictions. Despite the frequency with which it is challenged, our traditional philosophy of liberal policies toward foreign investment still makes sense.

III

Political Dimensions

8

ALAN V. DEARDORFF

ROBERT M. STERN

American Labor's Stake in International Trade

Free trade and the consumer. Labor in the export market. Mobility between industries. Subsidiary and nontrade industries: the effects of trade liberalization. The community and changes in trade patterns. The effects on labor of trade legislation, lobbying, and policy implementation. Protectionism and the AFL–CIO. Income redistribution and adjustment assistance.

The attitude of American labor toward international trade has changed over time, as economic conditions at home have fluctuated and as the pattern of trade has shifted. In recent years that attitude has become more protectionist, and the

U.S. labor movement has become an ardent lobbyist for insulating the U.S. economy from the effects of foreign trade. To help in understanding this change, we look in this chapter at the variety of ways that labor may be affected by trade. The historical record then suggests which of these effects have been of greatest concern to the labor movement. The results also suggest the manner in which trade policy should be formulated and implemented.

There are four ways in which workers are affected by trade, each of which is associated with a particular role that the worker plays in the economy. First, as consumers, workers participate in the national gains from trade by enjoying lower prices for the imported goods they consume. The extent of this gain depends on their pattern of consumption, and workers of different incomes may therefore benefit unequally from a move to free trade.

Second, as suppliers of factors of production, workers compete with similar factors abroad when trade is free. Employment and real wages in various occupations will therefore be affected differently by trade, depending on the relative scarcity of these factors at home and abroad.

Third, as members of industries, in the short run workers share in the fortunes of their employers as trade causes their industries to expand or contract. Since some industries gain from access to foreign markets while others suffer from foreign competition, we will again find diversity within the labor force in short-run gains and losses from trade.

Finally, as residents of geographic regions, workers participate in local labor markets and are affected by the performance of all industries located in their communities. To the extent that trade-oriented industries tend to be concentrated in particular locations, labor's stake in trade will also be geographically diverse.

Each of these four effects needs to be examined more carefully. As we do so, we will marshall such empirical evidence as is available to indicate how the gains and losses from trade are distributed across the labor force.

THE WORKER AS CONSUMER

Since the classical argument for free trade is given elsewhere in this volume, we will not repeat it here. Although trade increases the total welfare of a country, any move toward freer trade will tend in fact to benefit only certain groups in the population and to harm others. Most economists nonetheless regard the aggregate gain as a valid case for free trade, since theoretically the gainers can compensate the losers and still remain better off. Our concern here is to consider who, precisely, the losers will be.

In evaluating the gain or loss from trade for particular workers, the general argument is useful in focusing attention on two things. On the one hand, trade changes the terms on which a worker may exchange income for goods; on the other, trade can change incomes themselves. While worker incomes usually attract most attention, the terms on which incomes may be exchanged for goods are also important. This leads us to look first at the worker's role as consumer.

When a country moves toward freer trade (through tariff reductions, perhaps), prices of imported goods will tend to fall relative to those of exported goods. Given the complexities in a modern economy, this effect does not apply universally to each specific good, but it is valid as a general pattern. The effect of this change on consumers, assuming no change in their income, depends on their consumption patterns. Consumers of imported goods will tend to benefit from reduced prices, while consumers of exported goods will suffer. To assess the effect of trade on workers as consumers, therefore, one must know consumption patterns of different workers and the extent of their reliance on imported and exported goods.

Fieleke (1971) studied this problem by examining the budgets of low-, medium-, and high-income U.S. consumers, and by computing the added costs that tariffs impose on these groups as a percent of their total consumption. Using post-Kennedy Round (1972) tariffs, he found these percentages to be 1.7, 1.5, and 1.4, respectively, thereby concluding that the U.S. tariff structure is slightly biased against low-income consumers in favor of high-income consumers.

Unfortunately, Fieleke's computations are extremely simplified. He assumes, for example, that tariffs have no effect on the prices of nontraded goods—an assumption which is questionable. In support of his conclusion, however, he also examines the correlation between tariffs and unit values for 163 groups of closely comparable goods, and concludes that U.S. tariffs tend to be highest on low-quality items—that is, on items that low-income consumers tend to buy. This supports his conclusion that the U.S. tariff structure impinges most heavily on low-income consumers; liberalizing trade would therefore benefit them, as consumers, the most.

THE WORKER AS SUPPLIER

The effect of trade on labor income has traditionally been studied in the framework of the Heckscher-Ohlin model, under the assumption that factors move freely among industries within a country. Thus, a market wage or rental is established for each factor of production independently of where it is employed, and we can study how trade affects these prices.

Stolper and Samuelson (1941), who produced the best-known result here, showed that trade would increase the real wage of a country's abundant factor and lower that of its scarce factor. In the United States, which is presumed to be abundantly endowed with capital relative to labor, we would conclude that labor will lose from trade due to a reduction in its real wage.

Unfortunately, another implication of the Heckscher-Ohlin model is that the U.S. should be exporting capital-intensive goods, but attempts to verify empirically this trade pattern have generally failed. Leontief (1954) was the first to discover that the U.S. exports labor-intensive rather than capital-intensive goods, and other investigators have repeatedly duplicated this result.

Attempts to resolve this paradox have led to a variety of revisions and extensions of trade theory. For our purposes, the most interesting of these stems from the recognition that labor is not a single homogenous factor of production. Rather, workers are differentiated from one another by the level and nature of their skills, and workers who differ in skill are hardly regarded as perfect substitutes by potential employers.

Dividing factors of production into three—unskilled labor, skilled labor, and capital—provides the easiest way to capture this distinction among workers. Although the theoretical implications of such a division are not fully understood, it has proved much more successful in empirical applications than its two-factor counterpart. The United States, for example, is well endowed with physical capital, but even better endowed with highly skilled labor. And studies of U.S. trade patterns verify that the United States is an exporter of goods that require large amounts of skilled labor in their production. The scarce factor in the United States, then, is not labor as a whole, but only unskilled labor; only unskilled labor, therefore, should be harmed by trade. Skilled labor, or at least part of it, should benefit.

Some empirical evidence indicates this is true. Based on 1962 data, Ball (1967) found a significant negative correlation between U.S. effective tariffs and average annual wages across thirty-one U.S. industries. Assuming that average wage differences across industries reflect labor skill differences, this means that U.S. tariffs give greater protection to unskilled workers than to skilled workers. Cheh (1976) correlated the proportion of unskilled workers in an industry with measures of nominal tariffs, effective tariffs, and nontariff barriers, finding significant results only for nominal tariffs. Thus, while there is disagreement over which tariff measure is most highly correlated with a particular measure of labor skills, existing evidence nevertheless suggests that unskilled workers have the most to lose from a move to free trade.

Among skilled workers, who as a group will gain from trade, the distribution of those gains is uncertain. There are many kinds of skills, and aptitude for one does not imply an aptitude for another. Thus, even in the long run, workers may not be able to transfer skill from one occupation to another, and we should regard even skilled labor as comprising a wide variety of separate factors of production. If the U.S. abundance of skilled labor generally is not reflected in abundance within each skilled occupation, then there may be certain occupations which will lose, rather than gain, from trade.

While particular individuals may differ in their aptitudes, one could argue that the distribution and level of aptitudes across the population will be approximately the same for all countries. If so, the relative abundance of skilled labor in the United States would be explained by our well-developed educational system. If entry to various occupations were free, our abundance of skilled labor would be shared equally by all occupations, and their stake in trade would be roughly the same.

In fact, of course, entry to many occupations both in the U.S. and abroad is severely limited by institutional constraints such as trade unions, government licensing, and in some countries the dictates of custom and tradition. It is thus quite possible for particular occupations with limited entry to enjoy unusually high wages in the United States, despite the general abundance of skilled labor. And workers in these occupations may lose from trade when their products come under increased competition from the products of their more abundant counterparts abroad.

The effects of trade liberalization upon different occupational groups in the United States are discussed by Baldwin (1976), who estimated the employment effects of a 50 percent reduction in tariffs by the U.S. and the seventeen other major industrial countries, using data on occupations classified according to the 367-industry breakdown of the 1967 U.S. input-output table. With all sectors subject to the 50 percent reduction—except agriculture, textiles, and oil, which are covered by nontariff barriers—Table 1 shows that trade liberalization raises demand for highly educated technical workers and farmers, farm managers, and farm laborers, and lowers demand for skilled, semiskilled, and unskilled labor. This reinforces the idea that relatively high levels of education and abundant supplies of agricultural land underlie the U.S. comparative advantage in international trade.

THE WORKER AS MEMBER OF AN INDUSTRY

The effects of trade will be uniform across all suppliers of a productive factor only after enough time has elapsed for them to move from industry to industry. In the shorter run, however, workers cannot move, and are affected less by the national market for their services than by the performance of the industry in which they are employed. A skilled machinist, for example, may ultimately benefit from trade as the demand for skill-intensive products expands and the wages of skilled workers are bid up. But if he is currently employed in an industry which suffers from import competition, then the immediate effect of trade on him will be a reduced wage or, more likely, a greater probability of being laid off. To assess the immediate impact of trade on most workers, then, we must determine which industries will expand and which will contract as a result of trade liberalization.

This issue is complicated by interindustry trade patterns and by the need to take account of changes in exchange rates and of tariff changes abroad as well as at home. Over the last several years we have developed a model of world trade and production that takes all of these things into account (see Deardorff, Stern, and Greene 1978). In its current form, the

Table 1

Estimated Changes in U.S. Employment by Occupational Group Due to 50 Percent Reduction in Tariffs by the 18 Major Industrialized Countries[a]

Occupation	Percent of Industry Employment in 1970	Thousands of Workers
1. Research and development	0.14 %	1.6
2. Professional and technical	0.08	1.4
3. Management and administrative	−0.03	− 1.9
4. Craftsmen	−0.05	− 4.6
5. Sales workers	−0.03	− 1.4
6. Clerical workers	−0.02	− 2.8
7. Operatives	−0.14	−16.3
8. Laborers, except farm	−0.08	− 2.7
9. Service workers	−0.01	− 0.4
10. Farmers, farm managers, and laborers	0.46	12.1

Source: Adapted from Baldwin (1976:66).

[a]Assumes no reduction in tariffs on agricultural products, textiles, and oil, which are all subject to nontariff barriers.

model includes eighteen major industrialized countries and twenty-nine sectors, twenty-two of which involve tradable goods and the remainder nontradables. Table 2 shows estimates, based on 1970 data, of effects on employment in twenty-nine U.S. industries due to complete removal of tariffs and other trade barriers in all countries. Regarding labor's stake in trade, in the short run workers in industries with the greatest decline in employment have a clear stake in maintaining barriers.

One would expect the greatest trade effects on employment in those industries whose products are traded. Table 2 shows this to be the case. The major tradable industries in which employment would rise with complete tariff removal include agriculture, forestry and fishing, chemicals, nonelectrical and electrical machinery, and transport equipment. Employment would decline in textiles and wearing apparel, leather and footwear, pottery, china and earthenware, iron and steel, and nonferrous metals.

Industries whose products are not traded will also be affected by trade liberalization. This is particularly true for wholesale and retail trade, transport, storage and communication, finance, insurance and real estate, and community, social, and personal services. There are two reasons for this. The first arises from interindustry interaction. A nontraded industry whose product is sold as an input to traded industries will share in the fortunes of its customers. If the product is used primarily in export industries, demand for it will increase with trade liberalization and employment will expand. The reverse will be true if its industrial customers compete with imports.

If supply of inputs to industries engaged in trade were the only reason for trade effects on nontraded industries, one might expect a worker whose product is a nontraded *final* good or service to be immune from trade effects. But this is not the case. As trade is liberalized, the prices of traded goods—both exports and imports—tend to fall relative to the prices of nontraded goods. This occurs because trade acts

Table 2

Estimated Changes in U.S. Employment by Industry Due to Complete Tariff Removal on All Industries by the 18 Major Industrialized Countries[a]

Industry	Percent of Industry Employment in 1970	Thousands of Workers
Tradables:		
Agriculture, forestry, and fishing	0.56 %	19.3
Food, beverages, and tobacco	0.03	0.5
Textiles	−1.32	−14.7
Wearing apparel	−1.48	−17.2
Leather and leather-and-fur products	−2.34	− 2.0
Footwear	−1.26	− 2.6
Wood products	0.03	0.1
Furniture and fixtures	0.09	0.3
Paper and paper products	0.15	1.0
Printing and publishing	0.10	1.1
Chemicals	0.63	7.1
Petroleum refineries and coal products	0.43	0.6
Rubber products	0.27	0.7
Pottery, china, and earthenware	−0.70	− 3.0
Glass and glass products	−0.11	− 0.2
Iron and steel	−0.10	− 0.9
Nonferrous metals	−0.49	− 1.5
Metal products	0.05	0.7
Nonelectrical machinery	0.56	11.3
Electrical machinery	0.34	6.0
Transport equipment	0.71	12.0
Other manufactures	0.18	2.1

[a]Assumes no reduction in tariffs on agricultural products, textiles, and oil, which are all subject to nontariff barriers.

very much like a technological innovation, permitting transformation of one traded good into another and thus making all of them less expensive to obtain. The effect of this change in relative prices is to cause consumers to substitute away from nontraded goods toward traded goods. Thus, when trade is liberalized, output falls and workers generally suffer in nontraded industries (see Table 2).

Note that the positive and negative employment effects shown in Table 2 are all comparatively small in both absolute and relative terms. Therefore, normal employment growth in individual sectors and overall could probably handle much of the displacement that might occur if tariffs were removed multilaterally. The overall net and gross employment effects are also shown to be small. Existing programs offering employment compensation and job retraining would surely mitigate most worker hardships. At the same time, it would not appear to be costly were the government to make special adjustment assistance payments to displaced workers or, alternatively, to subsidize employers to encourage the hiring of these workers.

THE WORKER AS RESIDENT OF A COMMUNITY

In the short run, geographic immobility may make it impossible for a worker to participate in gains from trade enjoyed by suppliers of the same productive factor elsewhere in the country. To do so would require relocation to another community where new jobs or higher wages are appearing. Since moving costs and the time required may be substantial, there may be a long delay in equalizing wages and unemployment rates for a given category of labor across the nation. At the same time, a worker who ultimately suffers from trade may postpone that loss if other industries in his community are booming and if migration into the community is slow.

Thus for many workers the primary determinant of benefits or losses from trade is the performance of the principal local industry in their community. If trade expands that industry, both the industry's employees and other residents working in other industries will gain. Conversely, if trade harms the major local industry, workers laid off will compete with other workers in the same community and thus spread the loss to them. This effect is likely to be most pronounced in local service industries, whose workers not only compete with other workers more directly affected by trade, but who also depend on sales to these other workers. Therefore, if trade causes unemployment in the community to rise, these sales will suffer.

Naturally, this short-run effect will be most pronounced in communities with only one or a few industries. If no single industry dominates the local labor market, then losses in one industry will be cancelled by gains in another, leaving the rest of the community unaffected. But many U.S. cities and regions are known for their specialization in one or a few products—tires in Akron, cars in Detroit, and textiles in the Carolinas. In these places, the industry's stake in trade extends beyond its own workers to others in the community at large.

Baldwin (1976) has estimated the effects of trade liberalization on U.S. employment by region, as summarized in Table 3. The New England, Mideast, Southeast, and Great Lakes regions all show employment declines, while the Great Plains, Southwest, and Far West regions show increases. Of course, as noted already, the effects are all comparatively small.

THE ATTITUDE OF AMERICAN LABOR TOWARD TRADE

Labor's attitude toward trade will depend on the importance of the workers' various roles. Expanding trade will affect

Table 3

Estimated Changes in U.S. Employment by Region Due to a 50 Percent Reduction in Tariffs by the 18 Major Industrialized Countries[a]

Region	Percent of Industry Employment in 1970	Thousands of Workers
New England	−0.06 %	−3.1
Mideast	−0.03	−5.6
Southeast	−0.03	−3.5
Great Lakes	−0.02	−5.4
Great Plains	0.01	0.9
Rocky Mountain	–	–
Southwest	0.01	0.6
Far West	0.01	1.0

Source: Adapted from Baldwin (1976:68–70).

[a]Assumes no reduction in tariffs on agricultural products, textiles, and oil, which are all subject to nontariff barriers.

both consumption and production in the export and import competing industries, and these effects may not always be beneficial to industry employees. In addition, workers will be affected by overall conditions of employment, and by the rate of inflation in the economy, and these effects in turn will color their attitude towards trade.

We shall confine our attention to American labor attitudes toward trade since World War II. Lacking direct information, we will assess these attitudes through politics: congressional voting on the periodic renewals of trade legislation, labor and industry lobbying efforts, and actual implementation of trade policies.

Baldwin (1976) has divided the postwar period into four subperiods. In the first (1945–1950), the Reciprocal Trade Agreements Act, first proposed in 1934, was renewed three times—in 1945, 1948, and 1949. While Republicans generally opposed the Democratic versions of the trade bills, the Truman administration invoked foreign-policy arguments to support its liberal trade policy, and these were effective in the immediate postwar environment. Some concession was made in 1947, however, when President Truman directed that all future trade agreements should include an escape clause permitting the United States to modify or withdraw a concession if increased imports threatened an industry with serious injury. Organized labor apparently supported a liberal trade policy during this period, since it did not actively oppose the renewal of the trade legislation.

In the second subperiod (1951–1961), there was a noticeable erosion of Democratic support for continued trade liberalization. In 1951 a peril-point provision set a limit on tariff reductions the president could negotiate. This provision was supported by many Southern congressmen who were concerned with the effect of increased textile imports on industry in the South. Northern support reflected textile interests as well as the coal, lead, and zinc industries. In 1953–1954, with Eisenhower in office, the traditional Republican protectionist sentiment was combined with stronger protectionism among Democrats, as reflected in the near passage of a trade bill amendment calling for import quotas on petroleum, lead, and zinc. Invocation of the escape clause was made easier in 1955, and the president was empowered to impose quotas on the grounds of national defense. Congressional opposition to the 1958 renewal legislation was lessened by voluntary import quotas on oil and textiles. The administration also invoked cold war arguments in favor of expanding trade among the noncommunist countries and increasing presidential authority to negotiate further tariff reductions with the newly formed European Common Market. It thus appears that during the 1950s the major protectionist interests of American labor were concentrated in particular industries, especially textiles, coal, and oil.

From 1962 to 1967 there was a partial reversal of the protectionism of the 1950s, manifested in the Trade Expansion Act of 1962 which empowered the president over a five-year period to negotiate reductions in tariffs and nontariff barriers. The peril-point provision was considerably weakened, and the escape-clause criteria made more stringent. For the first time, financial adjustment assistance was to be provided to workers and firms injured by increased imports as a result of trade liberalization. To secure passage of the act, the Kennedy administration mollified textile and oil interests by extending mandatory import quotas, and further concessions were offered to the lumber, carpet, and glass industries.

Having paid these political prices, the Kennedy administration went to great lengths in seeking support for the legislation, and it was highly successful. Foreign policy objectives were greatly emphasized, especially the need for authority to negotiate with the Common Market. With special interests—particularly in the textile, oil, and coal industries—having been accommodated, the remainder of organized labor generally appeared to support the administration's initiative. It is also noteworthy that this was a period of very rapid economic expansion coupled with price stability, so that real wages increased substantially.

In the final subperiod (1968 to the present), protectionism again increased, and in recent years it has become extremely powerful. This can be explained in part by the rapid import penetration that began increasingly to affect many industries in the late 1960s. These increased imports were due to a variety of factors, among which were excess demand and increased inflationary pressures, the overvaluation of the U.S. dollar in the waning years of the Bretton Woods System, and increased marketing efforts in the United States by foreign manufacturers, especially those in West Germany and Japan. Also contributing to the rise in protectionism were the increased foreign direct investment activities of many U.S. manufacturers, sometimes resulting in increased imports, other times creating the impression that American workers were being displaced by investments made abroad rather than at home. The 1969–1970 recession also did not help.

By 1970 the AFL–CIO strongly favored a system of import quotas limiting foreign import penetration; until that time it had always supported a liberal trade policy. The AFL–CIO was not only concerned with job displacement. It was also disenchanted with the administration of the adjustment assistance program, whose provisions were interpreted so narrowly that not a single favorable decision affecting labor was made between 1962 and late 1969. The steelworkers were among the most important unions embracing protectionism in the late 1960s. Combining their interests with those of management, the industry was successful in obtaining voluntary export restraints from the Europeans and Japanese in 1968.

Not all the unions supported protectionism at this time, however. This is indicated in Table 4, which shows the positions of both labor and management. Each industry's trade balance in 1967 is also given, marking individual industries as net exporters or importers.

Of the thirty-three industries listed, management preferences were nine for freer trade, eighteen for protectionism, four in between, and two not available. The preferences of organized labor for freer trade coincided with management

Table 4

Positions of Management and Organized Labor on U.S. Trade Policy as Expressed in May/June 1973 Congressional Hearings

Industry	1967 Trade Balance (million $)	Management Position[a]	Organized Labor Position[a]
Poultry	$ 41	F	n.a.
Dairy	– 1	P	n.a.
Distilling	– 416	P	P
Soybeans	320	F	F
Tobacco	130	P	F
Textiles	– 418	P	P
Apparel	– 486	P	P
Paper	– 632	F	F
Chemicals	81	P	P–M
Plastics	527	P	P
Petroleum	– 505	F	P
Rubber	92	M	P–M
Rubber shoes	– 82	P	P
Leather	– 364	P	P
Shoes	– 471	P	P
Stone, etc.	12	P	P
Iron and steel	– 1,923	P	P
Lead and zinc	– 137	M	n.a.
Aluminum	– 95	F	M
Cutlery	– 16	P	P?
Hardware	38	P	P
Machinery	4,029	F	F
Tractors	146	F	F?
Machine tools	25	M	P
Bearings	23	P	P?
Business equipment	– 21	P	M?
Electrical	701	M	P
Cars	– 1,730	n.a.	P
Trucks	1,203	F	F
Aviation	1,695	F	F
Bicycles	– 296	P	n.a.
Watches	– 126	P	P
Toys	– 51	n.a.	P

Source: Adapted from Magee (1977).

[a]F = freer trade; P = protectionist; M = in between; ? = guess of author; n.a. = not available.

preferences in six of the nine cases. With respect to protectionism, labor and management preferences coincided in fourteen of the eighteen cases. Evidence thus suggests that organized labor is more protectionist than not, but that there is significant support for freer trade, particularly in some important durable goods industries.

In view of increasing protectionism since the late 1960s, it is surprising that the Nixon administration could get Congress to agree to the Trade Reform Act of 1974, which gave the president further substantial authority to negotiate reductions in tariff and nontariff barriers. In part, this can be explained by the strong leadership role that the administration took on trade policy, together with the blunting of some key protectionist forces, particularly in the textile and steel industries where import quota arrangements were renewed and extended. In addition, the administration stressed the need for further negotiating authority to strengthen U.S. economic interests, to combat foreign protectionism, and to guarantee supply access to foreign-produced raw materials. It also pressed for liberalization of adjustment assistance to deal with job displacement resulting from increased imports.

The granting of presidential authority to negotiate reductions in tariff and nontariff barriers gave new life to the Tokyo Round of multilateral tariff negotiations, scheduled to end in 1979. Protectionist forces nonetheless continued to mount in the United States and elsewhere, in part because of the pronounced slowing down of economic activity that occurred here and abroad beginning in 1974. This made it more difficult for certain industries to respond to import competition, and in several instances management and labor interests applied pressure to institute import restrictions. Thus, while the U.S. has been engaged in a further round of trade liberalization, voluntary export restraints and orderly market arrangements have been imposed in such important industries as shoes and color televisions. Also, a trigger-price system for limiting steel imports into the United States was introduced in early 1978.

Our review of U.S. trade policy since the end of World War II has revealed a pronounced change in the attitude of American labor towards trade. Protectionism was important in the textile, coal, oil, and certain other smaller industries during the 1950s, but organized labor was otherwise favorable to a liberal trade policy. In the early 1960s the Kennedy administration succeeded in obtaining unprecedented authority to pursue multilateral trade liberalization, and it was able to halt and in part reverse some of the protectionist forces that had gathered strength in the 1950s.

Beginning in the late 1960s and continuing until the present, there has been a marked increase in protectionism, responding both to increased imports in many sectors and to the alleged job displacement associated with overseas investment activities of American companies. Management and labor in import-competing industries have combined forces in seeking protection against imports, whereas in several export industries the two groups have been favorable to a liberal trade policy.

Consumer interests have in recent years become increasingly vocal in criticizing import restrictions for raising prices to consumers. On the one hand, consumer benefits from liberal trade policies are spread over the population as a whole, and these benefits vary according to levels of income and consumption of domestic and imported goods. In contrast, workers in particular industries, regions, and occupations may be displaced because of increased imports; it is therefore not surprising that labor's attitude toward trade is shaped primarily by its role in production rather than in consumption.

CONCLUSION

The effects of trade on labor are far from uniform. They will depend for particular workers on (1) their consumption patterns, (2) the relative abundance of services they supply compared to their availability in the rest of the world, (3) the exposure to trade of their industries of employment and of other industries which buy their products, and (4) the exposure of other major employers in their community. It is quite possible, then, for a significant part of the labor force to be adversely affected by trade, either in the short run, the long run, or both.

This result does not contradict the traditional economic proposition that free trade is beneficial for the country as a whole. For that proposition has long been regarded as valid only if a move to free trade can be accompanied by a suitable redistribution of income, so that those who would otherwise lose from trade can be compensated by those who would gain. And we continue to regard that proposition—which essentially says that such redistribution is, in principle, possible so as to leave everyone better off—as a persuasive case for free trade as a long-run policy objective. To maintain restrictions on trade indefinitely is to incur a permanent loss of economic efficiency, and this loss will be a cost not only to the current generation, but to all succeeding generations as well.

But the move to free trade is costly for certain individuals and groups within the economy, particularly in the short run. Indeed, this is true of any change in trade or trade policy. Such costs should be considered in deciding how best to pursue the objective of free trade. And they are important even if free trade is never attained, since they suggest policy tools for restricting trade that minimize adverse effects.

Costs and benefits of trade to individual workers are of two kinds. Some are temporary, and arise from the inability of workers or firms to adjust rapidly to changing market conditions. Most of the effects discussed in the sections on labor in industry and in the community, and some of those discussed in the second section, are of this kind. They last only until workers move among locations, industries, or occupations sufficiently to equalize the wages of all workers of comparable ability. Other costs and benefits, however, are permanent and will not disappear, no matter how long we wait, for they represent changes in scarcity returns (economic rents). Unskilled workers in the United States, for example, through their scarcity, achieve a higher real wage than their counterparts elsewhere in the world, so long as trade is restricted. This is a "rent" which they will lose if they are forced by free trade to compete with the vast pool of unskilled labor around the world. Likewise, particular individuals who happen to have an unusual preference for goods produced abroad gain a kind of rent as consumers when free trade gives them access to a cheaper supply of those goods. And finally, members of an occupation who, through a labor union, restrict entry into their occupation, earn a scarcity rent that will be lost if trade is free.

This distinction between temporary and permanent costs and benefits is not, of course, clear cut. Where costs of training are high, for example, one might regard a change in the wage of a particular skilled occupation as permanent, since a member of that occupation is unlikely to recoup such a loss in his lifetime. But if we take a longer view and recognize that training must begin anew with each succeeding generation, then wage differentials among occupations must return to levels which just compensate for differences in costs of training.

It might seem logical that the permanent rather than temporary costs of trade liberalization would cause most concern to the affected workers. But this need not be the case, since the present value of permanent costs may be small compared to the immediate temporary costs. And in fact, as we have seen in our historical discussion, the temporary costs do seem to give rise to the most vocal worker objections. Traditionally, workers have voiced less concern over their long-run interests as consumers, or over the relative wages of skilled versus unskilled workers, than they have over the more immediate effects on their community, their industry, or their occupation. It thus seems reasonable to focus our policy analysis on ameliorating these temporary costs.

Since the topic of adjustment assistance is dealt with elsewhere in this volume, we will limit our remarks to the simple observation that even if adjustment assistance can be administratively feasible and effective, it can at best solve only part of the problem. For if adjustment costs are real to the workers themselves, they are also a real cost to the economy as a whole. Adjustment assistance merely transfers the burden of these costs from particular individuals to the economy at large, and will do nothing toward reducing the costs themselves.

To reduce these costs, trade policy should be managed in such a way as to make changes in trade occur only gradually and predictably. Gradual changes can be accommodated at little or no cost if achieved through normal turnover in the labor market. Many workers change jobs frequently and of their own volition, and often these moves include changes in location and/or industry of employment. So long as adjustment requires no greater movement of workers than the number who would be moving anyway, it entails no extra costs.

Even gradual adjustment, however, can be costly if it is not predictable. Workers decide where to move in part on the basis of current or expected conditions in various labor markets. If a change cannot be predicted, then actual wages or employment must change to provide these signals, and the economy must bear this additional cost of adjustment. If, on the other hand, it is known in advance that, say, employment will need to decline in a particular location, industry, or occupation, then this information by itself can discourage workers from entering that market, and the decline can be achieved through turnover without any decline in the wage or increase in the unemployment rate.

Thus, if we are to pursue the goal of free trade by reducing tariffs and other barriers to trade, these reductions should be spread out over a considerable period. The timing of reductions should be determined and announced well in advance. If possible, their effects on the trade patterns, production, and employment should be accurately forecast and publicized in order to permit workers to plan for the future and accommodate themselves to the changes without significant dislocation.

A second policy implication follows from this analysis, and seems to suggest an argument for protection. The costs we have discussed as resulting from trade liberalization arise as well from other changes in trade patterns. Therefore, to reduce adjustment costs arising from other disturbances, it would seem that we should actively seek to smooth out the effects of these disturbances and to make them more gradual. One could thus argue that a surge in imports should be met with increased protection, to be removed gradually over time.

This argument is questionable, however, for two reasons. First, as with almost all arguments for protection, trade restriction provides only a second-best tool for achieving the desired result. Since adjustment poses a problem only in the labor market—adjustment in consumption being accomplished much more readily—the appropriate tool here is a subsidy to employment rather than a tariff. Second, if such a policy were pursued with either a tariff or other policy tools, there would be danger that the public would perceive it as preventing adjustment rather than as facilitating it. The plan to remove protection gradually over time would attract much less attention and credibility than would its initial imposition. As a result, the crucial feature of predictability would be lost and a reduction in adjustment costs might not be achieved after all.

Finally, we would note that if a country chooses to maintain protection indefinitely in spite of the usual economic arguments against it, the interests of labor and the costs of labor-market adjustment should be considered in deciding which policy tools to use. The principal tools of protection in use today are tariffs, quotas, and negotiated export restraints. These tools differ in the extent to which they permit changes in the domestic and world economies to be accommodated gradually and predictably.

No clear case can be made among these policies in terms of the gradational changes they permit. Quantitative restrictions, which include both quotas and export restraints, generally insulate domestic markets from changes originating abroad more effectively than do tariffs. But quantitative restrictions also tend to contain, and thus exaggerate, the effects of disturbances originating domestically. Thus an increase in supply of imports will not affect domestic markets if a quantitative restriction is in place, but will depress prices and output of import-competing goods under a tariff. A decline in domestic demand for a product, on the other hand, can appear partly as a decline in imports if no quantitative restriction is currently binding, but must be fully reflected in a reduced domestic output if a quantitative restriction is already in place and effective. The choice among policies depends, therefore, in part on whether disturbances are expected to originate at home or abroad.

For predictability, however, we feel that tariffs are preferable to the other alternatives. First, continual change in world and domestic markets, plus the general growth over time of the world economy and trade, necessitate repeated changes in the quantities of imports to be admitted under a quota or negotiated as an export restraint. These changes are unlikely to be predictable, and will certainly not be announced far in advance. Thus they serve poorly as a guide to planning by any market participant. Tariffs, on the other hand, are simple percentage taxes on imports and need not be changed frequently at all. Their effects can therefore be predicted much more readily in planning for the future.

9

MALCOLM D. BALE

Adjustment Assistance: Dealing with Import-Displaced Workers

The effect of trade liberalization on income redistribution. The Trade Expansion Acts of 1962, 1974. Benefits and problems of free trade. Unemployment, counseling, and retraining. Justification of assistance—efficiency, equity, politics. Profile of the displaced worker. Financial penalties of displacement. Adjustment assistance legislation in 1978.

The elimination of trade-protection devices in general increases a country's real income. Yet, while significant progress toward reducing trade impediments between countries has been made, many barriers still remain. The most likely reason is the income redistribution that accompanies trade liberalization. Consumers benefit when a tariff is lowered, but firms and their workers producing domestic substitutes are made worse off.[1] This results because displaced labor and capital are not immediately absorbed into alternative uses, and also because they may earn less in subsequent employment. Although it is possible for the gainers to compensate the losers and still end up as gainers, full compensation usually is not provided.

This chapter will focus on trade adjustment assistance, the various ways in which government assists the victims of foreign competition and encourages them to adjust to a change in the economy. We will begin by outlining criteria for receiving adjustment assistance for workers, and discuss why it is preferable to alternatives. We will then review the U.S. experience with worker adjustment assistance, and consider current benefits available under U.S. law. Finally, we will consider why, despite the help given many thousands of workers, adjustment assistance is still controversial in the eyes of organized labor—and what might be done about it.

COMPENSATION UNDER TRADE ADJUSTMENT ASSISTANCE

Adjustment assistance for workers and firms injured by foreign trade was first introduced in the Trade Expansion Act of 1962. Since there was no precedent either in the United States or abroad for a program that compensated domestic interests injured specifically by international merchandise movements, the 1962 program was a radical departure from previously accepted trade policy.

Partly because of the uncertain costs of the program and partly because of its novelty, eligibility criteria for assistance were made very restrictive and few petitioners actually received any benefits.[2] In the first eight years of its life, no workers or firms were found to be eligible; before it was replaced, total assistance amounted to only $69 million and involved only 47,000 workers (Haberler 1950:131).

As a result of unworkable eligibility criteria, the requirements were relaxed considerably in the Trade Act of 1974, and workers' benefits were expanded. Tables 1 and 2 summarize eligibility requirements and program benefits under the new and old trade acts, respectively. The primary change is that workers no longer must prove that increased imports are the major cause of their unemployment, and that the increased imports result primarily from prior trade concessions. Under the 1962 act, if factors or business conditions other than trade concessions could be shown to have caused increased imports and unemployment, the petitioners were denied assistance. The 1974 act softens this condition considerably, and only requires that prior concessions be a "cause which is important but not necessarily more important than any other cause."

Because criteria for obtaining assistance have been relaxed, and because of major competitive changes occurring in world trade, the number of successful worker petitions has substantially increased. As of 28 February 1978, approximately 50 percent of 2,300 completed worker petitions have been declared eligible for assistance. In fiscal year 1976 alone, more than 435,000 workers received allowances amounting to more than $1.3 billion (USDL 1978). This dramatically increases the average annual expenditures, which were less than $6 million under the old trade act.

THE RATIONALE FOR ADJUSTMENT ASSISTANCE

Tariff reductions and quota liberalizations are typically "staged." Changes occur in announced steps over a number

Table 1

Worker Eligibility Criteria for Trade-Adjustment Assistance

Trade Expansion Act of 1962	Trade Act of 1974
1. Imports	
Articles like or directly competitive with those produced by the applicant are being imported in increased quantities.	Articles like or directly competitive with those produced by the applicant are being imported in greater absolute or proportional quantities.
2. Displacement	
Sales or production at the workers' firm must have declined. Workers concerned must be unemployed or underemployed, or threatened with either.	Sales or production at the workers' firm must have declined. A significant number or proportion of workers in a firm have been or are threatened with total or partial layoff.
3. Causation	
Increased imports must be the major factor causing unemployment or underemployment. Increased imports must be in major part the results of trade concessions granted under the trade agreement.	Imports must have contributed importantly to the separation of workers.

Source: Paraphrased from the statutory language of 19 U.S.C. Sec. 1901 and Sec. 221, P.L. 93–618.

Table 2
Worker Benefits under Trade-Adjustment Assistance

Trade Expansion Act of 1962	Trade Act of 1974
1. Adjustment Allowance	
A weekly adjustment allowance of 65 percent of the workers' average weekly wage, but not to exceed 65 percent of the average weekly manufacturing wage, for up to 52 weeks with up to 26 weeks extension for workers in training or workers over 60 years old.	A weekly adjustment allowance of 70 percent of the workers' average weekly wage, but not to exceed 70 percent of the average weekly manufacturing wage, for up to 52 weeks with up to 26 weeks extension for workers in training or workers over 60 years old.
2. Employment Services	
Training, testing, counseling, and placement services provided under other federal laws.	Training, testing, counseling, placement services, and other services through cooperating state agencies.
3. Relocation Allowance	
If a worker has a job offer in another area and the worker is a family head, then a relocation allowance covering family moving expenses plus a lump-sum payment of 2.5 times the average weekly manufacturing wage will be paid to the worker.	Workers who wish to move to another area may receive a relocation allowance of 80 percent of the necessary relocation expenses plus a lump-sum payment of 3 times the worker's average weekly wage, up to $500.
4. Other Allowance	
For travel to distant training centers grant 10 cents per mile plus a $5 per day subsistence allowance.	Job-search allowance of 80 percent of a worker's job-search expenses up to $500.

Source: Trade Expansion Act of 1962, Secs. 321–330, and Trade Act of 1974, Secs. 231–238.

of years in order to lessen firm and worker displacements in any one year and facilitate their adjustment. Staged liberalization, however, does not eliminate the case for adjustment assistance, since adjustment still must occur, albeit at a slower rate. Affected labor and business organizations have characterized staging as a process of "slow torturing to death." And firms will often remain in production rather than adjust, in hopes that protection will be restored if they can demonstrate the severity of their experience with the initial staged reductions.

Reduced trade barriers mean increased trade. This change will have the effect of reducing employment in import-competing industries and transferring workers into export and nontraded industries where they are more efficiently employed. The problem, therefore, is essentially temporary. But even temporary employment problems are not painless. Some workers may be unemployed for long periods; many workers may find that their skills are insufficient in today's labor market; other workers may have to relocate to find suitable employment. In short, the problems that displaced workers face cannot simply be assumed away.

Adjustment assistance confronts this problem. It mitigates the shocks of lowered trade barriers. It also distributes the benefits of freer trade more equitably between those who gain as consumers and those who bear the cost as producers.

There are at least three grounds on which adjustment assistance programs may be warranted. The first is that of efficiency: when the loss to society caused by a worker being unemployed exceeds the loss to the worker himself (see Bale [1976:245], Feldstein [1978:155] for examples). Assistance may also be justified on equity or distributional grounds, when government compensates individuals or groups because they have been injured by a specific government action. The final ground is political—to achieve larger social objectives, and to remove obstructive retaliatory voting and lobbying by those injured. In the case of an expansionist trade policy, a viable worker adjustment program is necessary to receive even lukewarm support by organized labor.

Eligibility criteria should differ for each of these justifications: When the justification is economic *efficiency,* assistance should be given when expenditures increasing worker employability are cost-effective (the direct cause of unemployment should be immaterial). When the reason is political, assistance should be given to neutralize political opposition and on the basis of political clout.

When compensation is given for reasons of equity, identifying the cause of injury becomes critical. If a government is to compensate a party for injury that the government has caused, then that cause or injury must be demonstrated. Under the Trade Expansion Act of 1962, eligibility depended on a showing that imports had increased because of trade concessions granted by the government, and that the increased imports were the major cause of unemployment. This double linkage between cause and effect and between effect and injury was very restrictive, and it indicated that the primary motivation for assistance under the old act was equity.

Under the existing legislation, efficiency criteria are emphasized, and equity considerations have become considerably less important. Yet the legislation could go considerably further than it currently does if efficiency considerations are paramount. Although Congress clearly intended that the program facilitate reemployment, the major program expenditures have been in the form of supplemental unemployment benefits rather than in the form of retraining and relocation expenditures. While unemployment compensation does facilitate job-search, it is perhaps a less effective—and certainly a less direct—means of securing reemployment than is retraining and relocation. The political pressures exerted by organized labor on policymakers are also apparent in the legislation and in recently suggested changes. The 1974 act is considerably more flexible, allows for more rapid delivery of benefits, and provides for somewhat more generous payments than did the earlier program.

CHARACTERISTICS OF TRADE-DISPLACED WORKERS AND THE REEMPLOYMENT PROCESS

Since U.S. adjustment assistance programs for workers have existed for more than a decade, it is now possible—from case studies on workers laid off in the early 1970s by firms engaged in manufacturing shoes, pianos, stainless-steel flatware, textiles, glass products, and radio electronics—to identify characteristics typical of trade-displaced workers and to evaluate the program's effectiveness on worker adjustment.[3]

Typically, workers displaced by imports have a low level of formal education—more than 60 percent have not completed high school—and occupy such low-skill occupations as machine operators, assemblers, fabricators, and the like. A few are clerks, foremen, and salesmen. The average age of import-displaced workers (about forty-four) is higher than the average age of the national work force. Many of the workers are over sixty. An unusually high proportion, sometimes as much as half, are female.

The profile which emerges is that trade-displaced workers possess characteristics which make them less employable than average U.S. production workers. They come from traditional, low-skill, high-labor industries, they are older than the average U.S. worker, a high proportion are females, and they have minimal formal education. The mean duration of unemployment is around forty weeks—nearly four times the national average.[4] Some workers fail to find reemployment after being displaced for more than one year, others become discouraged and cease to actively seek work, and a few take early retirement.

The situation is sometimes exacerbated by the fact that the firm from which workers are displaced is the sole major employer in a small community. Opportunities for reemployment in that community are, therefore, minimal. This is the case, for example, in several New England communities where footwear firms have ceased production.

THE EFFECT OF ADJUSTMENT ASSISTANCE

What effect did the adjustment assistance program have on trade-displaced workers? Interesting but contradictory results emerge from different studies.

One early study (Bale 1976:245), using regression techniques to control on socioeconomic characteristics, found that otherwise identical displaced workers who received counseling and training experienced longer durations of unemployment and found lower-paying employment than those workers who did not receive the benefits. This occurred at a time when the program was in its infancy, and when delays in the delivery of benefits were occurring. The explanation proposed for these results was that the more employable or more motivated workers (characteristics not detected in the regression) did not wait for assistance services, but sought reemployment on their own. Only those workers who were severely disadvantaged remained unemployed until they received the benefits.

A more recent work (Bale and Miller 1977:13) compared the experience of workers who received adjustment benefits within one month of layoff with workers who experienced longer delays in receiving benefits. The study confirms the importance of expeditious delivery of those benefits. Displaced workers came from two footwear firms located in small New England cities, and the members of each group were identical in many respects, with the exception of their adjustment experience.

Since footwear firms have been declining in the United States, and especially in the Northeast, displaced workers were forced to find other occupations at the outset. Of workers who received benefits rapidly, 27 percent participated in retraining programs and 81 percent accepted individual job counseling and testing. They currently hold employment as sheet-metal workers, food processors, construction workers, nurses, secretaries, plastic workers, and truck drivers. The most dramatic result of the analysis, in which other explanatory variables were controlled, was that workers who received counseling and adjustment payments punctually following layoff from their trade-impacted firm, received $1.03 per hour more in their new employment than did otherwise equivalent trade-displaced workers, and their mean current wage was higher than when they were employed at the footwear firms. At the same time, they remained unemployed for a much longer time than other workers sampled—which suggests that training itself increased their measured duration of unemployment, that the adjustment payments allowed them time to conduct a more thorough job search, and that they did not need to accept their first job offer. The last factor, of course, would also account for part of their higher wage in relation to nonassisted workers.

Two strong conclusions emerge. First, adjustment benefits must be delivered to workers promptly after their layoff in order to effectively provide assistance during the transitional unemployment period. Second, training and relocation benefits are crucial to program success, since the typical trade-displaced worker comes from a low-skill industry, and skills acquired in the trade-impacted job frequently cannot be transferred to other occupations. The relocation benefits are important, because it may be necessary for workers to move from areas of economic stagnation to areas of growth. This aspect becomes especially relevant if the trade-impacted industry is geographically concentrated so that many firms of the same industry in one region are forced to close.

PECUNIARY LOSSES OF TRADE-DISPLACED WORKERS

Workers displaced by foreign imports appear to suffer considerable financial lossess—which government compensation usually does not entirely counterbalance.

A primary cause of a worker's loss occurs during the period of transitional unemployment. One study (Bale and Mutti 1978:278)* of workers displaced from the footwear industry found that, during his period of transitional unemployment, the average worker forfeited wages of $3,899 and received an average of $2,426 in adjustment allowance and unemployment insurance. This left him with a net loss of $1,473.[5]

A second cause of the displaced worker's loss is that his wages fall. The study shows that the displaced worker suffers an annual loss of $1,805 in reduced wages when he finds reemployment, a loss which occurs despite an additional two hours per week worked in the new lower-paying position. To calculate the total loss to the displaced worker, the annual loss must be discounted and summed over the remaining twenty years of his productive life.

The absolute size of the annual loss will depend upon the growth rate of real wages in the shoe industry versus wages received in alternative employment. The study presents evidence that the growth rate of wages in manufacturing was slightly lower than that for shoes, and if this relationship continues into the future, the absolute difference increases. If the displaced worker is fortunate enough to find a job in a sector with faster growing wages, such as trade and services where the real wage growth was more rapid, continuation of these growth rates would result in a smaller loss and conceivably in some monetary gain to the individual. Discounting these flows at 6 percent, the present value of the loss to the displaced worker will be $24,311 if his wage in alternative employment grows at the average rate for all manufacturing, and $23,181 if his wage in alternative employment grows at the average rate for trade and services.

Adding the loss from unemployment to this figure yields a significant personal financial loss to the displaced worker. Trade adjustment assistance payments have not adequately

*Information used with permission from the *Journal of Human Resources*.

compensated the shoe worker for the loss incurred during his transitory unemployment, let alone indemnified him for lost earnings over the rest of his lifetime.

Other studies, one using a sample of workers from several industries (Bale 1976:245) and the other using a case study of a footwear firm (Bale and Miller 1977:13), have found that in certain cases workers *have* been adequately compensated for their financial losses, especially those who have found higher paying jobs. This, however, is probably an atypical outcome which the adjustment assistance program should strive to achieve. Even though program benefits are limited to the period of unemployment, counseling services and readjustment allowances should promote more careful and efficient job search, thereby minimizing the wages lost. Retraining should increase employment skills, conceivably allowing workers to receive even higher wages. For a variety of reasons, these goals have not always been realized.

THE FUTURE OF ADJUSTMENT ASSISTANCE

Over the years, the trade adjustment assistance program has been sharply criticized by labor and business as providing "too little too late" for those injured by increasing imports. Some labor leaders have even suggested that "trade adjustment assistance as a meaningful answer to jobs lost from imports is an idea whose time has passed" (Biemiller 1972). But like any new program, adjustment assistance changes with time, as experience and constituent demands indicate areas of need and improvement.

The Trade Act of 1974 provided for more generous benefits, easier eligibility, and more streamlined delivery than did the Trade Expansion Act of 1962. In April 1978 a bill to further improve the operation of the adjustment assistance program was reported out of committee, but died in the final days of the 95th Congress (USHR 1978). It proposes steps for simplifying the procedure for applying for assistance, and clarifies the wording of various clauses. It also would allow the Secretary of Labor to file an application on behalf of workers, and instructs him to provide full information to affected workers on the benefits available under this and other federal programs. The bill enlarges benefits by extending adjustment allowances an additional fifty-two weeks for workers taking retraining, and reimburses 100 percent of job search and relocation costs, up to $600 per worker.

Sentiment for reform of the adjustment assistance provisions is still strong, and reintroduction of this or a similar bill may be anticipated in the next Congress. The job for economists, program administrators, and interested labor groups is to design, improve, and perfect a program that meets the legitimate needs of displaced workers and of society.

As in the past, periods of trade liberalization and periods of retrenchment from a free-trade posture will occur in the future throughout the world. Likewise, changes in the competitiveness of products from country to country will occur as an inevitable consequence of a dynamic world. Adjustments to changing conditions are, therefore, going to continue, requiring a continual need for adjustment assistance. Similarly, as economic conditions change and as more experience is gained with the adjustment provisions, so it will evolve toward a program that more closely meets the needs of workers. The ultimate objective of freer trade and adjustment assistance is to improve the commonweal of every individual in society.

10

ROBERT O. KEOHANE

The International Political Economy of the 1980s*

The linkage between economic interdependence and political power. National sensitivity and vulnerability in international transactions. Bretton Woods and trade liberalization. Shifts in international economic strength. Industrial and nonindustrial economies. Four possible scenarios for the 1980s. The new international economic order.

*An earlier version of this paper was given at an international symposium on "Southeast Asia in a Changing World," Institute of Developing Economies, Tokyo, 15–17 March 1978.

International politics and economics cannot be sharply differentiated from one another, because economic interdependence turns economic power into a potential source of political power. International economic regimes, which are affected by political as well as by economic factors, provide rules and norms within which economic transactions take place. The postwar international economic regimes currently are eroding as a result of changing power relationships among advanced states, new definitions by the United States of its leadership role, increases in the price of oil, and pervasive economic difficulties. Although a reconstruction of these regimes under some form of collective leadership is in the interest of governing elites in the major countries, it will be difficult to achieve. Indeed, retrogression toward more protectionist economic arrangements that discriminate against poor, weak countries seems more likely. Proponents of a "new international economic order" (NIEO) may therefore find the 1980s worse than the 1960s, rather than better, and even the rich countries may find it increasingly difficult to maintain a reasonably open and cooperative world economy.

Since at least 1971 the conventional but misleading distinction between "international politics" and "international economics" has become increasingly difficult to maintain, even as a convenient fiction. Economic transactions have always depended on the political structure of the world, and political developments have had to be consistent with trends of economic change.[1] During the late 1950s and early 1960s, however, this connection was obscured by a separation at the level of bargaining between political and economic issues among industrialized, capitalist countries. This two-track system allowed trade and monetary negotiations to take place without *explicit* linkages to politico-military issues (Cooper 1972–73). The separation between economic and political issues in the bargaining realm began to break down late in the 1960s—not only in North-South relations, with the formation of the United Nations Conference on Trade and Development (UNCTAD) and demands by poor countries for political action to construct new economic arrangements, but in negotiations among the advanced capitalist countries as well. The United States linked maintenance of its troops in Europe with German offset payments, and began to use its political power to alter Japan's financial and trade policies (Treverton 1978). President Nixon's monetary and trade "shocks" of 1971 dramatized the links between economics and "high politics," which were further reinforced by the Arab oil embargo of 1973–1974. Economists may attempt to ignore politics, and strategists may still conduct their esoteric discussions without taking economic developments into account, but neither group of experts can offer more than an arbitrary and conventional disciplinary justification for this separation. Top policymakers, and observers who want to understand contemporary world politics and economics, have to struggle with the relationship between the two.

The first struggle is to understand the setting of foreign economic policy—in particular, how economic interdependence is related to political power, and how these linkages operate in the contemporary world. These issues will be addressed in the first part of this chapter. The second part will consider the erosion of international economic regimes; it will be particularly concerned with political as well as economic sources of that erosion, and with what the advanced industrialized countries could do about it. We will then present four possible scenarios in world political economy that may be, to some degree, plausible for the 1980s. Finally, we will briefly look at implications for the nonindustrialized countries, and at their demands for a new international economic order: how much better will the NIEO be?

ECONOMIC INTERDEPENDENCE AND POLITICAL POWER

Between 1950 and the present, international economic transactions increased sharply. Countries such as the United States, that had been relatively insulated from foreign trade in the past, have shown the greatest recent increases in the ratio of trade to gross national product (GNP). In 1960 U.S. foreign trade (exports plus imports) accounted for only about 7 percent of GNP; in 1970 for almost 9 percent; and in 1976 for almost 14 percent. Until 1973, growth in trade as well as investment took place disproportionately among the advanced capitalist states, but since that year industrialized countries have been spending more of their available funds on imports of fuels and raw materials. Between 1973 and 1976, for example, the U.S. trade deficit for fuels more than quadrupled, from $6.5 billion to $29 billion, with a further rise to well over $30 billion in 1977. At the same time the positive balance for aircraft, computers, and other advanced goods has been increasing, while older industries such as textiles, other consumer goods, and steel have been under pressure from new Third World producers as well as other manufacturers in the industrialized areas of the world.

These trade figures understate the rise in economic transactions, since they are overshadowed by increases in borrowing and lending in the wake of the oil price rises of 1973–1974. At the end of 1976, external bank claims on nonbanks totaled $326 billion worldwide, up 60 percent from year-end 1974; borrowing in international capital markets doubled, between 1973 and 1976, to $60 billion per year. Between 1970 and 1976 nominal debt of less-developed countries increased by 140 percent; real debt by about 40 percent.[2]

We must be cautious in inferring from these figures that international interdependence has increased proportionately. Interdependence implies risk: countries depending on others for goods, markets, or funds will be damaged if trading or financial relationships are disrupted or if the terms of trade or finance become adverse. For transactions to imply interdependence, potential changes in the transaction patterns must involve costs for the parties involved. Without such costs, there is no dependence; hence the political implications of the relationship are sharply limited.

Most patterns of transactions indeed entail potential costs, but these are not necessarily proportionate to the financial magnitude of the transactions. For the industrialized countries, imports of manufactured goods that they produce themselves (such as automobiles) have quite different implications for interdependence than do imports of raw materials that they cannot produce (such as petroleum for Japan, most of Europe, and, increasingly, the United States). To analyze changes in dependence and interdependence, it is necessary to keep in mind a key distinction between *sensitivity interdependence* and *vulnerability interdependence*. Sensitivity is measured by the costly effects on a country of changes in international transactions *within an established framework of policy*. The more adversely a country is affected by a change before changing its own policies to react to it, the more sensitive it is to that change. Vulnerability, by contrast, can be defined as a country's liability to suffer costs of changes in international transactions even *after its own policies have been altered*. Vulnerability can therefore only be assessed in the medium to long term, since it is difficult to change policies quickly.[3]

If a country is sensitive to changes in its international transactions, but not vulnerable to them, it can avoid long-term costs of changes by adjusting its own policies. Thus it is not dependent in a politically profound sense; its fate is not determined by others. But a vulnerable country finds that its dependence is a threat to its political autonomy. This has long been recognized by observers in poor countries, and it is reflected in the *dependencia* school of writers, largely from Latin America.[4] But it is also true for an industrialized country such as Japan, which relies on imports for virtually all of its oil and on manufactured exports for foreign exchange. In general, we can think of *asymmetrical vulnerability interdependence* as a fundamental basis of political power for actors that are relatively less dependent than their partners, and as a source of weakness for those that are relatively more dependent.

Interdependence is thus not simply a benign economic phenomenon, despite some of the rhetoric on the subject that emanated from the United States between 1973 and 1976.

Most interdependent relationships are asymmetrical; if they involve significant vulnerabilities, they become instruments for manipulation, pressure, or even threats. As an instrument for power, Germany carefully constructed such asymmetrically interdependent relationships between itself and its smaller neighbors in the 1930s. The United States, in its relationships with Japan, has benefited politically from similar asymmetries, although there is no evidence that American policymakers deliberately set out to make Japan dependent for this purpose. The major oil-producing countries of the Organization of Petroleum Exporting Countries (OPEC) have benefited from a situation that was even less of their making; paradoxically, it was their *weakness* in the 1950s and early 1960s that led to low oil prices and increased dependence of the industrialized countries on imports of petroleum. Yet the result—asymmetrical patterns of interdependence that conferred political power on the less dependent—was the same for the OPEC countries as for Germany in the 1930s and the United States after World War II (Hirschman 1945, 1969).

The concept of asymmetrical vulnerability helps us to see the connection between economic interdependence and power as usually conceived in world politics. Economic interdependence does affect the ability of governments to attain their objectives by influencing the behavior of other states. Yet political bargaining in world politics takes place within a structure of relations that is only partially determined by economic factors. At any given time, *international regimes* may exist that embody implicit and explicit rules for state behavior in a particular issue area, such as trade or monetary affairs. These regimes are constructed through the use of political influence, and persist in part because of the continuing activities of governments and the international organizations to which they belong. Governments may regard these regimes as important to their own autonomy, prestige, or influence in the world—as well as to their economic well-being (Keohane and Nye 1977: Chapters 1, 3–6).

A tightly connected set of such regimes existed as the "Bretton Woods System" until 1971. Liberalization of international trade and capital movements had taken place within the context, since 1958, of convertibility at pegged exchange rates between major currencies and the convertibility (rather nominal after 1968) of dollars into gold. Since the late 1960s these regimes have been subjected to great stress, and have been substantially altered. Exchange rates fluctuate under a regime that provides only the most general guidelines for governmental and central bank intervention. Trade liberalization has been reversed, at least temporarily, during the last several years. The world political economy appears to be in flux, because the established regimes—the rules and norms for behavior—seem threatened with collapse, or at least with decay. The key question for world political economy today is whether these regimes can be maintained relatively intact, or whether a new set of regimes will be constructed. Otherwise, more intense conflict in world political economy is likely to ensue.

THE EROSION OF INTERNATIONAL ECONOMIC REGIMES

Since the end of World War II, international economic regimes have been favorable to advanced industrialized countries, and to industrializing countries such as Japan in the 1950s and South Korea in the 1960s and 1970s. The United States has benefited economically from the arrangements, and has had the further privilege of exercising political leadership; but its partners have experienced even greater economic growth. In the 1950s, and for the first few years of the 1960s, the United States facilitated this growth by being content to play the role of balancer in the international monetary system, adjusting to the desires for reserves and the preferred exchange rates of other states. The U.S. market was the most open of industrialized country markets to Japanese goods in the 1950s, and to other exports from poor but growing economies thereafter (apart from those having special trade relations with the European Economic Community [EEC]). The American military umbrella allowed a number of protected states, such as Japan, to concentrate virtually all their energies on civilian technology and production. United States domination of the Middle East helped to keep oil prices low. Europeans and Japanese were naturally uncomfortable with their subordinate political position, and they feared that erratic or rash American behavior might involve them in war. But from an economic point of view, the arrangements existing between 1950 and 1971 were unprecedentedly favorable for these countries.

One result of the growth of the European economies and of Japan in the 1950s and 1960s was a narrowing of the gap in power (as well as in wealth) between those countries and the United States. The United States remained the most important actor in world political economy, but it was no longer as dominant as it previously had been. With increased competition, the economic price paid for leadership appeared to rise; in the late 1960s, concern was increasingly voiced within the United States about balance-of-payments deficits and job losses. Certain states, particularly France, became more assertive, adding political annoyance to supposed economic loss. Observers in the United States began to argue that the U.S. was providing a "collective good" of international economic order for a large number of states, but was paying a disproportionate share of the costs. The Nixon-Connally decision in 1971, unilaterally to suspend convertibility of the dollar into gold, constituted an attempt to redress a supposedly adverse situation by providing the United States with greater international economic freedom of action, and by forcing its allies and economic partners to come to terms. This maneuver was politically successful, since new monetary arrangements that conformed to American preferences were eventually agreed to; but the attendant uncertainty and disruption had very high economic costs. The dollar standard that persisted after 1971 was not accompanied by stable financial conditions or by effective intergovernmental action to control world liquidity growth; the result was an immense increase in international liquidity which appears to have contributed to the world inflation of 1973–1974.[5]

Thus, by the early 1970s, one basis of support for the Bretton Woods regimes—an American conception of its leadership role that accepted substantial responsibility for stabilizing the system—had been undermined as a result of changes in relationships among the advanced industrialized states. This might have been easier for the major economic powers to handle if prosperity had continued despite the monetary instability. During the 1960s the future of capitalism had seemed assured by Keynesian demand-management policies which were to make issues of income distribution obsolete and bring an "end of ideology." Charles Maier (1978) has called this the "great conservative idea" of the last generation, referring to the role of growth as a solvent of social conflict within industrialized societies. But it played an equally important role internationally. In a period of rapid growth, mercantilist ideas seem obsolete: far from being threatened by the successes of others, each country benefits from the new demand generated by growth elsewhere. The prevailing faith in technological progress and demand management made U.S. leaders quite sanguine both about the development of the European Common Market and about manufacturing growth in the Third World, since these were seen as circumstances to be welcomed rather than feared.

The 1970s brought an end to the assumption that the industrialized countries would be blessed with unbroken prosperity and growth in the future. The economic difficulties of this decade were produced in part by actions of the industrialized states themselves, such as U.S. involvement in Vietnam and consequent inflationary pressures, the rapid growth in world liquidity that took place when the pegged-rate monetary regime was breaking down, and the sharp recession of 1975 created by governmental measures designed to deal with the inflation of 1973–1974. Yet the situation was aggravated by the large and sudden increases in oil prices precipitated by the Yom Kippur War in 1973. Prosperity in the advanced industrialized countries had depended to a great extent on access to the petroleum resources of the Middle East and other parts of the nonindustrialized world at prices that were far below those of available substitutes. In turn, access to these resources at such prices rested on Western power in the nonindustrialized world, especially in the Middle East. After the withdrawal of Britain and France from political/military roles following the 1956 Suez debacle, this meant reliance on the power of the United States. In this way, American military power and political influence constituted an important prop for the international economic system.

Unfortunately for the rich states, the United States in the 1970s found it increasingly difficult to use force to protect its economic interests and those of its allies. In the early 1950s the United States and Britain had used a combination of economic pressure and thinly disguised covert force to overthrow the government of Mossadegh in Iran and restore the Shah to effective rule. Nothing like this seemed feasible to most observers in 1974; the risks of effective action were too high. This was to some extent due to increased Soviet military power in the Middle East. But it was also due to some other changes that had taken place in world politics during the intervening two decades—in particular, to the increased nationalism and greater militancy of large numbers of people in the nonindustrialized world, including the Middle East. It would have been easier to land the marines than to extricate them. Military action against an Arab state would also have compounded the problem of arranging an Israeli-Arab peace settlement. Furthermore, the interests of American-owned oil companies in the area could have been grievously damaged.

Thus, by the mid-1970s, three important sources of support for the international economic regimes born at Bretton Woods had been undermined. Largely as a result of shifts in relative economic strength, the United States had become less inclined to define its interests in collective terms rather than in more narrowly national terms. The increasingly assertive oil-producing countries had quadrupled the price of petroleum. And, partly as a result of these two developments, assumptions that economic progress would continue indefinitely had been shattered.

How are international economic regimes to be reconstructed? From one perspective, the key problem is to facilitate a transition to new patterns of world leadership that will effectively support new regimes. Like Great Britain in the interwar period, the United States is no longer able to provide political and economic leadership alone. Japan, Germany, and to some extent Saudi Arabia, will have to carry some of the burden. None of them has become as important as the United States; but they have become significant enough to no longer act as "small countries" whose policies have negligible effects on the system as a whole. They can no longer be "free riders" on a system supported by others and expect that system, and the benefits it provides, to persist.[6] Unfortunately, however, "collective leadership" is more easily recommended than carried out. The United States in the 1920s and 1930s was no quicker to accept the burdens of a system-supporting role than Japan or Germany have been during the 1970s (Kindleberger 1974). Nor are the leading states usually particularly anxious to give up the prestige or the perquisites of being Number One. Like Britain during the interwar period, the United States is less willing to share the privileges of leadership (such as the ability to finance large current account deficits by printing more reserve currency) than its burdens.

It is an open question whether, even in a period of prosperity, the transition to collective or multiple leadership could be effected. Charles Kindleberger (1974:305) has argued that "for the world economy to be stabilized there has to be a stabilizer, one stabilizer." If he is correct, efforts to promote collective or multiple leadership will be in vain, and so will the Carter administration's efforts to promote closer policy coordination. Barring a resurgence in American power or the emergence of a new leader on the scene, international economic arrangements will degenerate into increasingly protectionist patterns.

The economic difficulties that accompany erosion of international regimes make collective leadership more difficult to develop. As international regimes erode, governments can be less confident that their partners and competitors will behave according to an established and fair set of rules. Compromise becomes more difficult, since the adverse effects of concessions are more severe in a situation of poor economic performance. Increased imports of steel, textiles, or color television sets are seen as implying not merely adjustments, as jobs and capital are shifted to other productive uses, but absolute losses of employment and profits. Each government becomes increasingly resolved to put the interests of its own people—and its own interests in continuing to govern—first. A vicious circle develops in which breakdowns in international regimes and political leadership contribute to economic difficulties which, in turn, make those regimes more difficult to reconstruct and their leadership more burdensome.

Governing elites in the United States, Germany, and Japan share an interest in maintaining a relatively open world capitalist system. According to this logic of *overall interests,* Germany and Japan should act to reduce their current account surpluses by stimulating domestic demand and—particularly in the case of Japan—encouraging imports. The United States should take strong action to limit its demand for imported petroleum. But all of these actions would be politically painful. Japan and Germany are being asked to adopt current U.S. economic theories, which stress demand management and the need to avoid large surpluses on current account by industrialized countries, and their people are asked to adjust their personal financial behavior to American habits—to spend more and save less. From the German and Japanese points of view, it appears that Aesop's fable is being turned on its head: the ant is being lectured for not being more like the grasshopper. On the U.S. side, it is unclear whether the Carter administration can implement an effective anti-inflation program, which would hurt some politically influential groups in the United States. The 1978 energy legislation was sufficiently weak to allow doubt of its efficacy in significantly reducing America's oil-import bill. Part of the problem is international; it is more difficult for governments to act together than separately. But the problem has domestic sources as well.

At this level, the issue is whether democratic governments in capitalist societies can formulate effective long-term political/economic policies in the face of particular, usually short-term, interests. This is hardly a new problem in world politics. Jacob Viner (1948:20) observes that in Holland during the seventeenth and eighteenth centuries,

> where the merchants to a large extent shared directly in government, major political considerations, including the very safety of the country or its success in wars in which it was actually participating, had repeatedly to give way to the cupidity of the merchants and their reluctance to contribute adequately to military finances.

During the Marshall Plan years, American administrators had to deal with the

> special demands of the American business and agricultural community that expected direct and early profit from the program—and who were well represented in Congress. . . . The general goals of multilateral trade were certainly in the interests of all these constituencies; yet they, unlike the State Department, were willing to undermine the achievement of the general aim for even the smallest immediate gain. [Kolko and Kolko 1972:444–45]

Effective policy coordination, or collective leadership, thus faces formidable obstacles. Governments of major capitalist states do not agree on what would be best for the international capitalist system. Even if they agreed, they would have different interests with regard to how the burdens of maintaining that system should be shared. And even if they came to a consensus on that point, it would be difficult for them to convince their publics to accept the necessary changes. Extensive networks for discussion of international economic issues remain in place, and many of them have been extended. But, in general, governments are talking more about policy coordination and accomplishing less. Disillusionment can all too easily turn to acrimony. The record of international economic negotiations during 1977 does not provide grounds for optimism that a smooth transition to collective or multiple leadership will take place.

THE INTERNATIONAL POLITICAL ECONOMY IN THE 1980s

The most optimistic interpretation of contemporary developments is that the world is still passing through the temporary disruptions occasioned by the inflation of 1972–1973, the oil price rises of 1973–1974, and the recession of 1975. Problems of inflation and unemployment are accounted for by

> an unusual bunching of unfortunate events unlikely to be repeated on the same scale, the impact of which was compounded by some avoidable errors in economic policy. In other words, the first half of this decade saw an upheaval in the economic affairs of the western industrialized nations that is unlikely to be repeated. [McCracken 1977:103, par. 98]

Economic conflict among industrialized countries is in part the result of these disturbances. Through sensible national economic policies and close international cooperation, the industrialized countries can return to full employment and price stability. According to this view,

> the fabric of international cooperation has held together extraordinarily well despite severe economic strains. . . . The general foreign policy challenge before us is not only to preserve this cooperative framework but to strengthen and extend it to insure global economic growth.[7]

Thus, according to the optimistic view, the 1980s may be a period of further institution-building and cooperation in a growing world economy. Newly wealthy states, such as the major oil-producers, will become closely linked to the industrialized countries, and may even join the Organization for Economic Cooperation and Development (OECD). Governments will become more and more willing to discuss their "domestic" economic and energy policies at international meetings, and policy coordination will therefore improve. World capitalism will emerge from its ordeal relatively unified and vigorous. Furthermore, prosperity will make the rich countries more willing to make at least some marginal concessions to the Third World. No one believes that the North-South conflict will disappear, under even the best of circumstances, but in this scenario it could be dealt with without fear of disrupting global politics or economics.

As indicated above, events of the last few years have not made this scenario seem more likely. Indeed, they have raised the specter of economic conflict and trade wars. According to the second scenario, then, the breakdown of the postwar economic regime will lead to progressive fragmentation and conflict in world political economy. Attempts at effective collective action will fail; international economic relations will become a Hobbesian "war of all against all." Industrialized countries will attempt to restrict their imports of types of manufactured goods produced by their own industries. Producers of raw materials will attempt to band together in cartels to raise prices of their primary products. Trade blocs will be created, linking powerful states with their dependencies. As a consequence of the breakdown of agreed-upon rules, asymmetries of power will become more directly important in determining economic outcomes. The strongest, least vulnerable states will be able to drive the hardest bargains. Thus everyone will be in a worse situation than before, but the United States would be hurt less than Germany or Japan, and the last two states would not be damaged as badly as less-developed countries that had begun to manufacture goods for export. In general, the lower on the political hierarchy a given country and the greater its reliance on the world economy, the more serious would be the consequences of this conflict system for its own society.

Since this scenario would be harmful to almost everyone, it would be likely to materialize only if elites in the most powerful countries lost control of the situation. More plausible, however, is a third scenario in which limited protectionism would take place, scaled according to the political and economic power of the victim. That is, powerful governments would attempt to protect vulnerable sectors within their societies by discriminating against weak countries. Thus the United States, Japan, and the European Community might develop agreements on steel and chemicals that would regulate trade among themselves, but would virtually halt the expansion of exports from Third World states. The advanced countries would maintain enough collective coherence to force adjustment costs onto poorer, weaker states. For this strategy to succeed, it would be necessary for the industrialized countries to separate major oil exporters from the rest of the Third World, which would be victimized. The major capitalist states would also have to cope with the consequences of dashing Third World hopes for improvement in the conditions of life: global agreements requiring widespread consensus, such as a law of the sea treaty, would become even more difficult to negotiate, and nuclear proliferation—as well as terrorism—might show a tendency to increase.[8] The world that resulted would be neither just nor peaceful. But the political logic—although not the moral justification—for this outcome can easily be explicated: power would be used by the privileged to protect their positions. And there is little doubt that the first round of an international struggle between rich and poor would be won by the rich.

Faced with the long-term consequences of this approach, elites in the industrialized capitalist states might prefer a fourth scenario, in which the costs of adjusting to change would be imposed on weak groups *within* their own societies rather than on governments and societies in the Third World. This would presumably require more conservative policies by governments of the advanced countries. Real wages would fall and social welfare benefits would be cut back. The vitality of capitalism would be restored by shifting resources to business profits. Relatively high levels of unemployment would be tolerated, at least in the short to middle run. The "crisis of democracy" would be solved by strengthening government, thus increasing the "governability" of modern industrial states.[9] However attractive this may be to established economic elites in the United States and elsewhere, it seems unlikely that such a political transformation will take place. There may well be some movement toward lower rates of growth of social welfare expenditures—but mostly as a reaction to economic necessity, not because of some profound political change. Organized labor and its allies in advanced societies are likely to remain relatively strong politically, and certainly more influential than the people or governments of poor countries in Asia, Africa, and Latin America. If forced to choose, governments of capitalist states seem more likely to attempt to impose costs on poor countries than on their own politically mobilized working populations.

HOW MUCH BETTER WILL A NEW INTERNATIONAL ECONOMIC ORDER BE?

For the last five years or so, nonindustrialized states have been demanding a "new international economic order" in various United Nations bodies and at the Conference on International Economic Cooperation in Paris. The specific demands include an integrated commodity program with a common fund; improvement of developing countries' terms of trade; better access to the markets of industrialized countries; improved access to modern technology; increases in official development assistance; and effective action to mitigate the debt burdens of developing countries (Gosovic and Ruggie 1976; UN Document E/L.1774 [1977]). Advocates of an NIEO contend that present international economic arrangements discriminate against poor countries in a variety of ways, and require systematic rectification.

There is undoubtedly much truth to this contention, although it may often be overstated for rhetorical purposes. The point here, however, is not to assess its validity, but to juxtapose demands for a new order with the analysis above and the scenarios just presented. If one looks first at the industrialized, capitalist countries, and at their economic as well as political problems, it is difficult to believe that they will accept a series of demands that would require further sacrifices and dislocations. On the contrary, the third scenario above seems more plausible: that the industrialized states will discriminate against the weaker members of the Group of 77, the negotiating bloc of the less-developed countries, while attempting to co-opt wealthy oil producers into the "rich men's clubs" centered around the OECD in Paris.

The universal rhetoric of equality does not, therefore, imply that the international economic regimes of the 1980s would be egalitarian (however that were defined)—any more than the Atlantic Charter or the Yalta agreements guaranteed that liberal democracy would prevail over the surface of the globe after the second world war. Unfortunately, it appears that substantial pressures are building up that may lead the industrialized capitalist countries to attempt self-protection at the expense of poor countries of the Third World. It is quite possible to imagine that the "new" international economic order of the 1980s will be less favorable to poor countries—particularly to the relatively efficient exporters of manufactured goods—than the much-criticized regimes of the 1960s.

CONCLUSION

From the perspective of the rich countries, it is difficult to be optimistic about the new trends in international politics and economics that we observe. The international order that emerged after World War II is breaking down, and its reconstruction is proving extremely difficult to achieve. The most positive features of the last few years have been the continued willingness of governments to discuss mutual concerns—even those traditionally considered "domestic"—in international arenas, and the evident reluctance of major governments to increase protectionism and dismantle the open world economy. Yet the major powers no longer seem to be in control of their political/economic destiny. No one seems adequately to understand the changes and shocks that we observe; even when there is private agreement among the elites on remedies, domestic politics often prohibits effective implementation of such agreements.

Conservatives lament this situation. We may wish to do so as well. Before we do this, however, it is wise to recall that the present world economy could hardly be defended as equitable, either between countries or—especially—within them. The distribution of rewards under capitalism has never been guided by principles of justice; this applies even more strongly to international political economy than to domestic society. Optimistic radicals may welcome a collapse, hoping that the new world will be better than the old one. Paradoxically, it is these radicals who behave like Joseph Schumpeter's (1934, 1951) entrepreneurs, relying on "creative destruction" to improve the world. Others, who may share the radicals' distaste for the inequities of modern capitalism but who fear the risks of upheaval and disorder, are relegated to fighting a "holding action," attempting to stave off disaster while rebuilding the system. For them, in the 1980s, there are likely to be more perils than opportunities.

IV

Case Studies

11

RICHARD JAMES SWEENEY

Energy, the OPEC Surplus, and the Future of the Dollar*

Reasons behind the devaluation of the dollar. OPEC's foreign assets. Energy problems and devaluation in Germany, Switzerland, and Japan. Conservation policies. The effect of economic growth. The Carter policy on oil. Free market policies and the balance of payments. OPEC wealth and Western financial markets. The 1978–1982 forecast.

Over the past two years the foreign exchange value of the dollar has hit new lows more than two dozen times against

*Written in autumn 1978.

the German mark, the Swiss franc, and the Japanese yen. Many observers have blamed this debacle on large U.S. oil imports, and on the lack of a U.S. energy policy to reduce these imports. Administration officials, in turn, have used the falling value of the dollar as a major argument in favor of supporting the energy programs they proposed.

The oil price increase by the Organization of Oil Exporting Countries (OPEC)[1] has, in fact, had a trivial influence on the international value of the dollar in terms of the mark, the Swiss franc, or the yen. The main causes of the dollar's problems are overexpansionary monetary and fiscal policies by the United States, and the only long-term cure is adoption of sound monetary and fiscal policies. Energy policies that cut down on domestic consumption and reduce imports are apt to have the short-term effect of increasing the international value of the dollar. For that matter, policies that restrict imports of coffee, cars, or anything else would have the same effect. While restrictive trade policies will have a once-and-for-all effect of improving the dollar, they cannot hold off the *continuous* downward pressure exerted by excessive monetary expansion and ongoing government budget deficits. Thus U.S. energy policy is largely a red herring in discussions of the cause and cure of the dollar's problems.

The net foreign assets accumulated by some (by no means all) OPEC nations gives them power, the way that wealth always enhances power. However, an ironic lesson of the post–World War II period is the frequency with which powerful nations are unable to use their power. It is not at all clear that its wealth gives OPEC much additional power beyond its ability to set international oil prices and to control oil production through general or selective embargoes. If no such embargo is threatened, shifts of funds out of the dollar in order to "punish" the United States will have negligible effects: relatively small changes in short-term interest rates and in exchange rates would induce offsetting shifts of funds into the United States. In contrast, if OPEC funds were shifted from the United States because of loss of confidence in the dollar, the negative impact on the value of the dollar would be dramatic, but then the OPEC shift would be an effect rather than a cause of the problem. It seems unlikely that attempts to "punish" the United States by shifts of funds would be successful.

This chapter forecasts the possible values of OPEC accumulations of foreign assets: these aid in judging the magnitude of the effect of loss of confidence in the dollar, and are of substantial interest in their own right. The OPEC accumulation of claims on Western nations over the next five years will apparently be a good deal smaller than many observers had forecast; OPEC's current account surplus is likely to vanish after 1982. Further, OPEC's net holdings of foreign assets will be concentrated in the hands of a few Arab countries, particularly Saudi Arabia. Thus, little of the dollar's woe is due to energy and energy policy. The "money weapon" is not particularly to be feared.

THE PRICE OF ENERGY AND THE FOREIGN EXCHANGE VALUE OF THE DOLLAR

In years of severe worldwide coffee shortages, the price of coffee rises dramatically, and so do the revenues of coffee-exporting nations. No wonder the Brazilian *cruzeiro* tends to strengthen relative to the dollar (not depreciate as fast) in such years. In the same way, the dramatic 400 percent oil-price increases of late 1973 and early 1974 strengthened the Saudi *riyal,* the Kuwaiti *dinar,* and other OPEC currencies against the dollar. However, the dollar's dismal exchange-market performance in 1977 and 1978 was not against the OPEC currencies, but against the currencies of Germany, Switzerland, and Japan.

Why this should happen because of the increase in energy prices is a bit of a mystery. None of these countries produces petroleum, and each is highly dependent on oil imports for its energy consumption—much more dependent than the United States, which produces more than half the energy it consumes. By contrast, Germany did not produce any petroleum, and produced only a small part of its total energy use. Looked at this way, Germany, Switzerland, and Japan were much harder hit by the oil-price increase than was the United States. These three countries, however, did use less energy per capita—and less per unit of output of gross national product (GNP). Their three currencies and the dollar could be expected to fall against OPEC currencies, and we would not be surprised to see them fall by about the same percentage. This, however, would leave them unchanged against each other, and we return to the question of how the energy price increases could cause the dollar to fall against the other three currencies.

U.S. monetary and fiscal policies—especially excessive monetary expansion—are responsible. It seems so obvious. But other explanations are advanced, and it is worthwhile to examine some of them.

Conservation and the Dollar

The major difference between the conservation efforts of the United States versus those of Europe and Japan may be the way the United States has tried to keep its domestic oil price below the world price by controlling the price of "old" oil. To the extent this program is successful in keeping the margin of cost to U.S. firms of a barrel of oil below the world price, it would tend to lower the value of the dollar by not letting the higher world oil price have its full effect on choking back U.S. oil demand. A number of economists argue that price regulation has not kept marginal cost below the world price. However, even effective price regulation would explain exchange-rate changes in 1974—not in 1977 and 1978. Apart from price controls, there seems to be little international difference in the effects of conservation efforts. Indeed, conservation efforts such as taxes on gasoline usage can be expected to have little effect, since one of the prime reasons for OPEC's success as a cartel is the very inelastic demand for oil.

The most impressive evidence of better conservation efforts abroad is the fact that U.S. oil imports have risen over the past few years while German, Swiss, and Japanese imports have not. A primary determinant of growth in energy use, however, is the overall real growth rate of the economy. The United States has grown significantly faster than these other countries; thus, we would expect to see U.S. oil imports rise more quickly. When these other nations achieve their potential growth rates, relative import performance is likely to change. Another consideration in judging relative import performances is that European nations have been able to meet much of the growth in their energy demand by bringing on line domestic energy sources, such as hydroelectric power. Such sources cannot be quickly, easily, or economically expanded much further, however, so when actual growth of the economies returns to its potential level, much of the increased demand for energy will fall on oil imports.

The Exchange Rate, Growth, and Energy Policy

The 1977–1978 experience of the dollar is difficult to rationalize in terms of energy policy during that period. Instead, some commentators argue that the poor performance of the dollar was based on (a) the superior growth of the United States, and (b) changes in expectations about future energy policy.[2] Explanations based on growth and on expectations of energy policy, however, are less persuasive than an explanation based on monetary and fiscal policy and on expectations of these variables.

Growth Weakens a Country?

It is quite unclear that low growth is the prescription for a strong currency, or that high growth leads to a weak currency. Can it seriously be argued that the Japanese yen would be stronger today if Japanese growth rates had been 2 percent lower per year since World War II? The United States was the dominant world economic power in the two decades after World War II because of its huge, powerhouse economy; a stagnating economy would not have made the dollar stronger.

The notion that high U.S. growth hurts the dollar is based on standard Keynesian analysis of two and three decades ago. This view ignores capital accounts and focuses on the balance of trade. It argues that as U.S. output and income rise, the U.S. demand for imports rises and causes the balance of trade to deteriorate. This, in turn, is supposed to put downward pressure on the dollar.

This story has two main flaws. First, the improved growth may well lead to an improved capital account. For one thing, a vigorous economy can make investment—financial, as well as that in plant and equipment—look attractive, and hence cause capital inflows.[3] For another, the story about differential growth rates implies that the dollar will strengthen when foreign growth rates revive. Thus, informed speculation should make the dollar start to rise now in anticipation of its future rise that will occur as foreign economies return to their long-run growth potential.[4]

Second, the resources and productivity of the economy are important determinants of the level of output. The faster these grow, the faster the economy grows and, with a given monetary policy, the lower is the inflation rate and the stronger is the exchange rate.[5] This view implies that growth strengthens the dollar, and is consistent with the experience that substantial growth performance makes a nation an economic power rather than a financial weakling.

Both these views of growth, however, place much of the blame for a weak dollar on monetary and fiscal policy. If growth is caused by expansionary monetary and fiscal policy, we would expect the dollar to weaken. But suppose that resource and productivity growth are mainly behind the economy's growth. If the fiscal and monetary authorities try to stimulate the economy to grow faster, they won't be very successful in accelerating growth, but they *will* weaken the dollar. Put another way, both approaches agree that monetary and fiscal stimulus will tend to weaken the dollar.

U.S. policymakers have argued that the stimulus has not really been excessive, but only what was necessary to get the economy moving. If the Europeans and Japanese had also expanded, their increased import demand would have kept the U.S. balance of trade from falling so far into the red. This puts the United States in the light of having a wise policy while other nations were not so wise, and rather self-servingly explains the fall of the dollar as induced by perceptive U.S. policy. But this view does not explain why the capital account did not serve to support the dollar. If the foreign exchange market viewed U.S. policy as wise and designed to strengthen the economy, it would presumably buy dollars. Instead, the market views the dollar—and dollar-denominated assets—as risky, and has caused the foreign exchange value of the dollar to drop. While some may argue that the market is simply in error—as, indeed, U.S. officials have increasingly claimed—on balance, the market's view seems a safer bet.

Expectations about Oil Policy

The view that differential growth rates play a large part in the dollar's performance is sometimes combined with the argument that expectations about U.S. oil policy also play a major role. But was the dollar hurt in 1978, when it became evident that Mr. Carter was not going to get everything he proposed in his energy program?

This is not clear, because there is little reason to believe his legislation would have been of much help to the dollar. To take one example, the president's proposed tax on gasoline might eventually drive up the price of a gallon of gasoline by as much as 10 cents. At an average price of 70 cents per gallon, the price of gas would rise 14.5 percent. If we rather generously assume that the demand for gas has a long-run elasticity of -0.5,[6] then gas consumption would fall by 7.5 percent in the long run. With the program phased in over several years, it would not even offset the effects of economic growth. It seems, then, that the dollar would have gained little from passage of the Carter administration's program. Failure to get some of the parts of the program thus can hardly have been much of a blow if the exchange market behaves reasonably. This point, however, is sometimes countered by the claims that either the market misunderstood how much the program would help, or took the fate of the program as a sign of how serious the administration is about the dollar's problems. Both claims seem very tenuous.

Misguided Balance of Payments Reasons for Energy Programs

Attempts to help the dollar by energy programs are misguided. There is no doubt that the embargo beginning in October 1973 revealed the dangers of U.S. dependence on foreign energy sources. But this has nothing whatsoever to do with the dollar's problems. Germany's problems of dependence on foreign energy, for example, are no less than before, are greater than those of the United States, and persist, despite Germany's payments surplus and the strength of the mark. Similarly, Germany was at least as hurt as was the United States by the oil price rise, but did not come to its present strong position through its energy policies. Although a judicious tariff program could help the United States to recapture some of the wealth that OPEC reaped by its monopoly power, this is quite independent of how well the dollar is doing.[7] Moreover, any temporary beneficial effect on the dollar of such a tariff could be quickly offset by overly expansionary monetary and fiscal policy.

The Case for Free Market Energy Policies

Some observers argue that demand and supply of petroleum—and of energy in general—are relatively unresponsive to price changes, even in the longer run, so oil and gas prices should not be decontrolled. To do so will raise prices, do little to help the balance of payments, and benefit producers. On the other hand, why not put a tariff or quota on energy imports to help the balance of payments?

First, the supply response to higher energy prices has been fairly impressive since 1974. Beyond this kind of supply response, free-market pricing turns on the efficiency of letting prices allocate supplies. The land parcels along Manhattan's Fifth Avenue are in perfectly inelastic supply, but free-market pricing remains the optimum way to allocate them, and this is the core argument for decontrol.

There is an optimum tariff argument for restrictions on energy imports, but this has nothing to do with the balance of payments. Further, in the short term, a tariff will reduce imports a bit and will help the balance of payments. Over a longer time, monetary expansion will have much more impact on the exchange rate. Indeed, it may well be the case that tariff-induced increases in oil prices might harm U.S. exports of goods that use energy and thus, on balance, weaken the dollar. Refusing to adopt free-market policies will do little good for the dollar—surely, not over a longer run—and may do harm.

OPEC'S WEALTH, THE "MONEY WEAPON," AND FUTURE ACCUMULATIONS

One of the hot topics of 1974–1975 was the question of how much wealth OPEC would accumulate from its oil-price increases, and what it would do with its new financial muscle. Many observers doubted that private financial markets could handle the task of recycling petrodollars to the hardest hit oil-importing nations. The OPEC countries, however, showed relatively little interest in direct recycling through lending to these nations.

Although the OPEC current account surpluses literally had to be invested somewhere abroad, it was feared that the OPEC nations would try to use their foreign investments to apply business and political leverage in the countries receiving the invested funds. There were some successful efforts at getting U.S. companies to honor the anti-Israel boycott. There was and is much feeling that "the Arabs" were "buying up" the United States and Western Europe.[8] Further, some observers feared that U.S. international policy would be swayed by pressure from Arab states.

The first few years after the oil-price rise and the tremendous increase in OPEC's wealth showed that Western financial markets could easily handle the recycling problem. Financial center banks and the Eurocurrencies markets played a crucial role. However, as OPEC foreign-asset holdings rose, observers became increasingly worried that these markets could be destabilized by shifts in OPEC funds, perhaps by purposeful shifts to use the "money weapon."

It is surely true that sharp oil-price increases or embargoes by OPEC could have serious destabilizing effects on Western economies. At the same time, the OPEC nations might well shift their funds from the United States or any other "targeted" country, thus adding to confusion and stress. But the real question is what they would add to the problems caused by oil-market changes. The answer is: not much. And the money weapon is unlikely to be used.

Financial markets are easily able to handle massive shifts of funds, with little disruption and little change in asset prices. If OPEC funds were shifted abroad, *and* if there were no change in underlying conditions, foreign funds would simply flow in to take their place, with only very small changes in asset prices or exchange rates (Logue 1976). However, if OPEC financial shifts are accompanied by, say, an embargo or a general loss in confidence in the United States, there would be large effects. The shifts in funds thus would not be a cause, but more like an effect. Given the difficulty of knowing underlying conditions, such shifts could add to short-run stress, but would have no real effect once underlying conditions became clear.

The money weapon presents little to fear. Indeed, given the possibility of "targets" acting to freeze OPEC assets, it seems unlikely that the weapon would even be contemplated.

While shifts of OPEC funds should not be a major worry, it remains true that OPEC investments—overwhelmingly by Arab nations—in the United States continue to rise. Although the resulting political pressures must be acknowledged and confronted, as with pressures from other foreign blocs, the problem of "buying up" the United States is exaggerated. As long as the U.S. current account deficit persists, some foreigners must be acquiring net U.S. assets—this is how the deficit is financed. OPEC's investments have gone principally to buying government debt rather than to acquiring private firms. There is no reason to discriminate in this regard against OPEC nations' investments here. Such discrimination breeds tremendous (and largely justified) ill-will. On the other hand, it is a mistake to think that the United States has much to gain economically from OPEC investments. If they were prohibited and went to, say, Britain, the United States would receive about the same amount of funds from other foreign sources. International capital markets function so smoothly that there would be little problem (Logue 1976; Sweeney and Willett 1977).

We have argued that the dollar's problems are principally due to overly expansive monetary and fiscal policies. As long as the United States pursues such policies, the current account deficit is likely to persist, and some foreigners will necessarily be buying up U.S. assets. Forecasts presented below, however, indicate that OPEC's wealth accumulations are apt to grow at a vastly diminished rate.

THE OPEC SURPLUS: FORECASTS FOR 1978–1982

Table 1 presents a baseline forecast, as of fall 1978, for the OPEC current account for the five years 1978–1982. The forecast was generated by the model described in the Appendix.[9] Of great interest to the topic of this chapter, Column (4) in Table 1 shows the OPEC current account surplus for this year and 1979 at somewhat over $15 billion, and then falling rapidly toward zero. The strategy is to discuss first the construction of this forecast, and then to show the variables to which it is sensitive and the bounds that can be placed on plausible real world outcomes.

Table 1 is based on forecasts of monetary and fiscal policy, and resource and productivity growth, of the major non-OPEC countries that give (a) inflation of perhaps 10 percent on average, and (b) a return to the economies' potential growth paths over the first three years. Thus, while Western prices continue to rise at an excessive rate, the forecast assumes that these countries recover to their real growth paths over the first three years and remain there. This Western inflation rate is reflected in the assumed time-path of the price of oil, which rises by 10 percent per year. This information on non-OPEC real growth rates, inflation rates, and the OPEC oil price allows forecasts of the world demand for oil (excluding OPEC nations' demand). The demand is measured in millions of barrels per day (MBD), and is forecast to grow on average about 3.5 percent per year.

To find OPEC's sales to the non-OPEC world, the non-OPEC supply of oil must be subtracted from the world demand for oil. The non-OPEC supply of oil is a consensus forecast, though perhaps a little higher than consensus for the last two years of the forecast. However, more optimistic forecasts would have the non-OPEC supply of oil up to 25 MBD in 1980, and perhaps to 29 MBD in 1982.

OPEC's oil sales are obtained as the difference between world demand and non-OPEC supply. These sales are then

Table 1

OPEC's Current Account

Year	(1) World Demand for Oil (MBD)	(2) Non-OPEC Supply of Oil (MBD)	(3) OPEC's Net External Assets ($ billions)	(4) OPEC's Current Account Surplus ($ billions/yr.)
1978	48.53	20.10	162.43	15.08
1979	50.37	21.10	175.71	15.45
1980	53.05	22.20	185.21	10.71
1981	53.97	23.30	190.05	7.71
1982	55.79	24.40	192.13	2.42

multiplied by the OPEC "take" (the share of the price/barrel that goes to the OPEC countries) to give the average of daily earnings on oil sales by OPEC, and the result is multiplied by 365 days to give yearly oil earnings by OPEC.

Beyond these earnings from oil sales, OPEC earns foreign income from its non-oil exports of goods and services, and from its earnings on assets held in foreign countries. Forecasts of non-oil exports are based on judgment rather than on statistics. The forecasts assume that real growth in OPEC's non-oil exports is positive, but averages about 3 percent per year, with 10 percent growth in nominal terms to keep up with world inflation. Interest earnings are forecast by the model. Starting with OPEC's holdings of assets abroad (its net external assets), the model applies forecast rates of return from these to give OPEC earnings on foreign investments.

OPEC's payments abroad include imports of goods and services as well as transfers abroad by private persons and agencies and by official entities. These payments are assumed to grow at a constant rate of 5 percent in real terms, which, when combined with the 10 percent inflation rate, gives a growth in dollar terms of approximately 15 percent per year. (In the Appendix, Table A-1 shows how the OPEC current account surplus is drawn from the net of its sources and uses of foreign earnings.)

On relatively reasonable assumptions, the OPEC current account surplus thus seems destined to vanish by the end of 1982 and, with continuation of the underlying assumption, OPEC's holdings of net external assets would cease to rise and would begin to fall from a level of somewhat less than $200 billion.[10] Furthermore, the approximate 10 percent inflation rate in the non-OPEC countries means the real value of OPEC's net external assets will be falling steadily, even while the money value of OPEC's net external assets rises at a rate falling from about 8 percent towards zero, and then becoming negative.

The course of OPEC's net external assets is of great importance, because the forecast implies OPEC will be relying on earnings from the assets to make up for the fact that by 1980 the value of OPEC's imports (including transfers) will exceed the value of OPEC's exports. In fact, after 1982 the interest earnings will be inadequate to bridge the gap between OPEC's foreign expenditures and its foreign earnings.

What are the major ways this forecast can likely be falsified? Oil demand in the forecast grows at between 3.33 percent to 3.66 percent per annum, based essentially on forecast real rates of growth in the non-OPEC world. An extended recession could hold this growth rate to zero or below for several years. Extensive fiscal and monetary stimulation could raise real growth and oil demand for several quarters or even a few years, but no longer. By themselves, either recession or boom can only change the timing of the forecast by hastening or delaying the time that OPEC's surplus vanishes. This is so because, over the longer run, oil demand will be determined by the potential real growth rates of the non-OPEC, non-communist world. If the country models are mistaken about potential growth, the forecast will be in error, up or down. On balance, referring to Table 1, both the country models and the oil-demand forecasting that lie behind Column (1) seem reasonable, and great surprises in Column (1) do not seem plausible.

OPEC's oil sales depend on Column (1) and, crucially, on the assumed time-path of the non-OPEC supply of oil, Column (2). Column (2) seems subject to much error. Some analysts envisage 25 MBD by 1980 and 29 MBD by 1982. This would radically affect the OPEC position and could, indeed, lead to the breakdown of OPEC as a price-setting body. On the other side, disappointing results in the North Sea, Mexico, exports from the communist bloc, and so on, could lead to a non-OPEC supply less than Column (2) forecasts. Significant shortfalls could strengthen OPEC's pricing power and lead to significant increases in the real price of oil—the price adjusted for inflation.

OPEC can affect its current account surplus by altering either its imports or exports. By far the largest scope for change is in imports of goods and services, plus official and private transfers. In effect, real receipts from oil income and OPEC non-oil exports are assumed to grow at perhaps 3.5 percent per year, while imports and transfer payments are assumed to grow at 5 percent in real terms. This is the cause of the forecast decline in the OPEC current account. Compared to the past few years, the assumed 5 percent growth is very moderate. Indeed, Saudi Arabia's imports grew at the rather astounding rate of about 70 percent in the years between 1974 and 1977, and its imports are estimated to be about $33 billion in 1978. However, these expenditures are at government discretion, and can be cut in response to growing foreign indebtedness on the part of the less wealthy OPEC countries and in response to the development plans of the rich OPEC nations. Note, though, that any such cutbacks can be severely restricted by internal political pressures. Indeed, real growth in transfers and imports may well be at rates above 5 percent, perhaps as much as 10 percent.

SUMMARY AND CONCLUSIONS

The dollar's problems over the past few years have been made at home. The dollar has done poorly against the mark, the Swiss franc, and the yen primarily because the United States has pursued overly expansive fiscal and (especially) monetary policies. The OPEC price increases transferred wealth from oil buyers to OPEC, and hurt Germany, Switzerland, and Japan to much the same extent as the United States was hurt. The oil-price rise explains OPEC's wealth accumulations, not the dollar's troubles. From this perspective, U.S. policy that is designed to cut back on energy use and/or oil imports will have a trivial impact on the foreign exchange of the dollar, compared to the effects of fiscal and monetary policies.

There are a number of good reasons for having a U.S. energy policy. None of them, however, have much to do with the value of the dollar.

Financial markets have worked quite well in handling the massive OPEC accumulations of wealth held abroad. "Recycling" has not been much of a problem. The "money weapon" has not been used, will likely never be used, and would, in any case, be an ineffective ploy. Much attention has shifted to the issue of whether Arab nations are using the oil wealth to "buy up" Western countries and thereby gain undue political influence. Only a few OPEC nations have substantial foreign assets, particularly Saudi Arabia and Kuwait. A great portion of their foreign assets is issued by governments; in other words, the OPEC countries are not gaining substantial control over private sectors of Western nations. All countries try to exert influence over other nations when they can. Restricting OPEC investments in U.S. assets would be highly discriminatory and would engender much ill-will. However, any funds kept out in this way would rather easily be replaced with non-OPEC funds because of the smooth functioning of international financial markets.

Forecasts reported above indicate that OPEC's net external assets should peak by 1982 at something under $200 billion. OPEC current account surpluses are likely then to vanish and become negative, causing OPEC net external assets to fall thereafter. Some individual OPEC nations—for example, Saudi Arabia—will be likely to continue to run surpluses, however. Over the next several years, until the OPEC surplus vanishes, OPEC's accumulation of net external assets will not keep up with the rate of inflation, and thus the real value of these assets will be falling even though the dollar value will rise through 1982.

12

GORDON W. SMITH

International Commodity Agreements

Commodity price fluctuations and the use of buffer stocks. The effects of market instability. Prebisch and the UNCTAD proposals. OPEC influence, the NIEO, and producers' associations. The economic effects of commodity agreements and compensatory lending. The impasse between industrialized countries and the LDCs.

The United States government is involved to an unprecedented extent in commodity negotiations and in the operation of international commodity agreements (ICAs). The latter have been tried before and were often found wanting, but many observers now argue that things are different, and that there are substantial gains being made from well-run ICAs operating through buffer stocks. But commodity policy is moving in a direction far removed from the ideal buffer stocks which are the foundation of most of the arguments favoring price-stabilizing commodity agreements. While there are those who argue that the idea of commodity agreements has arrived, the reality still lags far behind.

A LITTLE HISTORY

The prices of most primary commodities sold on open markets fluctuate a great deal, often spectacularly (see Figure 1). The problem is most serious for commodities with long investment lead times and high proportions of fixed costs in total costs (mining, tree crops), which tend to alternate between rather long periods of boom and depression. There is no question that producing a primary commodity for sale in more or less competitive markets is a very risky business.

The drive for government intervention to "improve" these market outcomes has spanned the whole of this century. As early as 1907, for example, the Brazilian government organized a coffee retention scheme to boost sagging prices. Great Britain sponsored the Stevenson Plan to restrict natural rubber exports during the 1920s. And government gave at least tacit support to many of the private producer cartels which arose earlier in the century. However, it was the Great Depression and the collapse it brought to commodity markets that encouraged the first widespread support for international governmental control of commodities.

Perhaps the most prominent of the activists was John Maynard Keynes, who envisaged large centralized buffer stocks on the pattern of Secretary Wallace's ever-normal granary. Not only would price fluctuations be damped by such buffer stocks, but purchasing power would be injected and withdrawn at proper moments of the business cycle. Keynes and others hoped that commodity agreements to stabilize

Figure 1
Annual Change in Economist Index
of Commodity Prices, 1861–1974

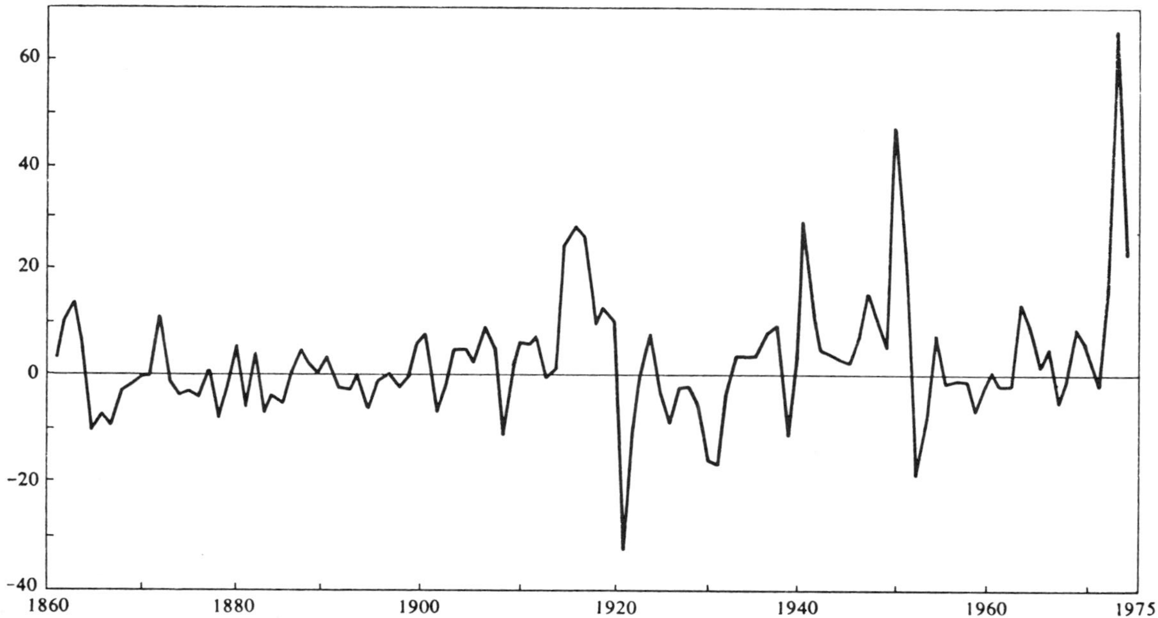

Source: Cooper and Lawrence 1975:674.

prices and incomes could be included in an international trade organization which would join the International Monetary Fund and World Bank in promoting growth and stability in the postwar world.

When the international trade organization failed to win U.S. support after World War II, the new world of stabilizing buffer stocks quickly receded into the background. Of the few commodity agreements finally negotiated—wheat, sugar, and tin—in the late 1940s and early 1950s, only wheat was particularly effective (see Table 2), and the coverage was too narrow to have much macroeconomic impact in the Keynesian manner.

To this point, the problems of primary commodity producers had not been considered an issue mainly of interest to "backward" or underdeveloped countries. But with national independence movements and the drive for economic development in the poorer nations and former colonies, this situation changed rather rapidly. Raul Prebisch, the Argentinian chief of the UN's Economic Commission for Latin America, was among the first (1949) to push primary commodities aggressively as a key less-developed country (LDC) issue. His concern was not so much with the instability of commodity markets, as Keynes's had been. LDCs could live with that. But Prebisch saw a secular tendency for the terms of trade to turn progressively against primary products. He argued that international trade was asymmetrical, that over each successive business cycle the primary commodities of the "periphery" (LDCs) bought fewer manufactured goods from the "center." Productivity increases in the "center" were captured by higher factor incomes, while productivity increases in primary products were passed on in lower prices, mainly because of the competitive nature of the markets involved and the slow growth in demand.

Prebisch's theory was not terribly convincing, and the empirical evidence has never firmly supported the factual assertion. Still, the belief that, unless there is intervention to prevent it, the terms of trade tend to move against primary prod-

Table 1

Principal Instruments Used in International Commodity Agreements

Instruments	Problems
Export Quotas	
Limits exports in periods of low prices. Quota levels are fixed to achieve market price targets. Usually are combined with ceilings on stocks producing countries may hold. When stock ceilings are reached, export quotas also become production controls, in effect.	(1) How to allocate quotas. (2) Stimulates production of nonmembers. (3) Does little to defend price ceilings in time of shortage. (4) Raises average price to consumer as a result. (5) Cheating on quotas is profitable.
Buffer Stocks	
Economically more respectable than export quotas. Tries to reduce price fluctuations by buying when prices are low and selling when high. Ceiling and floor prices are specified and defended by buffer stock. Ideally, prices should be stabilized around "long-run" trends. Application of sophisticated inventory control techniques has shown fixed ceiling-floor price scheme to be non-optimal. Buffer stock has always been combined with export quotas.	(1) How to determine appropriate price floors and ceilings. Errors can be costly. (2) How large a buffer stock is required? Underfinanced stocks can aggravate instability in some circumstances. Studies suggest, however, that for many commodities buffer stocks may have to be surprisingly large to achieve reasonable stabilization targets. (3) How will financial burden of buffer stock be allocated? (4) Private stocks will be greatly reduced for many commodities.
Purchase and Sales Agreement	
Parties agree to transact only within a certain price range.	Market supply and demand may dictate other prices.

Table 2

Major International Commodity Agreements since World War II

Agreement	Dates	Instruments	Success
Tin (5)	1956–present	Export quotas, buffer stock	Moderate: defended price floors; ceilings often penetrated
Sugar (4)	1953–1963 1968–1973 1977 (pending congressional approval)	Variable export quotas, minimum and maximum national stock targets. 1977 ISA has small buffer stock	Largely unsuccessful in achieving price targets
Wheat (5)	1949–1971	Multilateral agreements: some or all commercial transactions to take place within maximum and minimum prices	Early agreements successful due to U.S. and Canadian stock accumulation; 1967–1971 prices remained below minimum
Cocoa	1972–present	Export quotas, buffer stock	Prices above ceiling throughout agreement
Coffee (3)	1962–1972 1976–present	Variable export quotas	Raised prices in mid-1960s

ucts remains one of the tenets of those who believe that the international economy is biased against the poorer nations.

The first United Nations Conference on Trade and Development (UNCTAD, 1964) was a milestone in the escalation of concerted LDC demands on all fronts. In the mysterious ways of such things, the first UNCTAD generated a permanent international bureaucracy (the Secretariat) located in Geneva, the main function of which is to advocate what it conceives to be the common interests of LDCs. Its first secretary and leader of the first conference was—the Argentinian, Raul Prebisch. Comprehensive commodity agreements aimed at both stabilization and higher prices were pushed at this conference—even the development of synthetics was to be limited if necessary to accomplish these goals. At that time, the United States and other industrial nations strongly resisted most UNCTAD proposals, including those for generalized special preferences for the imports of LDC-manufactured goods. Indeed, it was then hard to take many of the proposals seriously, since they appeared so extreme.

Every four years another UNCTAD conference was held, and gradually some of the proposals began to appear more reasonable. But the real catalyst was the success of the Organization of Petroleum Exporting Countries (OPEC), and the commodity boom and bust of 1973–1975. With OPEC backing, LDCs *as a group* seemingly began to wield real power, and demands for a radical New International Economic Order (NIEO) were articulated in the UN in 1974 and 1975.

The centerpiece of NIEO demands was UNCTAD's Integrated Program to raise and stabilize the prices of seventeen commodities. To finance the program, a $6 billion "Common Fund" was proposed, from which individual commodity agreements could borrow. At the same time, producers' associations in several commodities threatened action to raise prices unilaterally. The International Bauxite Association, led by Jamaica, did indeed raise taxes severalfold on bauxite exports and linked the tax directly to the price of aluminum in the United States, effectively "indexing" them. Other producer associations were inactive or much less successful—e.g., the copper group (CIPEC), which failed in its attempt to arrest price declines through export controls. Still, such threats could not be discounted entirely. OPEC supported the demands of the Group of 77[1] in international meetings, and the Group of 77 refrained from attacking OPEC openly, even though several of its members were seriously injured by the oil price increases.

In this atmosphere of confrontation, the second big wave of commodity negotiations began in 1974. UNCTAD and the Group of 77 hoped to maintain the high real commodity price levels reached in 1973–1974 by indexing prices to inflation in the Organization for Economic Cooperation and Development (OECD) countries. UNCTAD shifted gears quickly. Western governments rejected the idea, and the collapse of many prices in late 1974 and 1975 reduced the cartel threat. Since then, price and revenue stabilization, rather than higher commodity prices, have become the immediate target of Third World supplier groups. The rhetoric has gradually shifted from confrontation to emphasis on gains which *both* consumer and producer nations could expect from price-stabilizing ICAs.

THE GAINS FROM STABILIZATION

The benefits of price-stabilizing commodity agreements are usually perceived as reducing the *costs* of "excessive" instability in unregulated markets. While some commodity markets may be inefficient and some private speculators too myopic or excessively risk-averse, correcting these distortions does not appear important enough to justify commodity agreements. Their only possible justification comes, rather, from the macroeconomic impacts of commodity instability.

Gains for LDCs

More than half of the non-OPEC less-developed countries depend on only two or three commodities for more than half of their export earnings. Some depend on only one commodity. Copper makes up more than 50 percent of the exports of Chile, Zaïre, and Zambia. Bangladesh earns about 80 percent of its foreign exchange from jute; Ghana, about 56 percent from cocoa; the Dominican Republic, about 50 percent from sugar. The export revenues of such countries fluctuate widely with price changes.[2] Since LDCs depend on imports for both capital and the intermediate goods necessary for growth, unstable foreign exchange earnings can wreak havoc with their economic development. Erratic, stop-go inflationary development can be the result.

Astute management of foreign exchange reserves over the commodity cycle, coupled with timely borrowing from private banks or from the International Monetary Fund, can greatly reduce the undesirable consequences of export instability. Unfortunately as the plights of Peru, Zambia, and Zaïre currently exemplify, such sophistication and restraint may be lacking in many LDCs.

Economists disagree about the seriousness of commodity instability for LDCs. Empirical evidence has not verified that export instability causes slower economic growth; it is not even uniformly accepted that export instability causes less stable growth. Certainly, the final impact of export fluctuations will depend upon each government's policy. Some have succeeded quite well; others, miserably.

There is also disagreement as to whether commodity agreements are a desirable way to deal with fluctuations in export earnings. If markets are otherwise operating satisfactorily, the Compensatory Finance Facility of the IMF, which lends to countries suffering temporary shortfalls in export earnings, may be sufficient to deal with the foreign exchange consequences of export instability.

What Might the Industrial Countries Expect from ICAs?

Less-developed countries are increasingly important markets for exports from the United States and other industrialized countries. In 1977 about one-quarter of U.S. and Japanese exports went to non-OPEC LDCs, while the figure was about 15 percent for Europe.[3] These percentages were higher in the recession of 1975, and it has been argued that LDCs' imports during the recession helped to stabilize the OECD countries. Policies which tend to stabilize the export earnings of LDCs around trend will contribute to the stable growth of the industrial countries' exports to the LDCs. But the question remains whether ICAs or compensatory lending would be best for this purpose.

In the 1970s a new advantage from more stable commodity prices was suggested. Greater stability will mean lower rates of inflation and/or unemployment in the United States. It is generally recognized—with extreme monetarists dissenting—that widespread, unanticipated price increases can raise the general price level. If the price increases are not perfectly accommodated by an increase in the money supply, unemployment and excess capacity will also result. Although primary commodities, excluding fuels, are not a large part of the various U.S. price indices, large increases spread over many commodities could have a significant impact (Popkin 1974:254). This does not happen often, but it did during the 1972–1974 period when, according to one estimate, 45 percent of the 1973 increase in the U.S. consumer price index resulted from increases in crude materials' prices (excluding petroleum) above their trend values (Popkin 1974:255-56). Such an economic shock, coupled with widespread downward price and wage rigidities, can set off a serious price/wage spiral. With the increasing incorporation of cost-of-living clauses in wage and other contracts, the United States is probably even more vulnerable to such a shock today than it was in 1973.

Clearly, large stockpiles of raw materials can prevent violent commodity price increases. If the stocks are accumulated gradually during periods of economic slack, the inflationary impact of the withdrawal of commodities from the market should be small.

This is not the same as price-stabilizing ICAs, however, even assuming that buffer stocks were to be their main instrument. But it is similar enough that the U.S. government is arguing that a principal benefit of ICAs will be reduced inflationary pressures in the United States.

To support this position, Assistant Secretary of the Treasury C. Fred Bergsten has used the so-called "ratchet effect" in pricing. He argues that although final goods prices are quickly increased to cover rising primary input prices, when commodity prices fall back to more normal or below-normal levels later on they are not reduced accordingly. In other words, because of asymmetrical price adjustments to primary input costs, fluctuating input costs ratchet up the price of final goods. Thus, according to this position, adding to a buffer stock in a period of low prices will not increase the prices charged for final goods, while buffer stock sales during shortages will keep final goods prices lower than they otherwise would have been.

While casual observation of retail coffee, sugar, bread, and other processed food prices does tend to support the ratchet hypothesis, thus far economic analysis has been inconclusive. Theoretically, however, its implication that profit margins increase with each commodity boom and bust seems unreasonable, if there is any degree of workable competition.

Still, if ratchet hypothesis is fully correct, potential gains to the United States from buffer stocks could be substantial. Jere Behrman (1977), for example, has estimated that the annual U.S. inflation rate from 1962 to 1973 would have been .4 percent lower had buffer stocks for eight important products stabilized prices within bands ±15 percent around trends during that period. And this period did not include the commodity boom years of 1973 and 1974. If one accepts a stable trade-off between inflation and output (through the Phillips curve and Okun's law),[4] another way of putting the gain is that gross national product (GNP) over these ten years could have been $15 billion 1975 higher in present value than it was, with no increase in the rate of inflation (Behrman 1977:39). This figure far exceeds any expected cost for the buffer stocks in that period.

Further research on ratchet pricing and the impact of various types of commodity agreements is necessary to be confident of results. Such research should certainly be undertaken, given the size of potential benefits.

WHERE ARE WE NOW? INDIVIDUAL COMMODITY AGREEMENTS

For several reasons, commodity agreements are not likely to produce anything close to optimally stable prices, even if stabilization is their goal. First, it is difficult to determine which prices should be defended, because long-run equilibrium prices are unknown and cost of production data are unreliable. Second, even if such prices would be known, there is no guarantee that a negotiated agreement would defend them; individual nations could be expected to do a good deal of jockeying to improve their gains at the expense of others. Decisions on prices and other matters, after all, result from *political compromise,* and considerations other than the economics play a role. In particular, the interests of producers and foreign policy establishments—those most affected by outcomes—are likely to receive excessive weight in political deliberations. Fourth, negotiated agreements have a way of coming unglued. And finally, buffer stocks, although economically more desirable, play second fiddle to export controls in most ICAs.

We can illustrate these points by brief examination of current and prospective commodity agreements.

North-South Agreements

At present, three commodity agreements exist in which almost all the producers are LDCs exporting primarily to industrial countries: the tin, coffee, and cocoa agreements. All of these are biased in favor of producers. Coffee, tin, and cocoa are far more important to exporting countries than they are to, say, the United States or West Germany. The cost of excessive prices to the latter is slight, while perceived benefits to the LDCs are substantial. And, of course, expected political gains may encourage consumer nations to acquiesce in producers' demands for higher prices.

The International Tin Agreement (ITA). The United States joined the tin agreement in 1976, after twenty years on the sidelines. While often cited as the most successful agreement in history, the ITA is actually fairly mild. Its buffer stock is much too small to be effective, and sales from the U.S. strategic stockpile provide most of the price stabilization on the upside. The ITA relies mostly upon export quotas to maintain floor prices.

The tin agreement could have substantial market impact if its buffer stock were enlarged. Unfortunately, ITA producers have been pushing aggressively and successfully for higher prices and, after 1977 and 1978 increases, real support prices are now considerably *above* long-run trends. The hard-line countries in the agreement—the United States, West Germany, and Japan—could have vetoed these increases. But rather than arouse animosity from the main producers—Malaysia, Thailand, Indonesia, and Bolivia—they went along with the key decisions. The agreement has thus taken on a definite pro-producer cast.

The International Coffee Agreement (ICA). The coffee agreements of 1962 and 1968 were clearly producer-oriented in that export controls were the agreements' only real instrument. Quotas were used rather effectively in the mid-1960s when, according to the General Accounting Office, nearly $500 million per year was transferred from consumers to producers of coffee. However, the second agreement fell apart in 1971 in a dispute over price adjustments to compensate for the devaluation of the dollar. Brazil then led the move to form a coffee *cartel,* which instituted more severe export controls than had been in effect in the coffee agreement. Brazil also formed a coffee trading firm, Café Mundial, to support prices in world markets. None of these moves was particularly successful.

Producers had second thoughts about going it alone, and in 1976 a new coffee agreement with U.S. participation took effect—again with export quotas but no buffer stock. The 1975 Brazilian frost drove green coffee prices well above \$3.00/lb., and as they fell back in 1977 to less than \$2.00, still about triple 1972 levels, Latin American producers—again led by Brazil—agreed to restrict exports until prices were pushed above \$2.00 again. This did not work. In September 1978 spot prices in New York had fallen to around \$1.50/lb. for the Brazilian product. In turn, producers demanded higher support prices from the coffee agreement—on the order of \$1.60 to \$1.80/lb., far above anybody's cost of production.

The International Cocoa and Other Agreements. The cocoa agreement, to which the United States is not a party, has been inactive since its inception in 1972. Its main tool is export quotas, and prices have been above established levels since then. The agreement is structured much like the coffee agreement, although it does provide for a small buffer stock. Negotiations are beginning for a new cocoa agreement, and the United States is pushing for a bigger buffer stock (as it did to no avail with coffee). If the U.S. does not succeed, we might expect a repeat of the producer bias of the coffee agreement.

Finally, mention should be made of negotiations for an agreement for natural rubber, which would rely principally upon *buffer stocks*. Producers say they will organize their own stockpile operation if consumer participation cannot be negotiated. For this reason, an ICA will probably result.

Close substitutes exist for natural rubber in many uses, and the buffer stock is intended to increase long-run consumption of natural rubber by guaranteeing a more stable supply. The potential for economic bias in favor of producers is still there, however, since most natural rubber production comes from Southeast Asia, a politically sensitive area to the United States and Japan.

Mixed Agreements

The new sugar agreement, and discussions of wheat and copper agreements, involve different issues. These commodities are produced in many industrial countries, unlike typical North-South commodities, so these agreements protect domestic producers while avoiding the quotas, tariffs, and subsidies of the past. The ICA, then, is an operational alternative to other forms of trade intervention which may preserve domestic producers' interests.

The International Sugar Agreement (ISA). Until the end of 1974, the domestic U.S. sugar market was largely isolated from the world market, with high prices for domestic sugar maintained through strict import quotas. However, the Sugar Act expired in 1974 at a time when prices were quite high, and the U.S. price coincided with the free market price. In 1976, however, world prices crashed to very depressed levels and have remained low since then.

The main U.S. objective in the new sugar agreement (pending congressional approval) is to prop the world market up to the levels which, with normal sugar tariffs and transactions costs, would allow domestic producers to receive 13 cents/lb. without deficiency payments and without extraordinary tariffs. Hence, the floor price of the ISA has been fixed at 11 cents/lb. and the ceiling at 21 cents. As in previous agreements, variable export quotas—along with nationally held target stockpiles—will be used to achieve price objectives. A very small international stock is also contemplated.

Relying on the ISA instead of tariffs to raise prices for U.S. producers should also please the LDCs, and if the ISA fails to operate effectively, the United States can always revert to the tariff.

Wheat. Sixty percent of U.S. wheat production has been exported in recent years, while many LDCs are heavy net importers. Thus, for this commodity, the North-South roles are reversed. Current discussions on a new wheat agreement revolve around three main issues: (1) exporters want freer access to the Common Market; (2) the U.S. wants importers to foot a greater part of the storage costs for the carry-over of surplus wheat for later sale; (3) the Common Market wants guaranteed floor and ceiling prices in the international market, while the United States favors more flexible "target" ceilings and floors to be achieved through internationally coordinated stockpiles.

By this time, a wheat agreement very well may be a reality. If so, it will probably avoid very high and very low prices, still leaving a good deal of market freedom in the middle.

Copper. Copper would appear to be a prime candidate for a commodity agreement based primarily upon a buffer stock. The market value is volatile, while the physical storage cost of copper is small. Several LDCs are important producers, while the U.S. copper industry has been in a semidepressed state for several years. A copper agreement would seem to serve the interests of all the most involved parties.

No agreement seems likely, however, in spite of on-going discussions. Two reasons stand out. First, the U.S. industry opposes it, despite an interest in higher prices, fearing that its interests might be sacrificed by U.S. negotiators for diplomatic gain with LDCs. Hence, the U.S. copper industry advocates strategic stockpile purchases of copper, and import quotas to bolster its profits. Second, econometric models of the world copper market indicate that a buffer stock in copper would have to be *very* large to be effective, and few countries seem willing to foot the bill.

THE COMMON FUND

The most "original" and far-reaching proposal of the current round of commodity negotiations is the UNCTAD Integrated Programme and Common Fund. The proposal includes seventeen commodities, of which buffer stocks are feasible for ten: cocoa, coffee, copper, sugar, cotton, jute, rubber, sisal, tea, and tin. Five of these commodities are governed by commodity agreements, or soon will be. The centerpiece of the proposal is a $6 billion common fund subscribed by exporters and importers. It would lend to individual buffer stocks, and supposedly would foster both new commodity agreements (e.g., copper), and greater reliance upon buffer stocks in agreements already functioning. If all agreements could be bound together in one package, UNCTAD assumed that logrolling increases the probability that individual ICAs would be negotiated or implemented. Moreover, by diversifying over a number of commodities, it was argued that a common fund could reduce total funding below that required if each ICA operated in isolation.

Whatever its merits—and they are not terribly convincing—there is practically no chance that the idea will be accepted by the key industrial countries. Much negotiating time and goodwill have been spent on this proposal, primarily because it has been the centerpiece of the Group of 77's NIEO demands. But the leading industrial countries support a case-by-case approach to ICAs, whereas UNCTAD insists that the exact uses of the $6 billion fund be determined only after commodity agreements are negotiated or modified. Also, the United States does not want UNCTAD to administer the money, and has proposed a much scaled-down version of common funding under which ICAs would contribute capital to the fund, which would then borrow on the open market to finance buffer stocks. Weaker agreements could benefit in money markets from pooling with stronger, more creditworthy agreements. The Group of 77 has rejected this approach, and the matter is now at an impasse.

CONCLUSION

Proponents maintain that well-functioning buffer stocks with lower inflation rates permit more stable growth in LDCs and create a more favorable climate for investment in raw materials production. However, none of the commodity agreements now in effect rely on buffer stocks, nor are many such agreements likely to be negotiated. Estimates of the buffer stocks required for stabilization are quite large. This size requirement, joined with obvious difficulties in operating buffer stocks, has made governments of both developed and less-developed countries reluctant to commit the necessary funds in most cases. Most international commodity agreements will continue to rely on export quotas to defend floor prices, and on small stocks to defend price ceilings—ineffectively. The bias against consumers is obvious.

13

MICHAEL W. KERAN

Japan's Trade Surplus and the Value of the Yen

The trade controversy between Japan and the United States. The real value of Japan's trade surplus. Elasticity of demand for Japanese exports. Factors affecting the dollar/yen exchange rate. Inflation, money supply, stock prices. Protection v. free trade. Japan's need for import liberalization.

Nothing in recent years has so upset the traditionally good economic relations between Japan and the United States as the international trade controversy. The focal points of this controversy are Japan's large and growing trade surplus and the U.S. trade deficit. This chapter will analyze the factors underlying the Japanese trade surplus, and will explain its relation to the appreciation of the yen. We will look at Japan's current trade surplus, and conclude that the primary short-run cause lies in the divergent stages of the business cycle in which the U.S. and Japan find themselves. Until recently, both countries were following divergent monetary policies—the U.S., an expansionary policy to reduce unemployment from its 1975 postwar high of 9 percent, while Japan was following a more cautious policy designed to reduce its inflation rate from its 20 percent high in 1974. This divergence in policy led to a divergence in income and import growth, and thus to a trade deficit for the United States and a trade surplus for Japan. A secondary cause of the Japanese trade surplus is the "J" curve phenomenon, whereby the yen appreciation has led to overstatement of the dollar value of exports and understatement of the yen value of exports. The result is a small overstatement of the real Japanese trade surplus.

The appreciation of the yen is then analyzed, and is shown to be primarily caused by the divergence in monetary policies followed in the two countries, rather than by the Japanese trade surplus. The trade surplus, instead of being a causal factor, has occurred coincidentally with the yen appreciation because both are related to a common third cause, i.e., divergence in monetary policies. The resulting rise in inflation expectations in the United States and fall in inflation expectations in Japan has been translated into a rise in value of the yen relative to the dollar.

Examination of the long-term Japanese trade surplus, of which the bilateral surplus with the United States is a major element, concludes that it is due to an assortment of formal and informal import restrictions intended to keep Japanese import growth low relative to export growth. If the Japanese do not correct this imbalance directly, through increased capital outflows and import liberalization, then the marketplace will correct the trade surplus indirectly by forcing a further appreciation of the yen. This market solution would benefit the consumer and those Japanese industries which are engaged in the internal distribution of goods. The cost of yen appreciation would be borne by the Japanese export industries, who would find their profits from export sales shrinking drastically. Given the Japanese government's revealed preference toward favoring export industries as a matter of national policy, there is a strong presumption that the Japanese will, for the first time in the postwar period, take import liberalization as a serious matter.

SHORT-RUN FACTORS BEHIND THE TRADE SURPLUS

In the short run, the single most important factor determining exports and imports is the business cycle. The Japanese economy has expanded at a modest pace since the 1975 recession; therefore, import growth has also been modest. At the same time, Japan's major trading partners such as the United States and Southeast Asia have had above average growth rates in the last three years, and Japan's export growth has been substantial. As a result, Japan's trade position, which was in approximate balance in 1975, moved to a reported $18 billion surplus in 1977.4.

Two adjustments need to be made to the reported surplus to determine its real underlying value. First, we must adjust the nominal export and import values for price changes to determine the real volume of exports and imports. Second, we must adjust the volume of trade for differences associated with the business cycle. The first adjustment will tell us how much of the trade surplus is real, and the second adjustment will tell us how much is permanent and how much is transitory—i.e., how much will be left when Japan returns to normal utilization of capital and labor.

Real versus Nominal Surplus

Table 1 shows that the growth in Japan's exports and imports is substantially different, depending upon the currency unit used for the measurements. Between 1975.4 and 1977.4 the *dollar* value of exports increased 51 percent, and of imports, 23 percent. In *yen* value, however, exports increased by a more modest 22 percent, and imports were virtually unchanged.

These differences reflect the approximately 23 percent appreciation of the yen relative to the dollar. To determine the real or physical volume of exports and imports, the nominal data must be adjusted for these exchange-rate changes.

The method of computing real exports and imports is described in the appendix to this chapter. A summary of the results of those calculations is given in Table 2. While the absolute growth rates of exports and imports vary substantially, depending upon the method of calculation, the implications for the differential growth rates are small. Only the dollar value of exports relative to imports is significantly larger (28 percent) than the yen and "real" values (22 percent). The dollar value overstates the size of the surplus for purely statistical reasons. When the yen appreciates relative to the dollar by 23 percent, the dollar declines relative to the yen by "only" 19 percent.[1]

The fact that the difference between exports and imports (in both yen and in real terms) is equal to 22 percent is somewhat of a surprise. It means not only that the Japanese yen price of imports declined by approximately 10 percent (the difference between the yen and the real increase in imports), but also that the Japanese yen price of exports fell by approximately 10 percent (the difference between the real and the yen export growth). The decline in import prices is to be expected, given the decline in the value of the dollar relative to the yen. However, the decline in export prices is surprising, and suggests that the Japanese exporters were selling goods abroad at a lower price than at home to maintain their foreign markets.

Table 1

Japanese Exports and Imports

Year	In Billions of Yen[a]					In Millions of Dollars[a]				
	Exports	% Change	Imports	% Change	Surplus	Exports	% Change	Imports	% Change	Surplus
1975.4	18,437		18,161		276	60,699		59,810		889
1976.4	22,260	20.7%	20,371	12.2%	1,889	75,802	24.9%	69,383	16.0%	6,479
1977.4	22,564	1.4%	18,158	−10.9%	4,406	91,457	20.7%	73,543	6.0%	17,914
1975.4 to 1977.4		22.4%		0.0%			50.7%		23.0%	

Source: *International Financial Statistics* (July 1978).

[a]At annualized rates.

On balance, therefore, the J curve phenomenon has tended to overstate the Japanese trade surplus measured in dollars, but apparently has not overstated the Japanese trade surplus measured in yen, because domestic prices have moved to at least temporarily offset the yen appreciation. This suggests that only a relatively modest J curve adjustment need be made to translate the nominal value of the Japanese trade into a real value. Approximately a $4 billion adjustment in the value of the trade surplus is estimated.

Cyclical Considerations

The Japanese economy is running well below normal capacity utilization. Real gross national product (GNP) from 1973 to 1977 averaged only 3 percent per year, versus an average of 10 percent in the previous ten years. The same observation applies to the growth in industrial production, which from 1973 to 1977 increased at an average annual rate of *minus* 0.3 percent, in contrast to the previous ten years which had seen increases exceeding 12 percent annually. This has been a major factor in the slow growth of imports and, therefore, in the substantial export surplus. For reasons discussed later, it is unlikely that Japan could have maintained 10 percent growth in real GNP or 12 percent growth in industrial production after 1973, no matter how stimulative government policies had been. But growth would certainly have been higher than it actually was.

If one assumes that potential output growth in Japan has declined from 12 to 7 percent since 1973, then industrial production in 1977 was approximately 30 percent below potential. Given that imports would grow about in line with income suggests that they are also approximately 30 percent below the full capacity level. The same reason suggests that exports were also below full employment levels in 1977, but to a much lesser extent. Japan's exports to North America and Southeast Asia were at full employment levels, given the strong growth in those areas. However, Japan's exports to

Table 2

Nominal and Real Exports and Imports (growth rates 1975.4 to 1977.4)

	Exports (1)	Imports (2)	Difference (1–2)
1. Dollar value	51	23	28
2. Yen value	22	0	22
3. "Real" value	32	10	11

(1) Percent increase in exports per 1 percent increase in income in the rest of the world.
(2) Percent increase in imports per 1 percent increase in Japanese income.

other industrial countries of Western Europe were probably significantly below potential, because of the slow growth in those countries. While these other industrial countries have a relatively high import elasticity of demand for Japanese goods (every 1 percent increase in income leads to a 2 percent increase in imports from Japan), they were also much closer to potential output, and represent a relatively modest 25 percent of the Japanese total export market. Thus, on balance, the "full employment" adjustment of exports is proportionately smaller. Total exports would probably have been about 10 percent higher on a full employment basis.

Adjusting the 1977.4 trade figures for the cyclical factor would have added approximately $16 billion to Japanese imports and $4 billion to exports, with the result that the trade surplus would be reduced by approximately $12 billion. Adding the two adjustments together, $4 billion for differences in prices and $12 billion for differences in the state of the business cycle, will reduce the nominal reported trade surplus from $18 billion to approximately $2 billion in 1977.4.[2]

The analysis suggests that much of the current trade surplus in Japan is a cyclical phenomenon which will tend to disappear when Japan returns to a more normal "full employment" level of output and demand for imports. This should *not* be interpreted as implying that there is no secular trade problem between Japan and the rest of the world, in particular, the United States. The nature and extent of that problem is discussed in a later section. Rather, it suggests that the divergent monetary policies of the United States and Japan have generated a divergence in the business cycle and import patterns. The rise in the yen value is not due to divergent trade balances, but to divergent monetary policies.

INTERNATIONAL VALUE OF THE YEN

Currency exchange rates are prices which represent the relative values of goods, services, and assets which can be purchased in related countries. These prices, like other prices, are determined by supply and demand. The demand for yen depends upon the desire of foreigners to buy Japanese goods, services, and assets, while the supply of yen depends upon the desire of the Japanese to buy foreign goods, services, and assets.

This definition of the supply and demand schedule behind the value of the yen suggests that all of the factors which will affect the balance of payments can affect the value of the yen. If the underlying balance of payments is in surplus, the demand for yen would exceed the supply and the value would rise. Conversely, if the balance of payments was in deficit, the supply would exceed the demand and the value of the yen would tend to fall.

If the value of the yen depends on the entire balance of payments, then exclusive focus on the trade balance would misrepresent the major factors that determine the exchange rates. Analysis usually focuses on the trade balance, because (1) it is a very large component of the supply and demand for yen, and (2) it is the factor which varies most in the short run over the business cycle. With fixed exchange rates, it is reasonable to base forecasts of balance of payments on cyclical variations in the trade balance. However, with flexible exchange rates, primary focus on the trade balance is misleading. A trade surplus such as Japan is now experiencing due to temporary business-cycle reasons would not necessarily lead to yen appreciation. Any tendencies for the yen to appreciate above its long-run equilibrium value would create an opportunity for speculators to make profits through selling the yen while it was temporarily high, and buying it back when the yen returned to its long-term value. Such arbitrage between financial assets in different currencies would tend to wash out strictly short-run or business-cycle fluctuations in exchange rates. Thus, the exchange value of the yen relative to the dollar would not necessarily fluctuate for business-cycle reasons.

The lack of a systematic relationship between trade surpluses and deficits and exchange-rate appreciation and depreciation since flexible exchange rates became widespread in 1973 certainly supports this conclusion. In terms of the recent Japanese experience, this analysis suggests that the current, cyclically induced, Japanese trade surplus which was discussed above is not a major factor in the current yen appreciation. It does, however, suggest that a long-term yen trade surplus could induce appreciation of the yen.

If trade developments have not been a major factor influencing the yen exchange rate, then the dominant factor must have been capital flows—a major increase in the demand for yen assets relative to the demand for dollar assets. Such a shift in portfolio preferences in favor of the yen is based on the belief that the future value of the yen-based assets will be higher than dollar-based assets, because the rate of inflation is expected to be lower in Japan than in the United States. Yen appreciation, in other words, has resulted primarily from monetary, not real, factors.

This analysis is based on the monetary theory of exchange rates, which depends on the following propositions:

(1) Purchasing-power parity theory of exchange rates. In the long run, the exchange rate will equalize the relative international purchasing power between the two currencies. If inflation reduces the domestic purchasing power of one currency, its international purchasing power will also be reduced proportionately via exchange-rate devaluation.

(2) Inflation is a monetary phenomenon. Changes in price levels are related to the difference between growth in the *nominal* money supply and *real* money demand.

These two propositions explain the movement in the dollar/yen exchange rate. An increase in the U.S. money supply relative to Japan will lead to higher inflation in the United States than in Japan, which in turn will cause the exchange value of the dollar to fall relative to the yen.

The real demand for money in Japan has historically grown faster than in the United States because the more rapid growth in Japanese real income has led to a higher transactions demand for money, and because the financial deepening in Japan has led to a rise in the average cash balances and a decline in the velocity of money.

On this basis, Japanese money-supply growth of about 7 percent greater than the U.S. money-supply growth would suggest the same rate of domestic inflation in the two countries. If 3 to 4 percent money growth is consistent with price stability in the United States, then 10 to 11 percent money growth would give price stability in Japan. If the Japanese money growth is more than 7 percent above the U.S. money growth, Japanese inflation would exceed U.S. inflation, and the exchange value of the dollar would rise relative to the yen. The opposite will be true when the Japanese money growth is less than 7 percent above the U.S. growth.

In Figure 1 we show the relative wholesale prices in the U.S./Japan, plotted on a monthly basis from 1971 to 1978. It also shows the exchange value of the dollar relative to the yen for the same period (both series are based on 1975 = 100). In 1971–1972, exchange rates were still fixed, and were way out of line with the underlying price levels.

Figure 1
Wholesale Price Index (WPI) and Exchange Rates, U.S. and Japan, 1971–1978

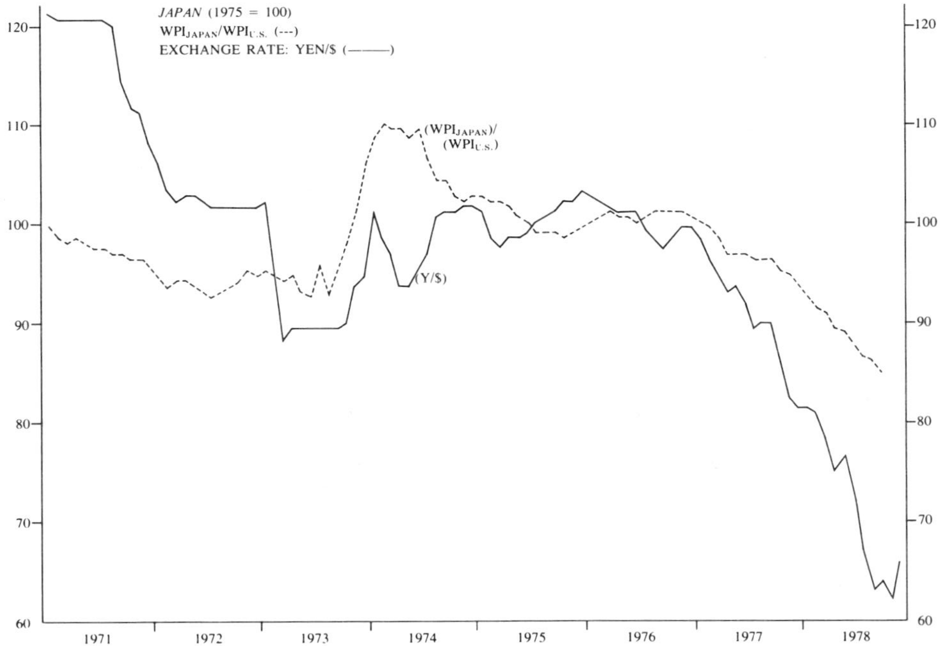

In the period August-December 1971, fixed exchange rates were realigned, but the change was not sufficient, and in March 1973 Japan, along with most other industrial countries, moved to a regime of flexible exchange rates. The initial market response to this new freedom was to undervalue the dollar relative to the yen. But by early 1975 exchange rates and relative prices were in line with each other.

Relative price levels in the United States and Japan (a measure of actual purchasing-power parity) have moved in close alignment with the yen/dollar exchange rate since early 1975. One can think of the exchange rate as a measure of "expected" purchasing power, in the sense that international investors wishing to preserve the real value of their portfolios will tend to shift their funds out of dollars into yen before the actual inflation-rate differential has reduced real purchasing power of the dollar assets relative to the yen assets. Because the exchange rate is determined in the short run by financial considerations, it will adjust relatively quickly to shifting portfolio preferences, while goods prices adjust more slowly to underlying monetary differences. Therefore, it is not unreasonable for exchange-rate movements, representing *expected* movements in purchasing-power parity, to precede *actual* changes in purchasing-power parity.

These inflation expectations could lead to movements in yen/dollar exchange rates which are disproportionate to actual differences in inflation. This would happen whenever investors expected the inflation gap to widen over the period in which they are planning to hold securities. They would sell dollars not only on the basis of the current inflation rate, but also on the basis of the expected inflation rate. While this would make the dollar "undervalued" relative to the yen in terms of current purchasing power, it would not be undervalued in terms of expected purchasing power.

Figure 2 suggests that there was good reason for investors to expect a widening of inflation differentials between the United States and Japan. It shows the differential money-supply growth rates from mid-1975 through the present period on a year-over-year basis. From mid-1975 until late 1976, the Japanese money supply grew somewhat more than 7 percent faster than the U.S. money supply. Over the same period, the exchange value of the dollar relative to the yen either rose moderately or remained unchanged. Starting in late 1976 and continuing through mid-1978, the Japanese money supply fell sharply relative to the U.S. money supply. This led to a decline in the expected inflation rate in Japan relative to the United States and, therefore, to a decline in the exchange value of the dollar relative to the yen. It also led, with a longer lag, to a decline in actual Japanese inflation relative to U.S. inflation. Thus, in summary, monetary developments affect the actual and expected inflation rates and, through this mechanism, the exchange value of the dollar relative to the yen.

If investors were shifting out of dollars into yen, we would expect that yen-denominated securities would rise relative to dollar-denominated securities. Figure 3 shows such a phenomenon was actually occurring in the U.S. and Japanese stock markets. In the period through mid-1976, when the Japanese money supply was rising by more than 7 percent faster than the U.S. money supply, Japanese stock prices increased less than U.S. stock prices. However, from late 1976 on, when Japanese money stock grew by less than 7 percent more than U.S. money, the Japanese stock prices rose substantially relative to U.S. stock prices. This suggests that in the earlier period the United States was a slightly more attractive investment location, while in the later period Japan was a substantially more attractive investment location.

This analysis also helps to explain an apparent anomaly in the Japanese and U.S. stock markets. Since the business cycle trough in 1975, the United States has enjoyed one of the most rapid growth periods in history. During the second half of that period, the U.S. stock market has declined rather than expanded, to the surprise of many analysts. The explanation is now clear. The rise in inflation expectations which has been associated with business-cycle expansion has been more

Figure 2
Year-over-Year Percentage Changes in Exchange Rates and Ratio of M2s,*
U.S. and Japan, 1975–1978

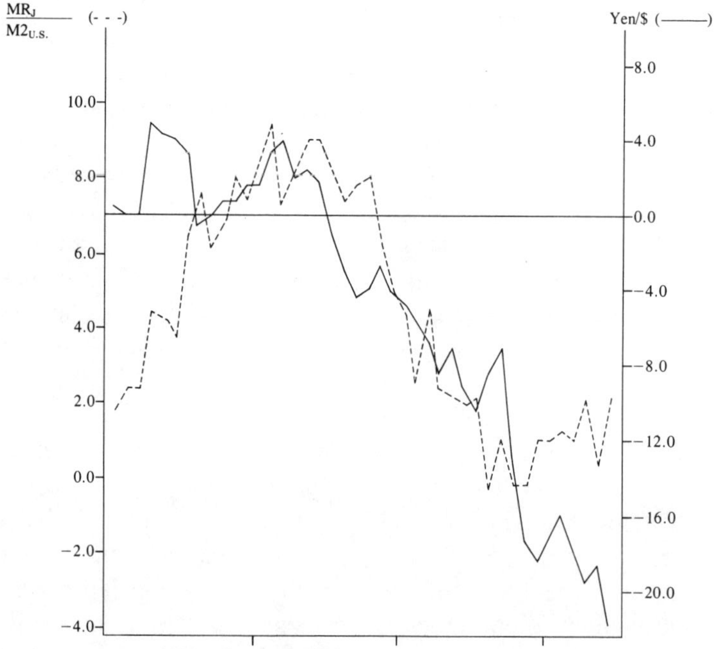

*M2 = Currency plus demand savings and time deposits of commercial banks.

Figure 3
Stock Market Values and Exchange Rates, U.S. and Japan, 1971–1978

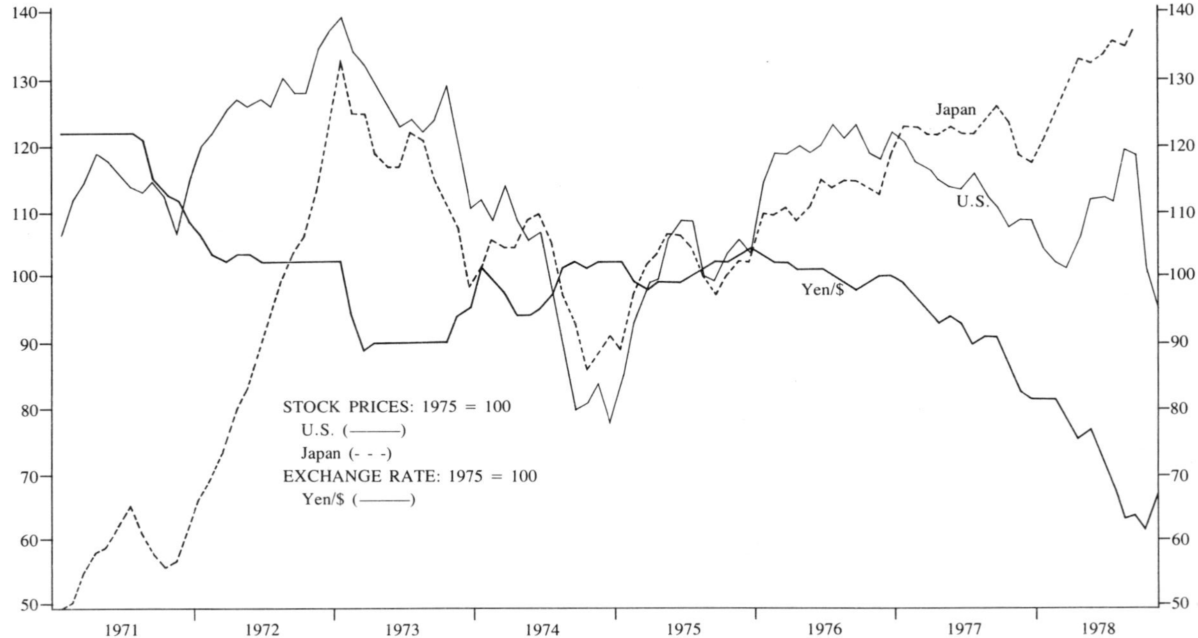

of a depressant on the U.S. stock prices than a rise in expected corporate earnings has been a stimulant. Conversely, the relatively slow recovery of the Japanese economy has been associated with strong recovery in stock prices, because the slowing in expected corporate profits was more than offset by the decline in inflation expectations.

This analysis suggests that the exchange rate is a measure of the expected inflation rate between the United States and Japan, and that inflation expectations depend upon the differential growth in the money supply in the two countries. The only way in which the exchange rates can be reversed, and the dollar strengthened, is for monetary policy in the United States to be less expansionary than it was in the past and for Japanese monetary policy to be more expansionary. There is already some tentative evidence that both countries have reversed their policies. The United States has succeeded in achieving its primary goal of full employment of labor and capital resources, while Japan has been successful in achieving its primary goal of reducing the inflation rate to levels observed in the late 1950s and 1960s. In Japan, wholesale prices have fallen at a 3 percent annual rate, and consumer prices have increased at only a 3 percent rate in the twelve months ending August 1978. It would be reasonable to expect Japanese monetary policy to become more expansionary in this environment. One would expect reestablishment of something close to a 7 percent differential between Japanese and U.S. monetary growth and, therefore, approximate stability in the dollar/yen exchange rate. Because inflation expectations have far outrun the actual inflation in the United States and Japan in 1978, the exchange value of the dollar relative to the yen could well recover substantially in the period ahead to bring it in line with the underlying purchasing-power parity value of the two currencies.

STRUCTURE OF JAPANESE INTERNATIONAL TRADE

Japanese international trade results directly from Japan's relative economic endowments of land, labor, and capital. Because of a long history of investment in human and physical capital, Japan currently has a large stock of wealth in the form of a highly skilled labor force and technically advanced capital stock. At the same time, Japan is small in size and densely populated. It is approximately the size of California, but with almost six times the population. In addition, except for low-quality coal, there are virtually no raw materials in the Japanese homeland. This natural endowment of an abundance of efficient labor and capital and a shortage of land and raw materials insures that Japan will tend to import food and raw materials and to export finished goods. Forty-four percent of Japan's imports in 1976 were fuels (including oil), 20 percent were raw materials, and 14 percent were foodstuffs. Thus, 78 percent of Japan's imports are of products which it would be either impossible or prohibitively expensive to produce domestically. On the other hand, 60 percent of Japanese exports are in the form of finished products, either machinery for business or automobiles, or televisions and stereos for households. In addition, 20 percent of exports are in the form of processed metal products such as rolled steel.

It should be recognized that this balance of "unfinished" imports and finished exports is natural for a country with Japan's economic endowments. The policy issue is whether this structure has been perpetuated longer or to a greater degree than the natural forces of the marketplace would have dictated. As Japan's per capita income approaches that of the industrial nations of Western Europe, and as discretionary income rises more than proportionately, one would expect that Japanese imports of discretionary consumer goods and nontraditional agricultural goods would also rise more than proportionately. But such a shift in Japan's imports has not occurred. As reported above, as late as 1976 (latest data available), 78 percent of Japanese imports were products which could not be produced in Japan at all, such as oil, or could only be produced at extraordinarily high prices. The remaining 22 percent covered all consumer, industrial, and other "discretionary" imports.

The policy which lies behind this pattern of imports is clearly protectionist in nature. It reflects itself in both formal and informal controls. In recent years, the range of formal controls on manufactured imports has been reduced, so that as of January 1978 Japanese residual import restrictions on industrial products stood at only five, compared to six for the United States, and as much as twenty for the Federal Republic of Germany and thirty-five for France. This is a relatively new phenomenon. As recently as the end of 1969 there were over a hundred commodities on the restricted list.

The removal or reduction in the number of formal import restrictions has not, however, significantly increased imports of finished—including consumer—products because of a wide range of informal restrictions, including an inefficient and costly distribution system. In spite of the declining cost of importing consumer and other goods because of appreciation of the yen, retail prices have continued to rise, roughly in line with the rise in prices of competing Japanese goods. To date, industries which distribute imported goods in Japan, not the final consumers, have been the principal beneficiaries of the yen revaluation.

Major, formal, protectionism still exists in agriculture. Japan currently restricts twenty-two agricultural and marine products, as compared with one for the United States. Most agricultural products, for which the United States has a traditionally strong comparative advantage and large export markets, are on the Japanese import restriction list. For example, the cost of producing rice in Japan is approximately five times the world price of rice.[3] Wheat, which is becoming increasingly popular in the Japanese diet, is also restricted in order to protect indirectly the rice farmers. The Japanese explain each restriction in terms of industry modernization, which imports would undermine. In other words, Japan's general trade policy is to liberalize imports only when they have established a domestic production sufficiently strong to compete with foreign imports. This same attitude applies in the one raw material that Japan has in abundant supply, i.e., coal. This is also on the restricted list, because its quality is inferior to U.S. coal which can be produced and delivered to Japan at a lower price.

While the Japanese import policy has been and continues to be protectionist, its export policy has always been for free trade. Export industries are the most rapidly growing industries in Japan. They have achieved major economies of scale in production by being able to sell in a world market rather than in the much narrower Japanese market. Because of her abundant supplies of skilled labor and modern capital, Japan has focused her export drive on technologically intensive commodities such as automobiles, colored television sets, and other types of consumer goods and, to a lesser extent, producer-durable goods which also have a relatively elastic demand. As a result, the growth in Japanese exports has been considerably faster than that of other countries, with its share of exports to industrial nations rising from 3 percent in 1958 to 12 percent in 1976.

This achievement has two dimensions: first, on the demand side, as discretionary income has risen faster than total income—especially in the United States, Western Europe, and Southeast Asia—the demand for Japanese technologically sophisticated consumer and producer goods has increased more than proportionately. On the supply side, with export industries growing and technological innovation occurring at a more rapid rate, the quantity of output has risen and production costs have fallen relative to total goods produced in Japan. Export industries have therefore been able to satisfy a growing foreign demand at stable or falling relative prices.

The growth in Japan's exports relative to its growth in foreign income is higher than that of any of the other major industrial countries (see Table 3). At the same time, its import growth relative to the growth in domestic income is the lowest of any major industrial country.[4]

This trade structure was a necessary condition to Japan's rapid economic growth through the mid-1970s. Japanese income growth averaged between 10 and 12 percent per year over the two and one-half decades from 1950—more than twice the rate of growth of other industrial countries. Under these circumstances, trade balance required that Japan's imports grow slowly relative to domestic income, and that its exports grow fast relative to foreign income. In this way, the growth rates of total exports and imports tend to be balanced, with only occasional periods of cyclical deficits.

In recent years, Japan's potential growth rate has declined from the 10 to 12 percent range to the 6 to 8 percent range. This decline is due to several factors, including: (1) the end of the technological catch-up phase, which permitted application of relatively low-cost technological innovations developed in the United States and other leading industrial countries; (2) completion of the transfer of labor from low-productivity agricultural and service industries to the high-productivity industrial sector, i.e., the elimination of "dual" economy; (3) reduced growth of the labor force with the maturity of the early postwar baby boom; and (4) reduced domestic investment from 30 percent to 20 percent of GNP.

The decline in growth of Japanese income will reduce the trend growth of imports proportionately. If the trend growth of exports is unchanged, it will permanently exceed the growth of imports, and Japan will have a secular and growing trade surplus. On the other hand, two factors will reduce export growth: there is likely to be some decline in income growth in Japan's major export markets; there will be a decline in Japan's export elasticity as its economy slows.[5] Neither factor is apt to reduce export growth to that of import growth.

This trade surplus can be dealt with in one of four basic ways: Japan can increase its capital outflow, liberalize its import controls, raise its inflation above inflation in the rest of

Table 3
Income Elasticities

	Exports (1)	Imports (2)	Net (1–2)
Japan	3.5	1.2	2.3
West Germany	2.1	1.8	0.3
France	1.6	1.7	−0.1
Canada	1.4	1.5	−0.1
United States	1.0	1.5	−0.5
United Kingdom	0.9	1.7	−0.8

(1) Percent increase in exports per 1 percent increase in income in the rest of the world.
(2) Percent increase in imports per 1 percent increase in Japanese income.

the world, or allow the yen to appreciate in the foreign exchange market.

Liberalizing Capital Outflow

There are good economic reasons to believe that Japan's capital outflow will increase in the future. The decline in the growth rate of the Japanese economy will naturally encourage Japanese savers to look for higher rates of return in other countries. However, the Japanese are basically an inward-looking people, and their willingness to invest abroad is probably insufficient for the size of the trade surplus which is likely to emerge. Furthermore, the eagerness of countries, especially in Southeast Asia, to accept a growing Japanese economic domination through capital ownership is limited, and this will limit a natural source of capital outflow. Finally, the opening up of the domestic financial market will induce a substantial number of foreigners to invest in Japan, and this would offset part of the capital outflow.

Eliminate Import Restrictions

As discussed above, Japanese imports consist mainly of raw materials, some agricultural products, and other inputs to the Japanese productive process. Few durable goods or agricultural products which compete directly with domestic producers are allowed into Japan. Liberalizing Japanese import restrictions, both explicit and implicit, would allow Japanese consumers to purchase high-quality foreign goods, especially consumer goods and nontraditional agricultural products. This would help reduce the export surplus in two ways: there would be a higher *level* of imports for the same level of income, and there would be a high *growth* rate in imports for every change in income. The first effect is the direct result of import liberalization. The second effect operates because most import restrictions are on goods with high-income elasticities.

Increasing Japanese Inflation Rate

Japan could offset the effects of rising export surpluses with an inflation rate greater than the rest of the world. This would discourage purchase of Japanese goods, even with the rise in foreign income, by making Japanese goods relatively less competitive. It is unlikely, however, that Japan would be willing to accept a higher inflation rate to deal with her surplus; that would be a classic case of allowing the tail to wag the dog. The Japanese are well aware of the economic cost of inflation, and have gone to considerable trouble to eliminate those costs over the last three years.

The Japanese can deal with their trade surplus unilaterally by each of the alternatives discussed above. If they do none of these, then the market will solve the problem in its own way—*by appreciation of the yen,* which will increase Japanese export prices just as a rise in domestic Japanese prices would, and thereby reduce their attractiveness abroad. By increasing prices in foreign countries, yen appreciation will limit severely the ability of Japan's most competitive and technologically advanced export industries to expand in foreign markets. The traditional export industries would have to look increasingly to domestic rather than world markets; and these industries would inevitably contract.

The foreign exchange market can and would impose this solution on Japan, because a large and growing trade and balance-of-payments surplus will create conditions under which the only way that the supply and demand for yen can be balanced is through yen appreciation. The Bank of Japan may resist appreciation by supplying yen to foreigners as the demand increases, but this is only a short-run expedient. Beyond the short run, the Bank of Japan will lose control of domestic monetary policy and be unable to contain domestic inflation.

On balance, then, Japan cannot stay with the *status quo*. In comparing the costs and benefits of voluntary action by the Japanese versus continued appreciation of the yen, it is clear that import liberalization would be the least costly course for the Japanese. Import liberalization would be least disruptive to Japan's most technologically advanced export industries, while it would disrupt its least advanced industries, those which compete with imports. Given Japan's long history of encouragement and support for export industries, the route of import liberalization seems to be the most likely.

CONCLUSION

The growing Japanese surplus has not been the major factor behind appreciation of the yen. Rather, both of these developments are due to a common third factor—Japan's relatively restrictive monetary policy in comparison with the monetary policies of its major trading partners. The same conclusion applies to the bilateral United States–Japan trade problems and the appreciation of the yen with respect to the dollar.

Over the last three years, Japanese monetary policy has been directed at reducing domestic inflation to a level equal to or less than that of the early 1960s. U.S. monetary policy, on the other hand, has been directed toward reducing unemployment to a level consistent with full employment of both capital and labor resources.

These divergent monetary policies have kept Japan's real growth rate and imports low relative to historic levels, while keeping U.S. growth and imports high. Thus, the trade surplus in Japan and the trade deficit in the United States are directly related to these divergent cyclical developments.

Over the long run, Japan's restrictive monetary policies have reduced actual and expected Japanese inflation, while the U.S. expansive policies have increased actual and expected inflation. Perceiving these different inflation trends, investors have increased demand for yen-based assets and reduced demand for dollar-based assets, thereby appreciating the yen in relation to the dollar.

The current Japanese trade imbalances will be reversed when the divergent business-cycle developments of the United States and Japan are brought more closely in balance, i.e., when Japan approaches full utilization of capital and labor resources over the next few years. However, reversal of the yen's appreciation relative to the dollar can occur only by reversal of the long-run monetary stances of the United States and Japan. As long as the United States pursues a monetary policy which generates progressively larger inflation rates, while Japan seeks low to zero inflation rates, the yen will continue to rise relative to the dollar.

There is some tentative and scattered evidence that the monetary policies followed by both countries will be reversed in the future, with Japanese policy becoming more expansionary and the U.S. policy becoming less so.

Besides monetary policy, there is an underlying structural or nonmonetary factor which could affect the future Japanese trade balance and yen value. This has to do with the fact that over the last twenty-five years the Japanese trade pattern has been based on 10 percent-plus domestic growth. In this context, Japan maintained trade balance with the rest of the world, which was growing more slowly, by exporting goods with high demand elasticities and importing goods with relatively low demand elasticities. This translated into exporting finished goods and importing raw materials—a pattern typical of a country with an abundance of labor and capital and a scarcity of land and raw materials. Now that Japan's growth rate is declining closer to that of other industrial nations, this trading pattern, if unchanged, could lead to secular export surpluses in the future. Japan can respond to this phenomenon either by increasing long-term capital exports, raising import demand elasticities by reducing import restrictions, increasing the domestic inflation rate, or allowing the yen to appreciate relative to other currencies.

For the Japanese domestic economy, the least disruptive solution would be increased imports, because adjustment costs would be imposed on the less-advanced industries. Next to inflation, the most disruptive alternative for the domestic economy would be yen appreciation, because adjustment costs would be imposed on the most advanced industries, which are big exporters. Thus, there are tremendous internal incentives to liberalize imports, as well as external incentives from the United States and other trading partners. Under the circumstances, it is reasonable to expect that the Japanese will respond positively to the demand for increased import liberalization.

14

ROGER D. HANSEN

Trade, the Developing Countries, and North-South Relations

Industrial priorities—domestic or international? The new emphasis in development strategies. Neo-mercantilism and Northern protectionist measures. Reform movements in international trade. Benefits of trade liberalization. Collective management and interdependence.

Political leadership in most developing countries—particularly in the more advanced countries of Latin America—entered the post–World War II period with the fundamental conviction that trade liberalization and a strong reliance on the mechanisms of the international economic system were *not* the most appropriate development strategies for them to follow. Rather, most of them shared a belief that a policy which came to be known as import substitution industrialization (ISI) was far more congruent with their developmental needs. As the phrase implies, production for the domestic market was given priority over production for international trade.

Several perceptions led to this policy choice. First, the impact of the Great Depression and World War II had led to the perception that dependence upon international market forces as an "engine of growth" was an unnecessarily risky element in a strategy of economic development. Second, as exporters of raw and semiprocessed materials rather than manufactured products, most developing countries also perceived that secular international economic trends were antithetical to their developmental needs. For they believed that the long-term forces of international supply and demand would inevitably produce a steady decline in the volume and value of their (raw material) exports relative to those of their (manufactured) imports. And third, they perceived that policies leading to rapid domestic industrialization would free them from these constraints imposed by the international economic system, and would accord them the political/economic strength and international status which seemed to be reserved for the industrialized states of the North.

For nearly twenty-five years, leading Northern economists, developmental agencies such as the World Bank, and governments have been trying to convince developing country elites that a fundamental policy choice in favor of the ISI strategy was a mistake, and have been arguing that development policies which remained closely linked to the international economic system and its price signals were the better policies to adopt. Again in oversimplified fashion, what Northern government experts and international agencies have been preaching to the developing countries has—in recent years—been captured by the phrase "export substitution industrialization." The *sine qua non* of this message has been:

Your emphasis on industrialization per se is not inappropriate; but the emphasis should be upon external market opportunities. The levels of effective purchasing power within your individual countries are far too low to support an *efficient* domestic industrial structure. That is why your levels of protection against foreign competition must be so high, why your industries are seldom cost-competitive internationally, and indirectly why your domestic industrial growth stagnates at high levels of underemployment and you face rising foreign debt and increasingly serious foreign exchange constraints. If, however, you alter your developmental policies to achieve a growing capacity for industrial exports, most of the present developmental problems you face will be significantly eased. With proper pricing of labor and capital your export sectors can grow rapidly, will help to absorb the underemployed, and will provide you with sufficient foreign exchange earnings to finance the essential imports you need to continue the process of rapid and balanced industrialization.

By the mid-1960s, many developing countries finally began to alter their development strategies to incorporate this new emphasis, and a few undertook comprehensive and coherent reforms to embrace the changed emphasis in its entirety.

THE PAST DECADE: THE FRUITS OF SUCCESS AND THE SEEDS OF FAILURE

The new emphasis of many Third World country (LDC) development strategies on export-oriented industrialization is reflected in developing country trade performance in recent years. Between 1960 and 1975, LDC exports of manufactures grew annually at an inflation-adjusted rate of approximately 12 percent. Particularly impressive were the performances of some eight to twelve countries in East Asia and Latin America, in which annual growth rates of manufactured products exceeded 20 percent. While much of this trade growth was accounted for by less than a dozen developing countries, recent statistics suggest that over the next five to ten years some twenty-five to thirty LDCs should have gradually combined the economic infrastructure and economic policies necessary to increase significantly their export of manufactures.

The last fifteen years have thus had a major impact upon the export profile of the LDCs, and upon their perspective on effective development strategies. Not only did the success of many developing countries in exporting manufactures give major support to the process of economic development; it also began to ease the dependence of a number of them on the export of raw materials to earn vitally needed foreign exchange. Eighty percent of LDC foreign exchange is obtained from export earnings, the rest coming from borrowings (commercial and concessional) and from foreign aid in the form of outright grants. Of that 80 percent represented by export earnings on the part of non–oil-producing LDCs, approximately 40 percent is now accounted for by the foreign sale of manufactured products, and this percentage continues to grow rapidly. The importance of this diversification is suggested by the fact that between 1960 and 1975 export earnings of LDCs depending primarily on raw materials averaged less than 5 percent per year, while export earnings from LDCs concentrating on manufacturing exports grew at an annual rate of 10 percent or better.

But for how long? Growing neo-mercantilist pressures in the North threaten to limit the access of LDC-manufactured products to their markets. If the issue has not yet created major tension, it is because new Northern protectionist measures have not yet had a major impact on LDC exports of manufactures. But a brief examination of present Northern protectionist activity suggests how close that activity is coming to producing major constraints on LDC export of manufactures. Since the issue of Northern neo-mercantilism, its origins and its likely evolution have been touched on in many of the preceding chapters, a brief analysis which focuses on the North-South aspects of the problem will suffice here.

By mid-1978 a very wide range of protectionist measures confronted LDC exporters of manufactured products to industrial countries. These measures include "orderly marketing arrangements'' and new import quotas (e.g., on developing country exports of footwear); the use of price floors in imports (as in steel and certain agricultural imports); new ''voluntary'' export restraints; increased use of countervailing duties against export promotion schemes quite prevalent in developing countries; and, of potentially major restrictive impact, subsidies to domestic industries to sustain levels of Northern domestic production in excess of those which would be dictated by the free play of market forces. All such measures adversely affect LDC exporters. It would appear that 1978 will be the first year in which Northern protectionist policies began to significantly limit LDC manufactured exports, as the following examples suggest.

An important example of recent limits on LDC exports is the present operation of the international Multi-Fibre Arrangement (MFA), originally negotiated in 1973. The arrangement provides for limitations on exports of clothing and textiles, and is based on a system of bilateral quotas—involving a quota on each group of textile products from any one country to another. As recently revised, the MFA provisions originally designed to protect exporters have been substantially weakened, and since 1977 much more restrictive quotas have been imposed. For example, new European Common Market quotas do not merely limit annual growth; they actually reduce past import levels for several countries and sharply limit any growth for others. The old norm was to allow approximately 6 percent per annum growth rates; in the European case, this has been lowered to a 0.5 percent/4.0 percent range. Most other Northern countries have introduced similar measures; the United States has recently decided to hold the 1978 export levels of its largest LDC suppliers at their 1977 rates, allowing for no growth. While such limits have often been overlooked in past years, it presently appears that this practice will not be repeated this year or in the immediate future.

Quotas have also been introduced in other categories of products of major interest to developing countries, with the probability that more will follow. Products already affected are footwear, monochrome television sets, and steel. Other products most likely to face increased levels of protection in one form or another, either of the import-restriction or the domestic-subsidy nature, include petrochemicals and a wide range of sporting equipment such as bicycle tires and tubes.

The very uncertainty within the international economic community created by these protectionist moves limits investment in LDC export sectors. In some cases, the potential investment thus affected is indigenous; in others, it involves activities of multinational corporations. In either case, the effect is to slow LDC export growth rates and most probably the process of domestic economic growth in the aggregate, and to raise the more fundamental question of the future of LDC development strategies which have—under Northern advice and, sometimes, Northern direct and indirect economic and political pressures—increasingly been oriented to industrial production for international trade. It would be ironic indeed—to say nothing of the equity considerations and the human costs involved—should the potential in Northern protectionist measures for undermining present Southern developmental efforts of the "export substitution" nature be realized after the very significant efforts which have been made to adopt them by Southern governments on the advice of their Northern counterparts.

WHY SO FEW EXPORTS CREATE SUCH A LARGE PROBLEM

At first glance, it is difficult to imagine why the exports of manufactured products from the developing countries should be the focus of so much protectionist activity within the North. The developing countries, containing well over 50 percent of the globe's population, account for only 9 percent of total global manufacturing production. They now produce only some 9 to 10 percent of all of the world's manufactured exports. Finally, it is estimated that *all of the developing countries' exports of manufactures did not reach 1 percent of the North's total consumption of manufactures before 1975*, and are unlikely to reach 3 percent much before 1990. How can such an infinitesimal percentage of world trade or Northern domestic consumption become the focus of such concentrated concern on the part of Northern private sectors and governmental circles? Two causes are generally apparent.

The first is the concentration of LDC-manufactured exports in specific product lines, a problem not illustrated by aggregate statistics. Seen from this perspective, it is clear that there is an issue of more significant magnitude, but one which would still appear to be of very manageable proportions without resort to protectionism. Except for very narrowly defined product groups—e.g., black and white television sets or radios, where about 50 percent of U.S. consumption is supplied by LDC exports—imports from the developing countries represent a very small proportion of the total supply in Northern countries.

Clothing, the product group that has perhaps contributed most to LDCs' export growth and that represents the highest increase in LDC market penetration, exemplifies the problem. In 1976 the developing countries still supplied less than 8 percent of the total consumption of clothing in the United States. Lumping textiles and clothing together, the proportion was even less—about 4 percent for the United States in 1974, 8 percent in Germany, and 2 percent in France in the same year.

The threat of Northern market innundation by manufactured exports from the developing countries is not substantiated by these statistics. The only real issue is the standard problem raised for liberal trade policy: will the adjustment costs which result from changing trade patterns be allocated in a manner which sustains support for continued trade liberalization? Will adjustment assistance programs be available for labor, capital, and those communities which feel the direct impact of the new international competition? Or will the potential gains to society as a whole from trade liberalization (see Chapter 1) be foregone in order to protect existing jobs and structures of production?

The second cause of concern would also seem to be based on a fundamental misconception, often phrased in Northern business circles as follows: "How many more Japans are out there?" The belief—to the extent that it is a belief rather than an easy excuse for protection—is that there exists a large number of LDCs that are on the verge of breaking into the international trading system with the same capacity to become a dominant global producer in many major industrial sectors that characterized Japan in the 1960s and the 1970s. Two brief observations are in order. First, this misconception reveals an extraordinary lack of insight into the cultural and sociological ingredients of the Japanese "economic miracle," and an equal lack of insight into the very different mix of traits within most countries of Asia, Africa, and Latin America. Second, changing rules and norms of international economic behavior since 1970 will not present developing countries with the same opportunities that existed in the 1960s and the early 1970s. Reforms in the international monetary system (e.g., floating exchange rates, International Monetary Fund [IMF] surveillance), which would create substantial obstacles to the replication of the Japanese international economic strategy and practices, have been continuously introduced since the collapse of the Bretton Woods system in 1971; reforms in rules and norms of the existing international trading regime are being worked on during the present Tokyo Round of the General Agreement on Tariffs and Trade (GATT) negotiations at Geneva. Taken together, the impact of these reform movements is likely to place substantial limitations on many of those monetary and trading practices of dubious legitimacy characteristic of the Japanese export drive of the past two decades, which led to the appearance of "*fair* trade" as a major issue in the politics of international economic relations over the past ten years, and which significantly undermined support for the liberal Bretton Woods system.

In summary, prevalent Northern concerns about the "threat" of LDC industrial competition are, for the most part, misplaced. The major developing-country manufacturing exporters—Taiwan, Hong Kong, and South Korea—account for close to 50 percent of all LDC manufactured exports. These three geographic entities are extraordinarily atypical developing countries, and their capacity to mount sophisticated and sustained export drives will not be matched quickly by other LDCs for reasons which are as much cultural and sociopolitical as economic in nature.

This is not to argue that industrial export competition from the Third World is not to be a growing phenomenon of the 1980s, for it certainly will be a significant issue in international economic relations. Countries such as Brazil, India, Mexico, Malaysia, and Colombia are already caught up in the process of rapid expansion of industrial export capacity, and many others will follow. But the crucial differences are likely to be those of *pace of change* in patterns of trade, and the *methods used* in influencing those patterns. Both differences should strengthen the analytical case for freer trade and the potential support for further trade liberalization.

The *pace of change* in each country should be slower than it was in the Japanese case for two reasons. First, the developing countries themselves are unlikely to be able to set and achieve export goals with the singleness of purpose which characterized a Japan or, for that matter, a Taiwan or a South Korea. Few other developing countries have either the private sector capacity or the governmental panoply of controls needed to operate in the "Japanese" fashion. Second, there should be a greater geographical spread of these new LDC exports throughout the North and other developing countries as well, rather than a simple targeting upon the U.S. market.

In addition, the *methods used* to expand LDC exports should be significantly different than those used in earlier periods, which bordered on unfair trade. Considerable international negotiating effort at Geneva is now being spent in an attempt to distinguish "fair" from "unfair" export promotion practices. Unless all such negotiations fail, it is quite probable that the rules of the game of fair trade will be marked by a greater clarity in the 1980s than they have been over the past fifteen years. The clearer the rules, the greater the potential to overcome neo-mercantilist pressures and to retain support for a liberal trading regime.

If it is counterproductive to consider North-South trading problems in terms of "future Japans," it is essential to think seriously about how trade policy, in the full panoply of economic and political policies, is involved in North-South relations. In policy terms, the ideal solution to problems already replete with conflict would be to use trade policy to reduce North-South confrontation and to begin a search for mutually beneficial rules of trade, rather than to allow growing degrees of Northern protectionism to exacerbate the conflict.

TRADE LIBERALIZATION: THE CASE FOR MUTUALLY BENEFICIAL ACCOMMODATION

International trade liberalization presents significant opportunities for mutual economic gain between countries. Even if the distribution of gains is uncertain, there is a strong presumption that under appropriate international rules all states should benefit. Domestically, effective adjustment assistance policies can also guarantee that the costs associated with trade liberalization are spread in an equitable manner.

Several recent studies of the so-called "Tokyo Round" of trade negotiations now taking place suggest how further trade liberalization could benefit both North and South. A recent study by the Brookings Institution, for example, estimates that Northern countries could gain over $8 billion annually in economic benefits from a 60 percent reduction in their tariffs; this estimate excludes some significant beneficial influences likely to accompany trade liberalization, such as the anti-inflationary impact of tariff cuts and the accompanying stimulus to technical change.

These same policies of trade liberalization could also prove to be of major benefit to the developing countries. It has been estimated that an annual increase of $2 billion in LDC export earnings would result from a 60 percent cut in most Northern industrial tariffs; the figure would double if cuts were to take place in the less-likely area of textiles' now controlled by the Multi-Fibre Agreement quota system discussed earlier. It cannot be too strongly emphasized that, for the developing countries, a more liberal international trading system would produce greater opportunities to earn foreign exchange through exports—particularly of manufactured products—and that the availability of this foreign exchange is, for almost all non–oil-exporting LDCs, vital for the purchase of imported capital goods and raw materials essential for sustained economic growth.

Again one notes the vast difference between literally all LDCs and Japan. As Japan became one of the world's leading exporters, it amassed and held huge amounts of foreign exchange; developing countries, on the other hand, spend almost every cent of foreign exchange they earn on increased imports—particularly on capital goods and agricultural products from the North.

Recent World Bank studies suggest that, if no new protectionist measures are allowed to limit trade flows, LDC earnings on manufactured exports could rise from $33 billion in 1975 to about $96 billion in 1985 in constant (1975) dollar terms. The importance of these earnings is suggested by comparing them with the much smaller foreign assistance volumes and receipts from international lending. Total foreign aid from the North in 1978 did not exceed $15 billion; total net disbursements on LDC commercial borrowing in international capital markets and such public institutions as the World Bank (1975) approximated $30 billion.

A second World Bank estimate suggests that if Northern countries were to dismantle existing trade barriers against LDC-manufactured goods, developing countries could earn $24 billion per year in addition to the amounts projected above. Finally, the World Bank estimates that if the LDCs could overcome their own supply constraints on manufacturing activity they could, under free trade conditions for manufactured goods, increase exports by yet another $21 billion. Thus, if fully rational economic policies were pursued by importers and exporters alike, developing country export earnings from manufactured goods might increase by $45 billion per year above those levels which would result from a continuation of present policies (incipient protectionist tendencies deleted).

The political processes presently influencing Northern trade policies clearly prohibit the tariff-cutting proposals upon which the World Bank's estimates were developed. They are cited simply to set the framework for thinking about North-South economic policies. And in doing so, the following points are also quite relevant. First, it should be noted that the North exports to the South well over three times the value of manufactured products that it imports from there. In 1977 the United States exported $18.5 billion in manufactures to the non–oil-exporting LDCs, and ran a $4 billion trade surplus with them. Including the oil-exporting countries, total U.S. manufactured exports reached $28 billion, and the trade surplus in manufactures was $13 billion. Clearly, Northern jobs lost and companies injured through increased LDC exports must be balanced against Northern jobs gained and firms strengthened by Northern exports to those same LDCs.

Second, while the so-called Generalized System of Preferences (GSP) now allows the duty-free importation of some LDC manufactures into Northern markets, it has accounted for no more than a minuscule increase in LDC exports of manufactured products. One of the largest estimates attributes an additional $500 million per annum in LDC exports to the program. In comparison with the $40 billion in earnings from

LDC-manufactured exports to the developed countries in 1976, and in comparison with the potential trade increases linked to global tariff reductions, the GSP program is, in the aggregate, a small and rather inconsequential policy issue in almost any economic sense.

In sum, all empirical studies of the North-South trade policy issue share the conclusion that both parties to the bargain can gain considerably from further trade liberalization. And almost all studies further emphasize the crucial nature of the contribution which trade liberalization can make to the development process—particularly for the so-called "upper tier," or semi-industrialized and relatively more advanced, developing countries. The added foreign exchange to be earned from the sales of manufactures permits them to repay unusually elevated foreign debts contracted during the global stagnation of the mid-1970s, to continue maintenance of acceptable international credit ratings, and to continue to import the necessary ingredients (capital equipment and raw materials) for the process of industrialization, sustaining aggregate growth rates of approximately 6 percent per year.

A successful outcome in this area of the present North-South economic dialogue will depend to a considerable degree upon the capacity of Northern governments to contain current neo-mercantilist domestic pressures, which not only oppose any further trade liberalization, but also seek to restrict present degrees of commercial freedom.

TRADE LIBERALIZATION: THE PRESENT NORTHERN POLICY DILEMMA

Trade liberalization is difficult for democratic governments to design and implement under the best of economic and political circumstances. This difficulty stems from the concentration and visibility of the costs of liberalization, most particularly in the forms of jobs lost and factories shut down. Since the benefits to both consumers and producers are far more diffuse and far less visible, supporters of trade liberalization tend to be less vocal and less systematic in the presentation of pro-liberalization views than opponents.

Historically, periods of successful trade liberalization seem to be positively related to the following factors: the international leadership of one major economic power willing to absorb short-term economic and political costs in the belief that they will be outweighed by long-term benefits, political as well as economic; the capacity of political leadership in that one country to link the issue of trade liberalization to the broad and ambiguous concept of "national interest"; and buoyant international economic conditions allowing for the rapid reemployment of those factors of production (especially labor) displaced by changing patterns of trade. The current absence of these factors suggests why significant trade liberalization of benefit to the LDCs will be difficult to obtain in the immediate future.

The United States has led the global trade liberalization effort throughout the post–World War II period. The U.S. was able to do so because of its strong competitive economic base, the ability of its political leaders to link trade liberalization and "national security," and favorable international economic conditions (rapid growth, low unemployment, etc.). In recent years, however, each of these conditions has altered rather dramatically. The growing economic strength of Europe and Japan, and an increasingly overvalued dollar, were among the major factors which gradually undermined the competitive edge of many sectors of American industry in the 1960s and early 1970s, creating growing domestic interest group opposition—particularly from organized labor—to trade liberalization.

That opposition was strengthened as the link between trade liberalization and the concept of national security began to weaken. As the cold war thawed and talk of détente lowered the perceived primacy of national security concerns within Northern states, it became increasingly difficult to defend trade liberalization as a necessary ingredient in a strategy which sought to bind the United States, Europe, and Japan against threats of Soviet expansion. Indeed, as the security issue diminished, intra-Northern economic conflicts became increasingly visible and highly "politicized." By 1971 those conflicts, and the policies of all Northern countries which had contributed to them, resulted in the break-up of the Bretton Woods system.

Thus, by the late 1970s no single country was willing (or able) to assume leadership in the fight for further trade liberalization. In this atmosphere, the relative bargaining power of domestic special-interest groups rose, thereby increasing the strength of protectionism. This growing neo-mercantilist strain was greatly strengthened by the general global economic conditions of the mid-to-late 1970s. With many Northern countries facing historically high rates of inflation and/or unemployment, low growth rates, and major degrees of international economic uncertainty (e.g., the price and availability of energy sources, the value and the future role of the dollar in the international monetary system), Northern governments found themselves locked into an international negotiation to further liberalize trade, while they were forced by domestic political and economic pressures to adopt and implement a growing number of protectionist measures.

There is wide disagreement concerning the likely outcome of the contemporary Northern economic policy dilemma. Optimists believe that "collective management" by a small group of OECD (Organization of Economic Cooperation and Development) countries can replace the leadership role of any single state, and that "the management of interdependence" can be accomplished by three or four leading Northern states in a manner which will avert any long-term shifts toward protectionism. Pessimists have far less confidence in the potential for novel forms of "collective management" to contain present pressures for a reversal of the international economic liberalization course set at the end of World War II.

To a considerable degree, the differences in viewpoint stem from differing projections of Northern economic growth rates. Those who believe that Northern countries can shortly resume more rapid growth rates typical of the 1960s and early 1970s are generally also inclined to believe that protectionist tendencies can be overcome. Most pessimists, on the other hand, doubt that there will be a return to such rapid and uninterrupted growth. They cite both domestic and international factors in arguing that the latter half of the 1970s is likely to mark an end to a lengthy period in which annual GNP (gross national product) growth dividends were able to suppress distributional conflicts, domestic as well as international.

In this period of economic uncertainty, attempts to hold support for present degrees of trade liberalization of importance to developing countries, or to further expand their market opportunities, will pose difficult hurdles for Northern political leadership. For despite the fact that present aggregate levels of LDC-manufactured imports are very low, they have expanded rapidly in very narrow product lines and are perceived (incorrectly) to have a significant employment impact, particularly in a depressed labor market. Thus, the aggregate benefits to the North of liberalized trade in Southern manufactures are lost sight of under present economic conditions and perceptions of "future Japans."

Despite the difficulties, continued trade liberalization, with more attention paid to the "rules of the game" and to the broad issue of Northern economic adjustment policies, may still be the best policy option available, and one that is politically viable if collective management can produce agreement on needed trade and monetary rules in the next few years. Success will require several critical policy ingredients. The first will involve a reconceptualization of the purpose and the content of programs of adjustment assistance in Northern countries. The concept must quite consciously take into consideration the projected evolution of productive capacity in developing countries, and must steer Northern workers and capital out of those labor-intensive, standardized-technology industries where growing LDC competitiveness can be foreseen. Northern countries need not move all the way to "indicative planning" in order to identify with a high degree of probability those industries and product lines which are likely to produce the most Southern competition in the coming decade. However, a very serious examination of what is generally referred to as "industrial policy" will be needed to determine the degree to which a variety of state policies can assist private-sector adjustment to changing international competitive patterns.

Second, GATT reforms must assure that the use of escape clauses and adjustment assistance programs is indeed for the purpose of phasing out lines of production which can no longer compete unless they continue to receive protection (external restraints on trade or domestic subventions). Without some form of international surveillance and reporting mechanisms, there is little hope that major abuses of temporary protection and adjustment assistance can be avoided, abuses which in effect turn adjustment assistance into "resistance" assistance.

Third, rules and norms clarifying the concept of fair competition must be developed far beyond their present stage. The history of the past ten years of international economic relations testifies to the need for major progress in clarifying for all parties—Northern and Southern states, exporters and importers—what constitutes fair trade. To take one example, consider the use of export subsidies. Almost all countries promote their foreign sales in one form or another. What forms of promotion are "fair" and what forms "unfair"? What actual subsidies should be acceptable? One recent policy proposal suggests that in order to help standardize the practices now in use, uniform export subsidies could be permitted to the extent of the average level of import duties for any given country.

Difficult as they may be, these are the types of hurdles that must be overcome if trade issues between North and South are to ease rather than increase the degree of strain already present in North-South relationships. If the hurdles are not overcome, there is a double risk to the present international economic system. The first is further exacerbation of North-South relationships, particularly between the North and the upper-tier Southern states which are developed enough to take rapid advantage of broader international trading opportunities. The second risk is to the capacity of Northern countries to manage interdependence in this period of strong neo-mercantilist pressures. An inability of Northern states to reach agreement on international monetary and trade reforms could further weaken present degrees of international economic liberalism.

A number of observers feel that the nation-state cannot live with the degree of restraint on national autonomy which is the concomitant of present degrees of international economic interdependence. One might agree more with their viewpoint were it clear what values each observer would like to see emphasized in the international community.

TRADE, HUMANITARIANISM, AND EQUITY: THE CRUCIAL BALANCE

It may seem strange to some readers that the issue of Northern humanitarian support for Southern economic development, and the impact of that support on Northern thinking about North-South trade relations, has not yet received any mention whatsoever. The reason is simply that the Northern humanitarian interest in the problems of poverty in the developing countries has very seldom been linked to specific issues of trade policy.

The Northern public interest in "assisting the developing countries" has registered in all public opinion research for the past quarter-century. Yet it is a very diffuse interest and, to a great extent, the one set of policies which generally respond to (and draw on) this diffuse support are policies of foreign aid. Despite the oft-repeated remark that foreign aid "has no constituency," and despite the annual congressional battle over the foreign aid budget each year, it is probably not far from the mark to suggest that monies are voted for foreign economic assistance throughout the North each year in considerable part because legislators are aware of this diffuse support. Of course, much of what is called foreign aid is a reflection of very special domestic interests, and much more is a reflection of executive branch foreign-policy goals which have nothing to do with the humanitarian concern for assisting the development process. Nevertheless, general public-opinion polling and survey data on legislators' views support the conclusion that there has, in addition, been a sustained interest in assisting Southern economic development which reflects values and norms of Western culture, and is not simply a reflection of special interests.

But this ingredient has not played any significant role in influencing Northern foreign trade policies, perhaps due to its very diffuseness as well as to a lack of understanding of the economics of the development process. Trade liberalization per se raises other public-opinion concerns which are *more salient* than the rather vague sentiment for assisting the South. If the average American perceives a choice between assistance to the LDC growth process and keeping open a major plant in Peoria, his sympathies go to the latter. And unless the *perception* of this choice is altered—through the introduction of more visible and successful adjustment assistance programs to aid the workers in that plant; through a better understanding of the diffuse benefits to the North of those Southern imports, for example, in terms of fighting Northern inflation; and through a more sophisticated understanding of the role those imports play in Southern economic development (thus connecting them much more concretely to the humanitarian concern issue)—protection for Peoria is increasingly likely to emerge victorious in present international economic and political circumstances.

Quite recently a much more specific issue has arisen which further weakens the humanitarian concern support for trade liberalization *vis à vis* the LDCs. It is the linking of that humanitarian concern to the concept which has come to be called "absolute poverty." As described by the president of the World Bank, absolute poverty "is a condition of life so characterized by malnutrition, illiteracy, disease, high infant mortality, and low life expectancy as to be below any reasonable definition of human decency." The term is generally applied to those 750 million–1.2 billion people in the South living at poverty levels so desperate that, even when they survive to adulthood, such factors as malnutrition, disease, and lack of education have, in effect, deprived them of anything we can label "equality of opportunity" to become productive members of their societies.

Within the past five years, development economists have begun to focus their attention increasingly upon the absolute poverty problem, its causes and potential remedies. Unfortunately, an overly simplistic approach to the problem on the part of some has given rise to the view that: a major contribution to the absolute poverty problem has been misguided LDC efforts at rapid industrialization; a radical altering of development strategies is needed to overcome the absolute poverty problem; industrial sector development should be given lower priority in the development strategy mix; and all Northern assistance should be allocated to the attempt to overcome absolute poverty.

To the degree that a growing Northern concentration on the absolute poverty problem contains the seeds of an anti-industrialization bias—a bias that can be strengthened when applied to export-led industrialization—it becomes increasingly easy for Northern special interests to turn this new concept in development thinking to their own purposes. If the view spreads that LDC industrialization—particularly for export—can often contribute to the magnitude of the absolute poverty problem in developing countries, then the humanitarian support for economic development prevalent within the

North will become even further detached from support for trade liberalization than it has been in the past.

The new emphasis on the problem of absolute poverty, and the attempt to develop a strategy to meet what are now called "basic human needs" in developing countries, is long overdue, and is of vital importance to the process of economic development. In questioning older development strategies, the new emphasis can be of significant assistance in further refining development policies, and in ensuring that development planners—North and South—are constantly forced to face the potential issue of equity trade-offs posed by varying development policies.

However, Northerners must bear in mind the extraordinary degree of economic and sociopolitical differentiation that exists within the developing countries. No single set of policies will be appropriate for all; the proper mix will be different for each LDC. Different economic factor endowments, different economic structures at the present point in their development, different sociopolitical strengths and weaknesses, different private-sector attributes, and different linkages with the international economic system will all tend to suggest varying emphases in the development strategies of each country. Indeed, there will be some LDCs in which export-oriented manufactures production may play a significant role in eliminating absolute poverty. Any aggregate Northern response to the absolute poverty problem that attempts to suggest that Bangladesh and Brazil should follow even vaguely similar development strategies will succeed, not only in destroying the potential international legitimacy of a concept (the meeting of "basic human needs") that deserves all the support it can acquire, but also in further exacerbating the entire range of North-South conflicts and further souring the current North-South dialogue.

A balanced Northern response to Southern developmental needs and desires must include policies which move well beyond an either/or choice concerning industrialization and absolute poverty emphases. Expanded access to Northern markets for Southern industrial goods will continue to be a critical ingredient in successful LDC economic development, as well as a significant benefit to Northern consumers and anti-inflation efforts. Difficult as the political task may be, the effort to hold onto and expand present levels of trade liberalization of benefit to the LDCs must be continued for reasons of Northern self-interest as well as international equity.

Northern commitment to such a trade liberalization strategy need not limit efforts to alleviate the absolute poverty problem. For years we have understood that the achievement of differing economic goals requires the use of different policy tools. The attack on the fundamental causes of absolute poverty requires policies *additional* to trade liberalization, not policies which *replace* that liberalization. While the appropriate mix and ordering of policies to achieve a more appropriate balance between growth and domestic equity is the subject for a different study, this concluding generalization is unlikely to be challenged as a result.

15

D. GALE JOHNSON

Agriculture in the International Economy

The increase in U.S. agricultural exports. Import duties on agricultural commodities. Reasons behind the trade surplus. The growth of factor productivity and of crop yields. The impact of domestic policies on agricultural exports: the United States and other countries.

The prosperity of American agriculture depends upon its access to foreign markets. The output from nearly a third of all cropland is exported, and were this market to significantly shrink, agriculture would be faced with severe adjustment problems. U.S. agriculture employs less than 4 percent of the total labor force and produces approximately 3 percent of the gross national product. Yet in recent years agriculture has accounted for a fifth of total commodity exports.

If it were not for the large surplus of agricultural exports over imports, the position of the dollar in the world money markets would be even more precarious than it is. While numerous other producing sectors have sought additional protection from the competition of imports, agriculture has continued to expand its exports.

U.S. agriculture has emerged as an important net exporter since 1960, and particularly since 1972—a period when its employment of labor and its share of national income produced have both declined. The country's emerging comparative advantage in agriculture has been due to numerous factors, perhaps the most important being that modern science and technology have been applied more fully to agriculture in the United States than anywhere else in the world. U.S. agriculture has become capital-intensive in terms of both physical and human capital per worker. More capital per worker is employed by agriculture in this country than by manufacturing, even when one excludes land from the measure of capital.

While the productivity of American agriculture is a necessary condition for a large net surplus in agricultural trade, the size of the surplus also depends on a gradual reduction in the extremely high trade barriers imposed by many other nations against key farm imports. In such countries as Japan and members of the European Community, these trade barriers often amount to 50 to 100 percent of the international market price.

Finally, our agricultural surplus depends on the willingness of the United States to follow a liberal trade policy. It will depend on a willingness to permit imports of those products for which our costs are not competitive. In the long run, our exports can only be as strong as our imports, which ultimately serve as payment.

The large surplus of American agricultural exports over imports—which has exceeded $10 billion annually since 1974[1]—is a recent phenomenon. In most years between World War I and World War II the United States was a net agricultural importer; although it enjoyed a modest export surplus during World War II and immediately after, throughout the 1950s the United States again imported more agricultural products than it exported.*

Every year since 1960 agricultural exports have exceeded imports, but even during that period, as in the 1950s, food aid and export subsidies were major factors in achieving actual export levels. In 1973 (ending 30 September) the agricultural trade surplus reached $7.2 billion, more than treble the previous year. And in every succeeding year, the surplus has exceeded $10 billion, reaching more than $13 billion in 1978 (FATSR 1974, 1977*a*; FATUS 1978:1).

COMPOSITION OF U.S. AND WORLD TRADE

Since the end of the Korean War, agriculture has declined as a percentage of world commodity trade from about 31 to 15 percent. During the same period, the U.S. share of nonagricultural exports declined from something over 20 percent to 11 percent, while, with some fluctuations, its agricultural exports have remained roughly constant at about 20 percent (FATUS 1976; the last year given is 1975). Thus, while the U.S. share of total world trade has declined significantly, the U.S. share of agricultural exports has remained quite stable. The result has been a significant increase in the U.S. agricultural trade surplus.

Increased U.S. import barriers for agriculture in recent years do not explain this change, which occurred largely after 1970. The most heavily protected farm products during the 1950s and 1960s, such as dairy products, are also the most heavily protected in the 1970s. Most of our agricultural imports enter either duty free (rubber, coffee, cocoa) or at rela-

*Unless indicated otherwise, all dates refer to fiscal year.

tively low rates. In 1976 the average import duty on dutiable farm products was 7.0 percent, in contrast to 10.8 percent a decade earlier. Import duties on dutiable products averaged 5.55 percent in 1974 and 1975 (FATUS 1977:4).

Only beef has experienced apparent significant increased protection in the 1970s. But even this increase is more apparent than real. Although we do have import restrictions on beef and veal in the form of voluntary export restraints, they have only reduced imports of beef and veal by about 15 to 20 percent in some years. During part of the 1970s, however, the restraints were removed, and in 1974 beef imports were below those permitted by the import control program. Many forms of beef—cooked and canned—are not controlled at all, and duties are very low.

The composition of U.S. agricultural exports has changed markedly in the past thirty years. In 1950 cotton and tobacco together accounted for 44 percent of agricultural exports, the grains for 29 percent, and oilseeds (including products), 6 percent. By 1960 cotton and tobacco had declined to 18 percent, and for the three years 1975 through 1977 they declined further to 9 percent, while grains accounted for 46 percent, and oilseeds and products, 23 percent (FATSR 1974 and subsequent issues). In recent years grains and oilseeds, especially soybeans, have eclipsed the role formerly held by cotton and tobacco as the critical factors in U.S. agricultural exports.

THE ROLE OF PRICES AND QUANTITIES

In 1971 agricultural exports amounted to $8.0 billion, with imports at $6.1 billion. By 1977 agricultural exports had trebled (with 54 percent due to increased quantity and 94 percent to increased prices), while imports had somewhat more than doubled (19 percent in quantity, 104 percent by price; FATUS 1978 [September]:111–14, [March]:45–46).[2] Thus, export volume grew almost three times as fast as import volume, while export prices increased somewhat less than import prices. The increased surplus, therefore, was due primarily to the substantial increase in exports.

Besides increases in grains, feeds, oilseeds, and products, there were increases in shipments of fruits, vegetables, animals, and animal products, each accounting for a relatively small percentage of total agricultural exports in 1971—7 percent for fruits and vegetables, and 12 percent for animals and animal products (FATSR 1977:1).

WHY THE TRADE SURPLUS INCREASED

Agricultural imports grew slowly with our slow population growth between 1971 and 1977 or 1978—a time when real per-capita income growth was also small. Moreover, the *income elasticities* of demand for several of our key imports are low. As noted, trade restrictions were not a major factor in restricting the growth of imports.

The increased trade surplus, therefore, must be explained by increased exports. World agricultural trade increased significantly in the years after 1971, and in that time the U.S. share increased from 17.7 percent in 1971 to 20.3 percent in 1976, the last year for which data are available (WEC 1977:23–28).

The most striking example of increased U.S. agricultural exports is in the grains. Between 1969–1971 and 1973–1976 world grain exports increased by 43 million metric tons, of which the United States supplied 36 million metric tons, or 82 percent (WEC 1977:26). Increased grain and products exports accounted for about half of the increase in total U.S. agricultural exports between 1971 and 1976–1978.

Two factors were primarily responsible for the remarkable increase in the U.S. share of world grain trade from 35 percent in 1969–1971 to 49 percent in 1973–1976. First, the

United States increased its grain production more than did its two major export competitors, Australia and Canada;[3] second, because the price system was permitted to work more fully in the United States than in its export competitors, the United States reduced its consumption of grain, especially for feed use, much more than did the other countries.[4] These two changes were not particularly large, but the United States exports a smaller percentage of its total grain production than its major competitors, and therefore small percentage changes in production growth and domestic use resulted in large absolute changes in export.

As already noted, increased exports of oilseeds and products were due to both increased volume and prices, with the latter dominating. The price of soybeans increased relative to feed grains from the early 1970s to the present. The relative price increase has been partly due to European Community policies which permit importation of soybeans (and other oil-bearing crops) duty free, while imposing high variable levies upon feed grains.

WILL THE SURPLUS PERSIST?

The continuation of the large American agricultural trade surplus depends on a number of factors, some of which are indigenous, while others depend upon events elsewhere.

There are three indigenous factors—our agriculture's productivity, growing domestic demand for our major export products, and our domestic agricultural and trade policies. The external factors are essentially two—the level of demand in the rest of the world for U.S. agricultural exports, and the policies followed by other important trading countries or areas.

In recent years the concern has arisen that the growth of factor productivity (output per unit of input) and of crop yields has been slowing. Grain yields increased little if at all during the first several years of the 1970s. Farm output per unit of all inputs in 1974 was little above the level of the late 1960s. However, a substantial increase in factor productivity began in 1975 and continued through 1977 and into 1978. Our measures of factor productivity do not reflect the effects of weather, which was quite adverse in important areas of the country each year from 1974 through 1976. As weather has returned to normal, crop production per acre has returned to its long-term upward trend despite a significant increase in total cultivated area. The increase involves land of less than average productivity, which would depress output per unit of land. And if farmers have adequate incentives to produce, farm production will continue to increase in the future.

Growing domestic demand for our major export products—especially the feed grains and oilmeals—could restrain our export growth. In 1977–1978 domestic use of grains was 16 million metric tons, or 9 percent below 1973–1974. Domestic use, which is primarily for feed, has gradually recovered from the level of 1974–1975, which was low because of sharply increased grain prices the preceding year. The recovery has been slow due to the continuing reduction in the cattle inventory through increased slaughtering rates, which added to the supply of beef and, until recently, reduced the profitability of feeding grain to beef cattle. As cattle numbers start to increase, it will pay to feed increasing amounts of grain to cattle. After declining somewhat in 1972 and 1974, domestic use of oilmeals has increased significantly in recent years and will probably continue to grow. However, since 1975 usage has grown only very slightly more than production. If domestic use of feed grains and oilmeal feeds increased at a rate equal to or slightly greater than production, it is likely that prices would increase somewhat and offset any small decline in exports.

Our domestic agricultural policies could have a significant impact on our agricultural exports. Current price policies for the grains have two major components—a target price, and a price support or loan rate. The target price does not directly affect market prices, since it is used to determine the payments, if any, to be made to producers participating in the commodity programs. Support prices, however, may affect market prices, since farmers can obtain a loan on their crops in the amount of the support price or can sell the grain in the market (Johnson 1978:188–207). When supplies are large and expected market prices low, farmers place a large part of their crops in the price support program. As supplies accumulate and market prices weaken to the price support level, that level begins to influence market prices and thus export prices. If this situation should occur—and the amount of grain in reserve has grown substantially in recent years—the United States will become a residual supplier. Other exporters can dispose of all their supplies simply by underselling U.S. exporters; U.S. exports will decline; U.S. grain stocks will increase; the treasury costs of the program will become large enough to force major efforts to reduce production. If this should happen, then the U.S. agricultural trade surplus could be adversely affected. Thus, the most worrisome domestic factors that could reduce the agricultural trade surplus is the level of price supports.

EXTERNAL FACTORS

Two external factors were noted: growing demand for our agricultural exports, and the policies followed by other countries. Obviously, these two factors are interrelated. If the high-income countries of Western Europe enacted major reductions in import barriers to grain, world grain exports would increase substantially and the United States would share in that growth. European Community grain imports have declined during the 1970s, and if current policies are maintained, imports will continue to decline. Since there is little likelihood that the agricultural policies of the European Community and other Western European countries will change significantly within the next few years, future increases in world grain trade will be due largely to developments in the centrally planned economies and the developing countries.

From 1970–1972 to 1977–1978 world grain imports increased by 47 percent, or 52 million tons, almost 50 percent of which resulted from increased grain imports of the centrally planned economies, and another sixth of which occurred in North Africa and the Middle East as a result of the increased foreign exchange available from increased oil prices. The remainder was taken by the low-income developing countries outside of North Africa and the Middle East (slightly more than a fifth), with a significant part going to such middle-income developing countries as South Korea, Taiwan, Malaysia, and Singapore; Japan accounted for most of the rest (WAS 1978).

It is reasonable to expect that the centrally planned economies will continue to increase their net grain imports. The factors responsible for the past growth continue to plague policymakers in these countries, especially in Europe. The demand for livestock products is increasing faster than the production of feed. Consumer resistance to increased food prices has made it impossible to slow the demand growth through higher prices for meat and milk. Thus, continued growth in grain imports can be expected, though it is not possible to predict future growth of import demand for grain. It is even possible that China could become a much larger net importer of grain in the years ahead, as family incomes are increased and the economy is modernized.

While international trade in grain and other food products will continue to grow in future years, rapid growth in the food imports of the low-income developing countries is unlikely. Several of these countries, including India, are now achieving significant rates of growth of food production. The middle-income developing countries, however, should continue to import increasing amounts of food.

CONCLUSION

The large surplus of agricultural trade has resulted primarily from the high level of productivity of American agriculture and the significant growth in demand for the major farm products produced at low cost in the United States. Our agricultural productivity can continue to improve in the years ahead. Maintaining the large surplus, however, will depend largely on the growth in demand for our exports and the appropriateness of our domestic policies for farm products. If farm output is not restricted for political reasons, and if markets are permitted to allocate available supplies between domestic and export markets, agriculture may continue its strong export surplus.

V

Conclusion

16

RICHARD JAMES SWEENEY

Policy, Trade, and the International Macroeconomy

The case for trade liberalization. The power positions of protectionist groups. The interdependence of trading policies. OPEC's influence. Politics and economics. Macroeconomics and trade negotiations. The need for sound monetary and fiscal policies.

Problems affecting the international economy fall into two general categories: macroeconomic issues and trade policy. Trade policy is an ongoing issue, fought out every day in Congress, the executive agencies, and the courts, as well as in international negotiations. The Tokyo Round of negotiations on the General Agreement on Tariffs and Trade (GATT) is only one of the more visible, current signs of this struggle.

Macroeconomic problems come and go. At present they include relations with Japan, evolution of the international monetary system, the Organization of Petroleum Exporting Countries (OPEC), and U.S. energy policy. Trade and macro issues, however, are closely related.

TRADE ISSUES

The essays in this book reflect the very strong consensus among economists in favor of trade liberalization. The case for free trade is based on the simple truth that voluntary exchange between two people is mutually beneficial—otherwise they wouldn't do it or continue to do it. Since free trade between two nations makes both better off, the question arises—why don't we have it? Why do such powerful political forces favor protection?

Although trade liberalization benefits a nation as a whole, it can hurt some members of that nation—even severely. Those who gain come out so far ahead that they could compensate completely those who lose and the gainers would still be ahead. The problem is that the losers typically are *not* compensated, because no "natural" mechanism ensures compensation. Instead, they must seek political redress (Cuddington and McKinnon, Chapter 1; Amacher, Tollison, and Willett, Chapter 3). Protectionism helps threatened industries and workers, but only at the cost of greater harm to the industries that would benefit from trade.

There is no doubt that trade liberalization can hurt some groups—in particular, unskilled labor (Deardorff and Stern, Chapter 8). Fairness, therefore, would seem to require a program such as adjustment assistance (Bale, Chapter 9).

For threatened industries, however, maintaining protection is the best way to handle compensation—by eliminating any need for it. For this reason, trade policies of Western nations are determined politically by the power positions of the pro- and anti-protection groups. Those favoring protection include industries that are threatened, those that might be threatened in the future, and their allies. Among allies, "labor solidarity" has encouraged some unions to favor protection in order to help out threatened workers. Further, individual consumers often see the damage done in particular cases by freer trade while they overlook the benefits of cheaper imports.

The freer-trade forces include consumers, who benefit from cheaper imports, and those industries that will gain with freer trade. It is often forgotten that many U.S. industries depend on imported materials and components. Over the longer run, moreover, other countries cannot pay for our exports except with funds earned by our imports from them. Since imports ultimately constitute payment for exports, barriers to imports also become barriers to exports. This has been obvious in GATT negotiations, where the United States cannot win freer access to foreign markets except at the "price" of allowing foreign countries to export more to us.

One of our success stories over the past ten years has been the performance of U.S. grains in international markets (Bale, Chapter 9). A major reason for this success has been superior technological progress, which traditionally has supported the American standard of living, and which plays a substantial role in explaining the composition of U.S. exports (McCulloch, Chapter 2). The U.S. steel industry, on the other hand, has lagged (Adams and Dirlam, Chapter 6), and has tried to get effective protection from foreign competition. These two industries put the conflict in clear terms: to increase exports of our high-productivity, low-cost goods, we must allow foreign imports to compete with our inefficient industries.

Governments treat trade as one element in the general set of international problems they face, not as a separate issue. Some of these issues, however, are similar to trade problems. For example, liberalizing foreign investment in an economy, as discussed by Tollison and Willett (Chapter 7), is similar to liberalizing trade for that country. As another example, one argument in favor of a tariff is that it exercises a country's monopoly power in international markets (the so-called "optimum tariff," discussed in Chapters 1, 3, and 11). Schemes to stabilize commodity prices (see Smith, Chapter 12) often have similar aims by organizing a type of cartel. The success of OPEC has inspired other primary product producers to emulate OPEC's actions, and an internationally organized and recognized price stabilization scheme would offer an excellent vehicle.

MACRO ISSUES

International trade and macro issues are never addressed in exclusively economic terms. Political considerations bear heavily on economic policy, and changes in economic interdependence can alter relative political power (Keohane, Chapter 10). Confrontations of nations from North and South take place along a spectrum that includes much more than economics (Hansen, Chapter 14). However, such key economic issues as protectionism and commodity stabilization programs can have major impacts beyond the narrowly economic (Hansen, Chapter 14; Smith, Chapter 12).

Trade is sensitive to the macroeconomic environment of inflation, unemployment, and real economic growth. Indeed, beginning with the OPEC oil price increases of 1973–1974, the price boom in commodities at around that time, and the recession starting in 1974–1975, macro issues have played a dominant role in international economic policymaking. Trade negotiations are substantially dependent on the macroeconomic state of economies. We cannot expect a significant new round of trade liberalization until there is greater and more widespread international prosperity. In this light, the Tokyo Round of GATT negotiations promises to be something of a disappointment, partly because it couldn't really succeed in the recent economic environment.

With the end of the Bretton Woods system in 1971 and the move to generalized floating in early 1973, a search began for new, recognized guidelines toward international monetary and financial behavior. On the supernational level in this evolving system, perhaps the central role of the International Monetary Fund (IMF) will be to encourage nations to run sound monetary and fiscal policies that minimize the harm done to other nations (Heller, Chapter 5).

A major issue in negotiations among nations is coordination of their monetary and fiscal policies (Arndt, Chapter 4). During its first eighteen months the Carter administration was obdurate in urging the Germans and Japanese to join the United States in running expansionary monetary and fiscal policy in order to pull the world out of recession—the "locomotive theory." These nations declined on grounds that such a policy would be inflationary and would have little effect on their real growth rates. While coordination of policies, if well done, remains an ideal, how will conflicts be resolved when nations disagree?

Macro and trade policies are closely linked in bilateral Japanese–U.S. economic relations as well as in U.S. energy policy. While the United States set record current account deficits in 1977 and 1978, it also ran record bilateral deficits with Japan. In part, these deficits were due to above-average economic growth in the United States—and thus an upsurge in imports—combined with below-normal Japanese growth, and thus subnormal Japanese imports (Keran, Chapter 13). One reaction in the United States was to press for liberalization of the rather protectionistic Japanese economy, though McCulloch (Chapter 2) argues that it is generally inappropriate to focus on bilateral deficits. But another reaction was to press for protection for such U.S. industries as steel (Adams and Dirlam, Chapter 6).

The 400 percent OPEC oil price increases of 1973–1974 caused massive transfers of wealth to the OPEC nations.

Some observers, including the Carter administration, have blamed U.S. energy policy for a substantial part of the dollar's debacle in 1977–1978 vis-à-vis the German mark, Swiss franc, and Japanese yen. Those countries, however, are far more dependent than the United States on foreign energy sources. The dollar's real problems are due to the United States' overly expansionary monetary and fiscal policies (Sweeney, Chapter 11).

CONCLUSIONS

It is notable that there is a strong consensus among economists in favor of liberalizing trade. Views on macro issues are much more diverse. It seems clear that many of the United States' international problems are due to domestic inflation, which will subside only with sound monetary and fiscal policies. Such policies alone can stabilize the U.S. economy, the dollar, and ultimately the international economy. The great size of the U.S. economy makes it a major determinant of international economic performance. Not until the United States gets its own house in order can genuine progress toward freer trade be expected. Until then, rising protectionism will continue to accompany macroeconomic disorder.

APPENDICES

5. H. Robert Heller: "The Changing International Monetary System"

Appendix A: Excerpt from Articles of Agreement, International Monetary Fund (Article IV, 1978)

Section 1. General obligations of members

Recognizing that the essential purpose of the international monetary system is to provide a framework that facilitates the exchange of goods, services, and capital among countries, and that sustains sound economic growth, and that a principal objective is the continuing development of the orderly underlying conditions that are necessary for financial and economic stability, each member undertakes to collaborate with the Fund and other members to assure orderly exchange arrangements and to promote a stable system of exchange rates. In particular, each member shall:

(i) endeavor to direct its economic and financial policies toward the objective of fostering orderly economic growth with reasonable price stability, with due regard to its circumstances;

(ii) seek to promote stability by fostering orderly underlying economic and financial conditions and a monetary system that does not tend to produce erratic disruptions;

(iii) avoid manipulating exchange rates or the international monetary system in order to prevent effective balance of payments adjustment or to gain an unfair competitive advantage over other members; and

(iv) follow exchange policies compatible with the undertakings under this Section.

Appendix B: Exerpt from Articles of Agreement, International Monetary Fund (Article IV, 1978)

Section 3. (b) The Fund shall exercise firm surveillance over the exchange rate policies of members, and shall adopt specific principles for the guidance of all members with respect to those policies. Each member shall provide the Fund with the information necessary for such surveillance, and, when requested by the Fund, shall consult with it on the member's exchange rate policies. . . .

These principles shall respect the domestic social and political policies of members, and in applying these principles the Fund shall pay due regard to the circumstances of members.

11. Richard James Sweeney: "Energy, the OPEC Surplus, and the Future of the Dollar"

Appendix: The Forecasting Model

In broad strokes, the model allows OPEC to affect the non-OPEC free world by the price of oil that OPEC sets. The price of oil, along with the resources, technology, and efficiency of the non-OPEC free world and the fiscal and monetary policies of these countries, will determine real growth rates as well as yields in financial markets there. In turn, these growth rates affect the non-OPEC free world demand, since economic growth increases the demand for energy. The financial market yields represent the returns OPEC countries can earn on the assets they hold abroad.

Thus, country models are used to determine behavior in the non-OPEC free world, and this gives the non-OPEC free world demand for oil. From this, the non-OPEC free world supply of oil is subtracted to give the demand for oil from the OPEC countries. These OPEC oil sales, times the OPEC "take," give OPEC's oil earnings from abroad. These foreign earnings are augmented by OPEC's sales of non-oil exports, and also by OPEC's income from the earnings on the assets it holds abroad. OPEC expenditures abroad include expenditures on goods and services, as well as private and official transfers, such as Saudi Arabia's development grants to non-OPEC less-developed countries. The balance of OPEC income from abroad and its outgo to abroad is the OPEC current account. The structure of the OPEC forecasting model is summarized in Table A-1. Table A-2 classifies the variables of the model into those that are determined within the model (the endogenous variables) and those that are not determined within the model (exogenous variables that influence the model's endogenous variables); the exogenous variables are subclassified into those that the model user can specify (such as the non-OPEC free world monetary and fiscal policies) and those that are embedded in the model (such as resources and technology).

Some of these points deserve more detailed comment. First, the country models used to generate output growth rates and financial yields are small models based on rational expectations, and paying primary attention to monetary and fiscal policies as driving variables. The models emphasize international linkages, including links through current accounts, international price competition, international financial market integration, and international influences on money supplies of those countries that intervene in foreign exchange markets to manage the values of their currencies.

Second, the "non-OPEC free world" consists of all countries that neither belong to OPEC nor to the communist world. (This usage is well established, though it bizarrely includes some fiercely totalitarian nations in the "free" world.) The non-OPEC free world supply of oil includes the net supply from communist nations to non-communist countries (perhaps 10 percent of the non-OPEC free world supply of oil). This non-OPEC supply is not forecast by the model, since it is felt that informed judgment yields at least as good results as statistical modeling.

Table A-1
Structure of OPEC Model

Fiscal and monetary policies: resources, technology, efficiency in non-OPEC freeworld (ex) and World oil price (ex)	→	Non-OPEC free world demand for oil (end)	−	Non-OPEC free world supply of oil (ex)	=	OPEC oil sales (end)		
OPEC oil sales (end)	×	OPEC "take" per barrel (ex)	=	OPEC oil earnings (end)				
OPEC net external assets (end)	×	Yield on net external assets (end)	=	OPEC interest earnings (end)				
OPEC oil earnings (end)	+	OPEC interest earnings (end)	+	OPEC non-oil exports (ex)	−	OPEC foreign expenditures on goods and services including official and private transfers (ex)	=	OPEC current account surplus (end)

Table A-2
Variables in OPEC Model

Endogenous Variables	
Non-OPEC:	OPEC:
• *Real growth* and *interest rates* in the U.S., UK, Canada, Germany, France, Japan, Italy, Australia, Brazil, Mexico • Free world demand for oil	• Oil sales to non-OPEC free world • Oil earnings • Net external assets • Interest earnings • Current account
Exogenous Variables	
Specified by User:	Not Specified by User:
• *Fiscal and monetary policies* in U.S., UK, Canada, Germany, France, Japan Italy, Australia, Brazil, Mexico • World oil price • Non-OPEC free world supply of oil • OPEC take/barrel as fraction of price • OPEC non-oil exports • OPEC foreign expenditures on goods and services, including official and private transfers	• Structure and parameters of country models for U.S., UK, Canada, Germany, France, Japan Italy, Australia, Brazil, Mexico • Resources, technology, and efficiency in non-OPEC world

Third, OPEC "take" per barrel is less than the delivered price paid in non-OPEC countries by transportation, insurance, oil company revenues, etc. The take is a variable percentage of the price, at this time perhaps 92 percent.

Fourth, OPEC non-oil exports are not estimated. A fair portion of them depends on political considerations. It is felt that informed judgment gives superior results to statistical forecasting of this variable.

Fifth, OPEC has net external assets—that is, assets in non-OPEC countries. These are net because the majority of OPEC countries is in debt to the non-OPEC world. For example, such OPEC countries as Indonesia and Ecuador remain quite far in debt to the non-OPEC world. Among OPEC countries, Saudi Arabia and Kuwait in particular are major holders of positive net external assets. The OPEC as a whole earns a positive yield, which depends on spreads between the rates paid on debt owed and the rates earned on assets owned. The return on net external assets will depend on how they are distributed across non-OPEC nations, since yields are different across these countries. The yields are forecast by the model. The model assumes net external assets are distributed in the same pattern as in 1977 and early 1978. In order to convert returns into dollars, exchange rate changes are taken into account. For example, if *Deutschmark* (DM)–denominated assets yield 5 percent but the DM appreciates 10 percent against the U.S. dollar, the percentage return of these assets is (approximately) 15 percent. The exchange rate changes are forecast by the model.

Sixth, OPEC imports of goods and services, as well as private and official transfers to the non-OPEC world, are not forecast by the model. Extensive experimentation with statistical forecasting models indicates better results can be obtained from using expert judgment. One reason for this is that imports as well as transfers are very greatly influenced by political decisions. For example, it was essentially decisions by the Saudi government that led to Saudi imports in early

1978 that were substantially larger than had been expected by analysts. Similarly, official Saudi transfers are a political variable. The late 1978 export and import performances of Iran were greatly affected by political disturbances. For the majority of OPEC countries that are net debtors, their imports are constrained by their governments' willingness to go even further into debt, and by their ability to obtain this extra financing.

Seventh, the world price of oil is not forecast by the model. The complex economic and political factors that influence OPEC pricing policy are better left to expert judgment rather than to explicit modeling. However, the model does provide a great deal of information for judging the pressures on OPEC pricing. For example, the model also produces inflation rates from the country models, and thus it is possible to see what is happening to OPEC income in real terms as well as in money terms. Further, the forecast level of OPEC oil sales will have implications for the necessary cutbacks or expansions in OPEC production and how they might be made. These, in turn, feed back into pricing decisions. Thus, a large enough fall in OPEC sales could well lead to a reduction in the price of oil in real terms.

13. Michael W. Keran: "Japan's Trade Surplus and the Value of the Yen"

Appendix: Measuring Real Exports and Imports

The easiest way to compute real exports and imports is to deflate the nominal values by their respective export and import price indexes. The import price index will reflect the foreign price of Japanese imports as well as any changes in the international value of the yen. In the two-year period 1975.4 to 1977.4, Japanese import prices fell 9 percent, which is approximately equal to the difference between the 10 percent rise in U.S. wholesale prices (a measure of the foreign price of Japanese imports), and the 19 percent fall in the value of the dollar relative to the yen.* This result is consistent with the standard economic assumption that Japan is a "price taker" for import goods—the price being determined in world (i.e., U.S.) markets, with the yen import price different only to the extent that the exchange rate changes.

Recall from Table 1 in the text that nominal yen value of imports was unchanged, while the dollar value of imports increased 23 percent between 1975.4 and 1977.4. Deflating the yen value of imports by the import price index gives a real import growth of 10 percent. Deflating the dollar value of imports by the U.S. wholesale price index (WPI) gives real growth of 11 percent. These results are consistent with each other, and also with the pattern of growth in Japanese import demand. As 80 percent of imports are raw materials and other inputs to the productive process—industrial production rather than real GNP is a better measure of demand. As shown in Table A-1, industrial production increased 15 percent in the period, which is roughly in line with increases in real imports. Equally important, the growth in industrial production in 1975 and 1976 is consistent with the yearly pattern of real import growth as shown.

Turning to exports, the yen value increased 22 percent and the dollar value increased 51 percent between 1975.4 and 1977.4. Deflating the yen value by the export price index gives a real export growth of 33 percent, substantially more than the nominal yen value. The reason is that the export price fell 8 percent, almost as much as import prices.

This result is surprising. It means that the substantial 23 percent yen appreciation against the dollar through 1977.4 was almost matched by an equal and opposite fall in Japanese prices relative to U.S. prices. Yen appreciation by itself would have *increased* the size of the nominal trade surplus (the "J" curve phenomenon). Lower inflation in Japan rela-

*While the yen appreciated by 23 percent against the dollar, the dollar depreciated by "only" 19 percent against the yen because of different base of calculation.

Table A-1

Production and Imports
(percent change)

	Industrial Production	Real Imports[a]	Real Imports[b]
1975.4/1976.4	12	10	11
1976.4/1977.4	2	0	0
1975.4/1977.4	15	10	11

[a]Import price index.
[b]U.S.—wholesale price index.

tive to the United States would *decrease* the size of the nominal trade surplus (the reverse of the J curve). The real trade surplus would equal the nominal surplus only when the change in the exchange rate between the United States and Japan was just equal to the difference in inflation rates in both countries. This does not seem to be the case with respect to either the consumer price index (CPI) or wholesale (WPI) prices. However, as indicated in Table A-2, it is true for export prices.

U.S. export prices have increased in line with wholesale prices, which is what is expected if export industries are faced with the same cost and productivity conditions as the average of all industry. In Japan, however, while wholesale prices have *increased* 5 percent, export prices have *decreased* 9 percent. This 14 percent spread is directly related to yen appreciation, and to the attempt of Japanese exporters to keep the dollar price of their goods from increasing faster than the wholesale prices in the United States.

While this pricing strategy will not eliminate effects of the yen appreciation in reducing the Japanese trade surplus, it could well lengthen the period of adjustment. This would occur because the adjustment would operate in the supply rather than the demand side of the market. If the yen appreci-

Table A-2

Prices: U.S. and Japan (percent change 1975.4 to 1977.4)

	CPI[a]	WPI[b]	Export Price
1. United States	12	10	9
2. Japan	13	5	−9
Difference (1–2)	−1	5	18

[a]Consumer price index.
[b]Wholesale price index.

ation had been allowed to raise export prices, there would have been a substitution by consumers of expensive Japanese goods for cheaper U.S. goods in the same product line (like automobiles). However, the reduction in export prices has kept Japanese export goods competitive with U.S. goods, which keeps export sales from declining, but cuts deeply into profits in export business. This will eventually induce Japanese manufacturers to switch sales to the more profitable domestic market.

NOTES

1. John T. Cuddington and Ronald I. McKinnon: "Free Trade versus Protectionism: A Perspective"

1. Summarizing recent reconsiderations of the classical theory by Bhagwati, Ramaswami, and Johnson, Gerald Meier (1973:7) concludes:

> In terms of international welfare economics, free trade is a preferable situation to no trade; restricted trade is also preferable to no trade; free trade is preferable to restricted trade, except that an optimum tariff is preferable to free trade. . . . The only first-best argument for tariff protection is that of *optimizing the terms of trade*. The other arguments have noneconomic objectives, or are for suboptimal policies, or are nonarguments for protection.

2. Kindleberger (1973:77–78) has an interesting discussion of the worldwide rise in tariffs and the League of Nations' attempt in 1927 to negotiate a tariff truce.

3. The interested reader is referred to Kindleberger (1973) for a detailed account of the deterioration in international trade and world output.

4. A counterexample, however, is the Cobden-Chevalier Treaty of 1860 between Britain and France.

5. The GATT, as initially negotiated in 1947, included only the non-communist, developed nations. Since that time most less-developed countries have become parties to the agreement. Under Article 18 of the GATT, however, they have been permitted to retain protective tariffs and import quotas "in order to implement programmes and policies of economic development designed to raise the general standard of living of their people." The industrialized nations thus allowed unrestricted importation of LDC products without demanding reciprocal concessions. This has greatly reduced the incentive for trade liberalization in the LDCs and, it could be argued, has been partly responsible for their highly restrictive trade barriers that evolved after World War II and have, on balance, been retained to the present day. As a result, most missed out on the world trade boom after 1947.

2. Rachel McCulloch: "Determinants and Implications of U.S. Trade Performance"

1. A smoothly functioning system of trade based upon comparative advantage will not necessarily allow the United States to continue its present level of production in any specific industry. Because each nation's comparative advantage shifts over time, trade along lines of comparative advantage—i.e., trade which produces greatest overall benefits—requires substantial internal adjustments. Typically, these include the redeployment of labor and capital between industries, a process often accompanied by lower earnings or unemployment for some factors in the declining sectors. On labor adjustment issues, see also Chapter 8 (Deardorff and Stern) and Chapter 9 (Bale).

2. These hypothetical costs are called autarky prices. Because trade tends to eliminate autarky-price differentials, indices of export prices are likely to measure differences in the composition of exports across countries rather than cost competitiveness.
3. There are significant lags between orders and production in many sectors, but these are short relative to the time horizon entailed in a U.S. foreign direct investment decision.
4. A U.S. trade balance deficit can be associated with lower *overall* employment only if two conditions are satisfied. First, the economy must fit the Keynesian framework—i.e., substantial excess capacity, so that higher demand tends to increase output rather than simply putting upward pressure on prices. Second, expansion through traded-goods demand must have some advantage over other kinds of expansionary monetary or fiscal policies. This would be most likely if excess capacity or unemployment tended to be concentrated in the traded-goods sector of the economy. (On the other hand, for an economy that is operating at or near full employment or with important supply bottlenecks, a trade deficit may serve as a desirable check on inflationary pressures.) It should be emphasized that the issue here is overall employment consequences, not sectoral adjustments. Unions sometimes muddle the distinction by talking about "jobs lost" to a particular industry without mentioning "jobs created" elsewhere in the economy. On the macroeconomic implications of the trade deficit, see also Chapter 4 (Arndt) and Haberler (1978).
5. Within the capital account itself, an important distinction is that between asset transactions undertaken for their own sake—virtually all private capital transactions and some government transactions—and those undertaken by national financial authorities specifically for balance-of-payments reasons, e.g., to influence exchange-rate movements.
6. The channels through which this occurs are discussed below in the section on industry competitiveness in general equilibrium.
7. If the United States has a comparative advantage in the production of R&D-intensive goods, the trade performance of R&D-intensive and non–R&D-intensive goods is likely to differ *more* than that of R&D-intensive and non–R&D-intensive industries, since a given *industry* will manufacture some *products* which are R&D-intensive and others which are not. For a discussion of the statistical issues, see USIER (1977).
8. The landmark study was that of Leontief (1954:3–32). For a survey and evaluation of other empirical evidence, see Bhagwati (1969).
9. Of course, some prices move more and others less than the average, so what matters for a particular industry or product is its own subset of prices rather than overall inflation rates. National average rates are useful, however, in describing overall trends, and when inflation rates are very high, deviations from the average are likely to be swamped.
10. Between 1971 and 1977 the United States maintained its percentage share of total Canadian and non–OPEC LDC imports, but lost ground to other foreign suppliers in the United Kingdom, West Germany, the European Economic Community as a whole, and the OPEC nations. See IMF (1978).
11. These arguments are not the same as the old debate concerning stability and the Marshall-Lerner conditions, but rather have to do with the political/economic pressures faced by monetary authorities.

12. Abroad, endogenous trade-policy developments will work in the opposite direction, as vigorous U.S. trade performance makes the case for protectionism stronger from the foreign viewpoint.
13. This is true even when overall slackness calls for fiscal stimulation, since not all industries will benefit equally from lower taxes.
14. On the U.S. experience with TAA, see Neumann (1978).
15. Obviously, the political and humanitarian problems of adjustment are thorny ones. Nevertheless, it seems vital to move adjustment assistance toward a greater focus upon *adjustment,* rather than allowing it to become an actual drag on the adjustment process. The plight of elderly, female, and minority workers, as well as those employed in geographically concentrated industries, should not be disregarded, but neither should the adjustment problem of a declining industry be allowed to perpetuate itself for the next generation to face anew.
16. Also see Chapter 11 (Sweeney).
17. However, the national security argument was pressed most vociferously by domestic producers with a direct economic stake in the issue.
18. Unusual weather conditions contributed to the 1977 volume increases and average daily imports were somewhat lower for 1978. However, by November 1978 the daily rate—this time without unusual weather conditions—had caught up to the 1977 average as imports climbed even higher, albeit at a slower rate than in the past.
19. Sweeney (Chapter 11) discusses the determinants of OPEC demand for dollar assets.
20. OPEC has discussed repeatedly a proposal to set the oil price in a stronger currency. To do so, however, would make more obvious that the price of oil has been declining in real terms.

3. Ryan C. Amacher, Robert D. Tollison, Thomas D. Willett: "The Divergence between Theory and Practice"

1. For discussion of the basic case for liberal trade policies and analysis of the AFL–CIO arguments for protectionism, see Amacher, Haberler, and Willett (1979), and Willett (1971), in addition to Chapter 1 in this volume.
2. Some of the leading pioneers in the development of public choice theory were Arrow, Black, Buchanan, Downs, Olsen, and Tullock. For extensive references to this literature, see Amacher, Tollison, and Willett (1976), and Mueller (1976).
3. The tendency for producer interests to dominate consumer interests in the determination of economic policies was emphasized by economists long before the development of public choice theory, but we believe that such theory presents a particularly useful framework for analyzing such issues. Previous discussion of the application of public choice theory to international economic issues includes Brock and Magee (1978), Caves (1976), Kindleberger (1975), Pincus (1977), Tollison and Willett (1976), Finger (1979), and Willett (1979*b*).
4. There are limits to expanding the coverage of protectionist bills, however. The typical voter is more sympathetic to concrete examples of restricting imports to avoid short-term losses in jobs than to across-the-board protectionism. As the number of protectionist measures linked together increases, so will consumer opposition to these measures. A bill containing the maximum number of protectionist measures thus does not necessarily have the greatest chance of passage.
5. We should stress that this is not meant as a general argument against vote trading.

What is bad about this form of logrolling at the national level is not that it acts as a means for revealing relative intensities of preferences on national issues, but that in its most blatant forms it is used to reveal relative intensities of preference on essentially local issues that never should have come before the national legislature. When restricted to positive-sum games, logrolling can become a beneficial means for revealing voter preferences on issues.

6. Recently, a number of protectionist measures have been undertaken administratively by the executive branch—for example, various informal quotas on textile, shoe, and television imports—but these have generally been undertaken in hopes that such concessions would keep Congress from passing even stronger protectionist measures.

7. Thus, while we agree with Kindleberger (1975) that there is no single, monolithic, public choice explanation of the historical record of trade policies, we feel that public choice theory is a useful aid in making sense of the various domestic and international forces which affect public policy toward international trade.

6. Walter Adams, Joel B. Dirlam: "Unfair Competition in International Trade"

1. For case studies of protectionism in several U.S. industries, see Mintz (1973).

2. As recently as 9 July 1976, in the *New York Journal of Commerce* (pp. 1, 6), Jacques Ferry, president of the French Steel Industry Association, stated that "a world steel pact is urgently needed to stave off chaotic market conditions." Such a pact, to be negotiated in conjunction with the ongoing multilateral trade talks in Geneva, would "involve major steel producing countries agreeing to orderly marketing procedures, with rules for resorting to production controls and import restrictions when these are justified by previously agreed criteria on levels of investment, employment, deliveries and the like." Not surprisingly, M. Ferry claimed "considerable support from . . . U.S. steel circles for such a pact."

3. The trigger price mechanism applied a series of modifications to estimates of production costs submitted by leading Japanese steel producers, selected because they were assumed to be the most efficient in the world. The product cost estimates, never publicly disclosed and inevitably arbitrary, were transformed into dollar prices below which any importer would be vulnerable to an antidumping proceeding. As the yen/dollar exchange rate moved upward, so did the quarterly revisions of the trigger prices.

4. See remarks of John Shenefield, Assistant Attorney General in charge of the Antitrust Division, before the financial analysts' federation, 29 June 1977, in *Forbes,* 20 February 1978, p. 31.

7. Robert D. Tollison and Thomas D. Willett: "Foreign Investment and the Multinational Corporations"

1. There is considerable debate over just how much economic interdependence has grown over the postwar period. There are, in fact, many different important types of economic interdependence, and different types have been changing at different rates. Perhaps the best-known treatment of growing economic interdependence is Cooper

(1968). For discussions of various types and measures of economic integration and economic interdependence, and references to the vast literature on this subject, see Tollison and Willett (1973), and Pigott, Sweeney, and Willett (1978).

2. One reason this was not more rapidly recognized was that in the most widely followed international statistics—those on our balance of payments—only capital transfers from the United States are included. Because of capital raised abroad, these figures understate the total increase in the amount of capital controlled abroad by U.S. multinationals. Furthermore, sales from these activities are often a multiple of capital stock figures. Thus, even though capital outflows from the United States were only a small fraction of exports in any one year, the sales resulting from U.S. investment activities overseas had become greater than export sales from the United States. For further discussion, see Herring and Willett (1972, 1973).

3. The terms "U.S.-related firms" or "U.S. firms" will be used to cover both foreign affiliates and subsidiaries of U.S.-based firms.

4. See, for example, Vernon (1971). This literature is surveyed in Gilpin (1975), and in Bergsten, Horst, and Moran (1978: Chapter 9).

5. On balance-of-payments effects, see Herring and Willett (1972) and references cited therein.

6. For further discussion of the AFL–CIO arguments, see Mitchell (1976) and Willett (1971), and references cited in those works.

7. For references, see Willett (1971). For general surveys of the economic literature on direct investment and on multinational corporations and their effects, see Bergsten, Horst, and Moran (1978), Hawkins and Walter (1979), Hufbauer (1975), Keohane and Ooms (1975), and Kindleberger (1968, 1970). See also the interesting piece by Baldwin (1970*b*) which discusses why we have both trade and capital movements.

8. For further discussion of current problems of international financial instability, see Willett (1977) and references cited therein.

9. An additional argument originally suggested by J. M. Keynes (1924) is that there may be a divergence between private and national interests in foreign investment as compared to domestic investment that is due to differential default risk. When a foreign railroad goes bankrupt, the investor and the nation lose, whereas when a domestic railroad fails, the investor loses but the nation still has the railroad. This type of national advantage argument would call for relatively more investment at home than calculations by private investors would yield.

10. In many industrial countries, the foreign operations of domestic companies are entirely excluded from domestic taxation. In the United States, domestic tax liabilities are maintained, but foreign tax payments are fully credited against these liabilities.

11. Empirical studies by Wassily Leontief have raised questions about the extent to which capital is relatively more abundant than labor in the United States; but despite the attention given to these findings of the Leontief paradox by international economists, they do not appear to have any influence on popular discussions of these issues. Thus, whether or not capital is really relatively abundant in the United States, the AFL–CIO behaves as if it is.

12. We are aware that there are objections to basing policies on assessments of motivations, but believe that in such a political economy context this type of approach is useful.

9. Malcolm D. Bale: "Adjustment Assistance: Dealing with Import-Displaced Workers"

1. The Stolper-Samuelson theorem, relevant for a long-run, competitive situation, predicts that in a capital-abundant country labor will become worse off and capital better off with free trade. In the short run, when resources are not mobile between industries and factor markets are not competitive, the effects instead are specific to resources in the impacted industries (see Baldwin [1970*a*] and Bale [1976]). Justification for assuming noncompetitive labor markets in the present analysis is given below.
2. See Bale (1974:49–79) for a discussion of the criteria for receiving adjustment assistance and the problems encountered by petitioning workers and firms.
3. See studies by Bale (1976:245), Bale and Miller (1977:13), McCarthy (1975), and Schriver, Bowlby, and Pursell (1976:547–56). The workers were surveyed in 1972 and 1973.
4. This figure is an underestimate, because the amount of time necessary to find employment for those still seeking work at the end of the interview period is not accounted for. Those who drop out of the labor force are not treated separately in the rest of the analysis, i.e., calculations implicitly assume that all workers remain in the labor force. Whether the losses suffered by those who drop out of the labor force are larger or smaller than the losses of those who remain in the labor force is not clear, given that there is no unambiguous indication of the opportunity cost of leisure time when labor markets are characterized by non–market-clearing wages.
5. His losses are actually smaller than this, since his wages are taxable, while unemployment insurance and trade payments are not. Additionally, special counseling and retraining benefits were provided to some displaced workers.

10. Robert O. Keohane: "The International Political Economy of the 1980s"

1. Marx, of course, made this point. See also Viner (1948) and Wallerstein (1974).
2. For the data in this and the preceding paragraph, see Katzenstein (1975), IMF Survey (1977), Morgan Guarantee (1977), and USIER (1977).
3. See Keohane and Nye (1977:8 19) for a more detailed discussion of interdependence as an analytical concept. The first clear statement of the notion of interdependence as vulnerability appears in Waltz (1970).
4. For an overview, see Gultung (1971). See also Caporaso (1979), editor of a special issue of *International Organization* on dependence and dependency.
5. See the discussion in McCracken (1977), a report to the OECD by a group of independent experts, henceforth referred to as the "McCracken Report."
6. For a discussion of this problem, see Hirsch and Doyle (1977). See also Whitman (1977), and Keohane and Nye (1977: Chapter 8).
7. Statement by Cooper (1977:4), as Under-Secretary for Economic Affairs Designate, before the Subcommittee on Foreign Economic Policy of the Senate Foreign Relations Committee, 18 March 1977.
8. For an interesting discussion, see Hansen (1978).
9. For a lament about ungovernability, see Crozier, Huntington, and Watanuki (1975), especially the essay by Huntington. The McCracken Report implies that stronger government is necessary for capitalism. See Keohane (1979) for a critique.

11. Richard James Sweeney: "Energy, the OPEC Surplus, and the Future of the Dollar"

1. OPEC members are Saudi Arabia, Kuwait, the United Arab Emirates, Iran, Iraq, Libya, Qatar, Algeria, Indonesia, Nigeria, Venezuela, Ecuador, and Gabon.
2. For an excellent exposition of these views, see Willett (1979*a*).
3. For example, many studies of capital flows find that an increase in growth will induce larger capital inflows, and this is often interpreted as being due to the country having more attractive investments and a larger number of them. For an early and influential study, see Miller and Whitman (1970).
4. This argument is based on the view that exchange rates will adjust today to reflect movements in rates that are expected for tomorrow. It is very much the same approach used in the "random walk" theory of stock market behavior. See Sweeney (1979).
5. This view is a major element of the monetary approach to analyzing international financial problems. See Johnson (1972).
6. While it is true that the long-run elasticity of demand for oil (or for energy in general) is greater than the short-run elasticity, the elasticity is still generally considered to be quite small. As an example—used because it is based on work done by and for the Federal Energy Agency (now in the Department of Energy)—see Marshalla (1977). The elasticity estimates reported there are relatively similar to those used for the forecast discussed below.
7. The optimum tariff argument depends on the country as a whole having some monopoly power in international markets. By cutting back on foreign sales, it can increase profits by raising its selling price; if exporters are not organized enough to do this, government can do it with tariffs and/or subsidies. Foreign governments are, however, likely to retaliate. For an application of this reasoning to the international oil market, see Sweeney (1977).
8. Such sentiments pop up weekly. For example, after this chapter was written, the 27 November 1978 issue of *Newsweek* ran a cover story, "The Buying of America," and the 24 November 1978 *Los Angeles Times* ran a front-page story on the reaction in the United States to Arab investments.
9. An excellent source of forecasts of the OPEC financial situation is Morgan Guaranty (1977 [November], 1978 [April, July]). Relevant sources include WAES (1977), CIA (1977), Moran (1978).
10. This is based on a relatively conservative estimate of OPEC's net external assets at the end of 1977 of close to $150 billion. While this is in the range of Morgan Guaranty estimates, other observers would place the estimate some $20 billion larger. This would raise the estimate of maximum net external assets by somewhat over $20 billion, and would make each year's current account surplus higher by perhaps $1 billion. It is important to note, however, that the general pattern of the surpluses' fall would be unaltered.

12. Gordon W. Smith: "International Commodity Agreements"

1. The Group of 77, the principal LDC negotiating bloc, now includes more than 110 countries, basically all the LDC members of the United Nations.
2. The demand for practically all primary commodities is inelastic in the short run, i.e., over a year or two. With industrial raw materials, demand fluctuations over the

business cycle are the primary source of short-run instability. In a recession, demand and price both fall, so total sales proceeds also must fall. In the case of agricultural products, fluctuations in output are due in good part to weather conditions or production lags (as with tree crops). Prices fall as production rises. Due to inelastic demand, the percentage decrease (increase) in prices is greater than the percentage increase (decrease) in production. So in this case, too, revenues fluctuate with prices.

3. If the European Common Market is treated as one entity, the percentage of its exports which went to non-OPEC LDCs would be higher than either that of Japan or the United States.

4. The Phillips curve relates the rate of inflation to the rate of unemployment, while Okun's Law relates the growth of output to the growth of employment. Both, particularly the Phillips curve, have been controversial items in the 1970s.

13. Michael W. Keran: "Japan's Trade Surplus and the Value of the Yen"

1. This results from the different base of calculating the charges. To give a simple example, if oranges and apples are $1 each, and the price of oranges goes to $2, then the price of oranges has increased *100 percent* relative to apples, and the price of apples has declined *50 percent* relative to oranges.

2. It is not at all clear whether it is correct to add the two adjustments discussed above to find the real underlying trade balance of Japan. If the Japanese had followed a type of monetary and fiscal policy which would have achieved full employment in 1977, the actual and expected inflation rate would have been higher and the yen would not have appreciated as dramatically as it did. If only the business cycle adjustments were made, the underlying trade surplus would have been approximately $6 billion versus the reported $18 billion.

3. The retail price of rice in Japan is "only" three times the world price. Farmers sell all of their rice to the government, and the government sells it to the consumers. The rice stabilization fund of the Ministry of Finance is a large deficit item in the government budget.

4. These results are taken from Houthakker and Magee (1969:111). While this study is somewhat dated, its results have not been significantly changed by later research. For example, the authors have somewhat higher export and import price elasticity for Japan than those estimated by others. However, the fundamental point, that Japan's export elasticities are much higher than other countries and her import elasticities are much lower than in other countries, holds for all studies of Japanese trade.

5. At least part of the high export elasticity of Japanese goods results from the fact that, in a rapidly growing economy, export industries tend to grow faster than the average of all industries because they benefit from a higher rate of technological innovation. We should expect that a slowing of Japanese growth would slow technological development in the export industry and therefore reduce the size of the export elasticity.

15. D. Gale Johnson: "Agriculture in the International Economy"

1. All references to years in this chapter are to fiscal years, unless otherwise indicated, with the ending year given. With the recent change in the federal fiscal year,

all data refer to fiscal years ending 30 September for recent years, and 30 June for earlier years.

2. Quantity indexes are for fiscal years; price indexes are for calendar years.

3. Data on production and domestic use from various issues of WAS.

4. Both Australia and Canada held domestic prices of grains below export prices. See Johnson, Grennes, and Thursby (1977:63).

REFERENCES

Adams, Walter, and Dirlam, Joel B. 1964. "Steel Imports and Vertical Oligopoly Power." *American Economic Review* (September).

Amacher, Ryan C.; Haberler, Gottfried; Willett, Thomas D., eds. 1979. *Challenges to a Liberal International Economic Order*. Washington, DC: American Enterprise Institute.

Amacher, Ryan C., and Sweeney, Richard James, eds. 1976. *The Law of the Sea*. Washington, DC: American Enterprise Institute.

Amacher, Ryan C.; Tollison, Robert D.; Willett, Thomas D., eds. 1976. *The Economic Approach to Public Policy*. Ithaca, NY: Cornell University Press.

Baldwin, Robert E. 1970*a*. *Nontariff Distortions of International Trade*. Washington, DC: The Brookings Institution.

———. 1976. "The Political Economy of Postwar U.S. Trade Policy." *The Bulletin* (NYU).

———. 1970*b*. "The Theory of Trade in Inputs and Outputs." *American Economic Review* (May).

Bale, Malcolm D. 1974. "Adjustment Assistance under the Trade Expansion Act of 1962." *Journal of International Law and Economics* 9.

———. 1976. "Estimates of Trade-Displacement Costs for U.S. Workers." *Journal of International Economics* 6.

———, and Miller, D. P. 1977. "Trade Adjustment Assistance: Provisions of the Trade Act of 1974 and Further Worker Experience." *Industrial Gerontology* 4.

———, and Mutti, J. H. 1978. "Income Losses, Compensation, and International Trade." *Journal of Human Resources* 13.

Ball, David Stafford. 1967. "United States Effective Tariffs and Labor's Share." *Journal of Political Economy* 75 (April).

Baranson, Jack. 1976–1977. "Technology Exports Can Hurt Us." *Foreign Policy* 25 (Winter).

Barnet, Richard J., and Muller, Ronald E. 1974. *Global Reach: The Power of Multinational Corporations*. New York: Simon and Schuster.

Behrman, Jere. 1977. *International Commodity Agreements: An Evaluation of the UNCTAD Integrated Commodity Programme*. Washington, DC: Overseas Development Council.

Bergsten, C. Fred. 1974. "Coming Investment Wars?" *Foreign Affairs* (October).

———; Horst, Thomas; Moran, Theodore H. 1978. *American Multinationals and American Interests*. Washington, DC: Brookings Institution.

———, and Krause, Lawrence B., eds. 1975. *World Politics and International Economics*. Washington, DC: Brookings Institution.

Bhagwati, Jagdish N., ed. 1977. *The New International Economic Order: The North-South Debate*. Cambridge, MA: MIT Press.

———. 1969. *Trade, Tariffs and Growth*. Cambridge: Cambridge University Press.

———, and Ramaswami, V. K. 1963. "Domestic Distortions, Tariffs, and the Theory of Optimum Subsidy." *Journal of Political Economy* 71 (February).

Biemiller, A. (AFL-CIO). 1972. *Statement at Hearings on Trade Adjustment Assistance before the Subcommittee on Foreign Economic Policy*. 92d Congress, 2d Session. Washington, DC: Government Printing Office.

Brenner, S. R. 1977. "Economic Interests and the Trade Agreements Program, 1934–1940: A Study of Institutions and Political Influence." Doctoral dissertation, Stanford University.

Breton, Albert. 1964. "The Economics of Nationalism." *Journal of Political Economy* 72 (August).

Brock, William A., and Magee, Stephen P. 1978. "The Economics of Special Interest Politics: The Case of the Tariff." *American Economic Review* 68 (May).

Canada, Statistics Canada. Various years. *Canada Year Book*. Ottawa: Information Canada.

Caporaso, James A. 1979. *International Organization* (Winter).

Caves, Richard E. 1976. "Economic Models of Political Choice: Canada's Tariff Structure." *Canadian Journal of Economics* 9 (April).

Cheh, John H. 1976. "A Note on Tariffs, Nontariff Barriers, and Labor Protection in United States Manufacturing Industries." *Journal of Political Economy* 84 (April).

CIA. 1977. *The International Energy Situation: Outlook to 1985*. ER 77–10240–U (April).

Cline, William R., ed. 1978. *Proposals for a New International Economic Order: An Economic Analysis of Effects on Rich and Poor Countries*. Washington, DC: Overseas Development Council.

Comptroller General of the United States. 1974. "Economic and Foreign Policy Effects of Voluntary Restraint Agreements in Textiles and Steel." *Report B–179342* (31 March). Washington, DC: Government Printing Office.

Cooper, Richard N. 1968. *The Economics of Interdependence*. New York: McGraw Hill.

———. 1977. "The International Economic Situation." Press release. Washington, DC: Department of State.

———. 1972–1973. "Trade Policy Is Foreign Policy." *Foreign Policy* 9 (Winter).

———, and Lawrence, Robert Z. 1975. "1972–1975 Commodity Boom." In *Brookings Papers on Economic Activity* 3. Washington, DC: Brookings Institution.

Council of Economic Advisors. 1978. *Economic Indicators*. Washington, DC: Government Printing Office.

Crain, W. Mark, and Tollison, Robert D. 1971. "The Influence of Representation on Public Policy." *Journal of Legal Studies* 6 (June).

Crozier, Michel J.; Huntington, Samuel P.; Watanuki, Joli. 1975. *The Crisis of Democracy*. New York: New York University Press.

Deardorff, Alan V.; Stern, Robert M.; Greene, Mark N. 1978. "The Sensitivity of Industrial Output and Employment to Exchange-Rate Changes in the Major Industrialized Countries." In *Trade and Payments Adjustment under Flexible Exchange Rates,* ed. J. P. Martin and M. A. M. Smith. London: Macmillan.

Dewald, W., ed. 1978. *The Impact of International Trade and Investment on Employment*. Washington, DC: U.S. Department of Labor.

FATSR. 1974, 1977*a*. *U.S. Foreign Agricultural Trade Statistical Report, Fiscal Year 1977*. Supplement to the monthly *Foreign Agricultural Trade of the United States* (FATUS) (April 1978). Washington, DC: Economics, Statistics, and Cooperative Service, U.S. Department of Agriculture.

FATUS. 1976, 1977, 1978. *Foreign Agricultural Trade of the United States*. Washington, DC: Economic Research Service, U.S. Department of Agriculture.

Federal Trade Commission. 1977. *Report on Steel*. Washington, DC: Government Printing Office.

Feldstein, Martin. 1978. "The Private and Social Costs of Unemployment." *American Economic Review* 68.

Fellner, W., ed. 1978. *Contemporary Economic Problems*. Washington, DC: American Enterprise Institute.

Fieleke, Norman S. 1971. "The Cost of Tariffs to Consumers." *New England Economic Review* (September/October).

Finger, J. Michael. 1979. "Trade Liberalization: A Public Choice Perspective." In *Challenges to a Liberal International Economic Order,* ed. Ryan C. Amacher, Gottfried Haberler, and Thomas D. Willett. Washington, DC: American Enterprise Institute.

Fisher, B. S. 1972. *The International Coffee Agreement: A Study in Coffee Diplomacy*. New York: Praeger.

Gilpin, Robert. 1975. "Three Models of the Future." In *World Politics and International Economics,* ed. C. Fred Bergsten and Lawrence B. Krause. Washington, DC: Brookings Institution.

———. 1975. *U.S. Power and the Multinational Corporation—the Political Economy of Foreign Direct Investment*. New York: Basic Books.

Gosovic, Branislav, and Ruggie, John Gerard. 1976. "On the Creation of a New International Economic Order." *International Organization* 30 (Spring).

Great Britain, Central Statistical Office. 1974. *Statistical Abstract of the United Kingdom, 1974*. London: Her Majesty's Stationery Office.

Gultung, Johan. 1971. "A Structural Theory of Imperialism." *Journal of Peace Research* 2.

Haberler, Gottfried. 1978. "Reflections on the U.S. Trade Deficit and the Floating Dollar." In *Contemporary Economic Problems 1978,* ed. W. Fellner. Washington, DC: American Enterprise Institute.

———. 1950. "Some Problems in the Pure Theory of International

Trade." *Economic Journal* 60 (June).

Hansen, Roger. 1978. *North-South Relations in the 1980s: The Necessity for Choice*. New York: Council on Foreign Relations.

Hawkins, Robert G., and Walter, Ingo. 1979. "International Investment and the Multinational Corporation." In *Challenges to a Liberal International Economic Order,* ed. Ryan C. Amacher, Gottfried Haberler, and Thomas D. Willett. Washington, DC: American Enterprise Institute.

Herring, Richard, and Willett, Thomas D. 1972. "The Capital Control Program and U.S. Investment Activity Abroad." *Southern Economic Journal* (July).

———. 1973. "On the Relationship between U.S. Investment at Home and Abroad." *Revista Internationale di Scienze Economiche e Commerciale* 1.

Hirsch, Fred., et al. 1977. *Alternatives to Monetary Disorder*. New York: Council on Foreign Relations.

Hirsch, Fred, and Doyle, Michael. 1977. "Politicization in the World Economy and Necessary Conditions for an International Economic Order." In *Alternatives to Monetary Disorder*, ed. Fred Hirsch et al. New York: Council on Foreign Relations.

Hirsch, Fred, and Goldthorpe, John, eds. 1978. *The Political Economy of Inflation*. London: Martin Robertson; Cambridge, MA: Harvard University Press.

Hirschman, Albert O. 1945, 1969. *National Power and the Structure of Foreign Trade*. Berkeley, CA: University of California Press.

Houthakker, Henrik S., and Magee, Steven P. 1969. "Income and Price Elasticities in World Trade." *Review of Economics and Statistics* (May).

Hufbauer, Gary C. 1975. "The Multinational Corporation and Direct Investment." In *International Trade and Finance,* ed. Peter B. Kenen. New York: Cambridge University Press.

———, et al. 1975. *U.S. Taxation of American Business Abroad*. Washington, DC: American Enterprise Institute.

IMF. 1978. *Directions of Trade Annual 1971–1977*. Washington, DC: International Monetary Fund.

IMF Survey. 1977 (various issues). Washington, DC: International Monetary Fund.

Imlah, Albert H. 1958. *Economic Elements of the Pax Britannica*. Cambridge, MA: Harvard University Press.

Johnson, D. Gale. 1978. "The Food and Agriculture Act of 1977: Implications for Farmers, Consumers, and Taxpayers." In *Contemporary Economic Problems 1978*. Washington, DC: American Enterprise Institute.

Johnson, Harry G. 1965. "An Economic Theory of Protectionism, Tariff Bargaining, and the Formation of Customs Unions." *Journal of Political Economy* 73 (June).

———. 1972. "The Monetary Approach to Balance of Payments Theory." *Journal of Financial and Quantitative Analysis*.

Johnson, Paul R.; Grennes, Thomas; Thursby, Marie. 1977. "Devaluation,

Foreign Trade Controls and Domestic Wheat Prices." *American Journal of Agricultural Economics* 59, 4 (November).

Katzenstein, Peter J. 1975. "International Interdependence: Some Long-Term Trends and Recent Changes." *International Organization* 29–4 (Autumn).

Kenen, Peter B., ed. 1975. *International Trade and Finance*. New York: Cambridge University Press.

Keohane, Robert D. 1979. "Neo-Orthodox Economics, Inflation, and the Role of the State: Political Implications of the McCracken Report." *World Politics*.

———, and Nye, Joseph S. 1977. *Power and Interdependence: World Politics in Transition*. Boston: Little Brown.

———, and Ooms, Van Doorn. 1975. "The Multinational Firm and International Regulation." In *World Politics and International Economics,* ed. C. Fred Bergsten and Lawrence B. Krause. Washington, DC: Brookings Institution.

Keynes, John Maynard. 1924. "Foreign Investment and National Advantage." *The Nation* 35 (August).

———. 1937. "The Policy of Government Storage of Foodstuffs and Raw Materials." *The Economic Journal* 68.

Kindleberger, Charles P. 1968. *American Business Abroad*. New Haven, CT: Yale University Press.

———, ed. 1970. *The International Corporation*. Cambridge, MA: MIT Press.

———. 1975. "The Rise of Free Trade in Western Europe." *Journal of Economic History* 35 (March).

———. 1973, 1974. *The World in Depression 1929–1939*. Berkeley, CA: University of California Press.

———, and Lindert, P. J. 1978. *International Economics*. 6th ed. Homewood, IL: Irwin.

Kolko, Joyce, and Kolko, Gabriel. 1972. *The Limits of Power: The World and United States Foreign Policy, 1945–1954*. New York: Harper and Row.

Krause, L. B., and Dam, K. W. 1964. *Federal Tax Treatment of Foreign Income*. Washington, DC: Brookings Institution.

Kreinin, Mordechai E. 1975. *International Economics: A Policy Approach*. 2d ed. New York: Harcourt, Brace, Jovanovich, Inc.

———, and Finger, J. Michael. 1976. "A Critical Survey of the New International Economic Order." *Journal of World Trade Law* 10 (November/December).

Law, Alton D. 1975. *International Commodity Agreements: Setting Performance and Prospects*. Lexington, KY: Lexington Books.

Lawrence, R. Z. 1978. "An Analysis of the 1977 U.S. Trade Deficit." *Brookings Papers on Economic Activity* 1. Washington, DC: Brookings Institution.

Leontief, Wassily. 1954. "Domestic Production and Foreign Trade: The American Capital Position Re-Examined." *Economia Internazionale* 7 (February).

Logue, D. E. 1976. "Does It Make a Difference Whether Petrodollars Are

Channeled to the Eurodollar Market or to U.S. Financial Markets?'' In *Eurocurrencies and the International Monetary System,* ed. C. Stein, J. Makin, and D. E. Logue. Washington, DC: American Enterprise Institute.

Lowinger, T. C. 1975. ''The Technology Factor and the Export Performance of U.S. Manufacturing Industries.'' *Economic Inquiry* (June).

Luttrell, Clifton B. 1978. ''Imports and Jobs—the Observed and Unobserved.'' *Review* (June). St. Louis, MO: Federal Reserve Bank.

McCarthy, J. 1975. *Trade Adjustment Assistance: A Case Study of the Shoe Industry in Massachusetts.* Report No. 58 (May). Boston: Federal Reserve Bank of Boston.

McCord, N. 1970. *Free Trade: Theory and Practice from Adam Smith to Keynes.* Newton Abbot: David and Charles, Ltd.

McCracken, Paul. 1977. *Towards Full Employment and Price Stability.* Paris: OECD.

McCulloch, Rachel. 1978. *Research and Development as a Determinant of U.S. International Competitiveness.* Washington, DC: National Planning Association.

McFadden, Daniel, and Oates, Wallace. 1978. ''Discussion.'' *American Economic Review* 68 (May).

Magee, Stephen P. 1977. ''Three Simple Tests of the Stolper-Samuelson Theorem.'' Working Paper 77–28, Graduate School of Business, University of Texas at Austin (February).

———. 1972. ''The Welfare Effects of Restrictions on U.S. Trade.'' *Brookings Papers on Economic Activity.* Washington, DC: Brookings Institution.

Maier, Charles S. 1978. ''The Politics of Inflation in the Twentieth Century.'' In *The Political Economy of Inflation,* ed. Fred Hirsch and John Goldthorpe. London: Martin Robertson; Cambridge, MA: Harvard University Press.

Malmgren, Harold B. 1970–1971. ''Coming Trade Wars? (Neomercantilism and Foreign Policy).'' *Foreign Policy* 1 (Winter).

Marshalla, R. 1977. ''Intertemporal Efficiency and the World Price of Oil.'' *Annals of Economic and Social Measurement.*

Martin, J. P., and Smith, M. A. M., eds. 1978. *Trade and Payments Adjustment under Flexible Exchange Rates.* London: Macmillan.

Mathias, P. 1969. *The First Industrial Revolution: An Economic History of Britain, 1700–1914.* New York: Charles Scribner's Sons.

Meier, Gerald M. 1973. *Problems of Trade Policy.* New York: Oxford University Press.

Miller, Norman C., and Whitman, Marina. 1970. ''A Mean-Variance Analysis of United States and Foreign Long-Term Portfolio Investment.'' *Quarterly Journal of Economics* (May).

Mintz, Ilse. 1973. *U.S. Import Quotas: Cost and Consequences.* Washington, DC: American Enterprise Institute.

Mitchell, Brian, and Deane, Phyllis. 1965. *Abstract of British Historical Statistics.* Cambridge: Cambridge University Press.

Mitchell, Brian, and Jones, H. G. 1971. *Second Abstract of British Histor-*

ical Statistics. Cambridge: Cambridge University Press.

Mitchell, Daniel J. B. 1976. *Labor Issues of American International Trade and Investment*. Baltimore, MD: Johns Hopkins University Press.

Moran, T. H. 1978. *Oil Prices and the Future of OPEC*. Washington, DC: Resources for the Future.

Morgan Guaranty. 1977, 1978. *World Financial Markets*. New York: Morgan Guaranty Trust Company.

Mueller, Dennis C. 1976. "Public Choice: A Survey." *Journal of Economic Literature* 14 (June).

Musgrave, Peggy B. 1969. *United States Taxation of Foreign Investment Income*. Cambridge, MA: Harvard Law School.

National Science Board. 1976. *Science Indicators*. Washington, DC: Government Printing Office.

Neumann, G. R. 1978. "The Direct Labor Market Effects of the Trade Adjustment Assistance Program." In *The Impact of International Trade and Investment on Employment,* ed. W. Dewald. Washington, DC: U.S. Department of Labor.

Pigott, Charles; Sweeney, Richard James; Willett, Thomas D. 1978. "Aggregate Economic Fluctuations and the Synchronization of Economic Conditions among Industrial Countries." *Revista Internationale di Scienze Economiche e Commerciale* 5.

Pincus, Jonathan J. 1977. *Pressure Groups and Politics*. New York: Columbia University Press.

Plott, Charles R. 1968. "Some Organizational Influences on Urban Renewal Decisions." *American Economic Review* 58 (May).

Popkin, Joel. 1974. "Commodity Prices and the U.S. Price Level." *Brookings Papers on Economic Activity* 1. Washington, DC: Brookings Institution.

Schiavo-Campo, Salvatore. 1978. *International Economics: An Introduction to Theory and Policy*. Cambridge, MA: Winthrop Publishers, Inc.

Schriver, W. R.; Bowlby, R.; Pursell, D. E. 1976. "Evaluation of Trade Readjustment Assistance." *Social Science Quarterly* 57 (December).

Schumpeter, Joseph. 1934, 1951. *The Theory of Economic Development: An Inquiry into Profits, Capital, Credit, Interest, and the Business Cycle*. Trans. Redvers Opie. Cambridge, MA: Harvard University Press.

Smith, Gordon W. 1979. "Commodity Instability: New Order or Old Hat?" In *Challenges to a Liberal Economic Order,* ed. Ryan C. Amacher and Thomas D. Willett. Washington, DC: American Enterprise Institute.

———, and Schink, George R. 1976. "The International Tin Agreement: A Reassessment." *The Economic Journal* 86 (December).

Stigler, George J. 1971. "The Theory of Economic Regulation." *Bell Journal of Economics and Management Science* 2 (Spring).

Stolper, Wolfgang F., and Samuelson, Paul A. 1941. "Protection and Real Wages." *Review of Economic Studies* 9 (November).

Sweeney, Richard James. 1977. "Alternative Tariff and Quota

Mechanisms in the Face of a Monopolistic Exporter of a Non-Renewable Resource.'' *Weltwirtschaftliches Archiv*.

———. 1979. ''An Introduction to Efficient Information Processing by Markets.'' In *Studies on Exchange Rate Flexibility,* ed. Richard James Sweeney and Thomas D. Willett. Washington, DC: American Enterprise Institute.

———, and Willett, Thomas D. 1977. ''Eurodollars, Petrodollars, and World Liquidity and Inflation.'' Carnegie-Rochester Conference Series 5. *Supplement to the Journal of Monetary Economics*.

———, and Willett, Thomas D. 1979. *Studies on Exchange Rate Flexibility*. Washington, DC: American Enterprise Institute.

Taylor, Lance; Sarris, Alexander H.; Abbott, Philip C. 1978. *Grain Reserves, Emergency Relief, and Food Aid*. Washington, DC: Overseas Development Council.

Tollison, Robert D., and Willett, Thomas D. 1976. ''Institutional Mechanisms for Dealing with International Externalities: A Public Choice Perspective.'' In *The Law of the Sea,* ed. Ryan C. Amacher and Richard James Sweeney. Washington, DC: American Enterprise Institute.

———. 1973. ''International Integration and the Interdependence of Economic Variables.'' *International Organization* (Spring).

United Nations. 1977. *Report of the Conference on International Economic Cooperation*. UN Document E/L. 1774.

U.S. Bureau of the Census. 1976. *Historical Statistics of the United States: Colonial Times to 1970*. Washington, DC: Government Printing Office.

———. 1975. *Statistical Abstract of the United States, 1975*. Washington, DC: Government Printing Office.

U.S. Department of Commerce. 1978*a*. *Overseas Business Reports*. Washington, DC: Government Printing Office.

———. 1970, 1978*b*. *Survey of Current Business.*. Washington, DC: Government Printing Office.

. 1976. *United States Foreign Trade Annual, 1969–1975*. Washington, DC: Government Printing Office.

———. 1978*c*. *United States Foreign Trade Annual 1971–1977*. Washington, DC: Government Printing Office.

U.S. Department of Labor. 1978. *Cumulative Summary of Trade Adjustment Assistance Cases*. ILAB/TAA 1976, and 28 February 1978.

U.S. House of Representatives. 1978. *Report No. 95–1061*. HR 11711 (April). 95th Congress, 2d Session. Washington, DC: Government Printing Office.

———. 1974. *Trade Reform*. Hearings before the Committee on Ways and Means, House of Representatives, on HR 6767. 93d Congress, 2d Session. Washington, DC: Government Printing Office.

USIER. 1976, 1977. *U.S. International Economic Report of the President*. Washington, DC: Government Printing Office.

U.S. International Trade Commission. 1975. *International Commodity Agreements*. Report to Committee on Finance of the U.S. Senate. Washington, DC: Government Printing Office.

U.S. Senate. 1974. *Trade Act of 1974*. Report No. 93–1298 (November). 93d Congress, 2d Session. Washington, DC: Government Printing Office.

U.S. Treasury. 1978. *Findings* (13 April). Washington, DC: Government Printing Office.

Urquhart, M. C., and Buckley, Kenneth A. H. 1965. *Historical Statistics of Canada*. Toronto: Macmillan.

Vernon, Raymon. 1971. *Sovereignty at Bay*. New York: Basic Books.

Viner, Jacob. 1948. "Power versus Plenty as Objectives of Foreign Policy in the Seventeenth and Eighteenth Centuries." *World Politics* 1 (October).

WAES. 1977. *Energy: Global Prospects 1985–2000*. Report of the Workshop on Alternative Energy Strategies. New York: McGraw-Hill.

Wallerstein, Immanuel. 1974. *The Modern World System: Capitalist Agriculture and the Origins of the European World-Economy in the Sixteenth Century*. New York: Academic Press.

Waltz, Kenneth N. 1970. "The Myth of National Interdependence." In *The International Corporation,* ed. Charles Kindleberger. Cambridge, MA: MIT Press.

WAS. Various issues. *World Agricultural Situation*. Washington, DC: Economic Research Service, U.S. Department of Agriculture.

WEC. 1977. *World Economic Conditions in Relation to Agricultural Trade* (August), WEC–12. Washington, DC: Economic Research Service, U.S. Department of Agriculture.

Weston, J. Fred, and Peltzman, Sam, eds. 1969. *Public Policy toward Mergers*. Pacific Palisades, CA: Goodyear Publishing Co.

Whitman, Marina von N. 1977. "Sustaining the International Economic System: Issues for U.S. Policy." *Princeton Essays in International Finance* 121 (June).

Willett, Thomas D. 1979*a*. *Alternative Approaches to International Surveillance of Exchange Rate Policies*. Boston: Federal Reserve Bank of Boston.

———. 1979*b*. "Challenges to a Liberal International Order: An Overview." In *Challenges to the Liberal International Economic Order,* ed. Ryan C. Amacher, Gottfried Haberler, and Thomas D. Willett. Washington, DC: American Enterprise Institute.

———. 1977. *Floating Exchange Rates and International Monetary Reform*. Washington, DC: American Enterprise Institute.

———. 1971. "International Trade Theory Is Still Relevant." *Banca Nationale del Lavora Quarterly Review* 98 (September).

Yeager, Leland B., and Tuerck, David G. 1966. *Trade Policy and the Price System*. Scranton, PA: International Textbook Company.

ABOUT THE AUTHORS

WALTER ADAMS, an internationally known economist and consultant to the federal government, is Distinguished University Professor and Professor of Economics at Michigan State University. He was president of MSU for a brief period ending in January 1970. In Washington, he served as consultant to the Small Business Committees of both the House and the Senate, to the Senate Judiciary Committee, and spent several years as a member of the U.S. Advisory Commission on International Educational and Cultural Affairs. Dr. Adams has taught in France, Austria, and Germany, and his books include *Is the World Our Campus?* (1960), *The Structure of American Industry* (1977), and *The Brain Drain* (1968).

RYAN C. AMACHER is Associate Professor and Chairman, Department of Economics, Arizona State University. He was consultant to the U.S. Treasury from 1972 to 1974 and again from 1975 to 1977, serving in the intervening period as Senior International Economist. He is the author of *Yugoslavia's Foreign Trade* (1972), "Eastern Europe's Stake in the Law of the Sea Negotiations" in *East-West Business: Theory and Evidence,* edited by Josef Brada (1978), and "International Markets versus the New International Economic Order: Challenges to the Independence of Nation States" in *Markets and Marketing: The East-West Nexus* (forthcoming), and of a number of other books and articles on sociopolitical subjects.

SVEN W. ARNDT, Professor of Economics at the University of California, Santa Cruz, is an authority on international trade and finance. As a visiting professor in Europe, he has given courses in disequilibrium analysis at the University of Mannheim and in economic integration at the University of Konstanz, both in Germany, and in international monetary economics at the Institute for Advanced Studies in Vienna. His books and articles include the forthcoming *Economic Interdependence: The Political Economy of Common Markets and Currency Areas,* "International Trade and Payments when Markets Fail to Clear" in *Equilibrium and Disequilibrium in Economic Theory,* edited by G. Schwoediauer

(1977), and "On Exchange Rate Dynamics" in the forthcoming *Asymmetries in the International Economy,* edited by E. Claassen and P. Salin.

MALCOLM D. BALE is an economist in the World Bank and Professorial Lecturer on international economics and trade policy at the School of Advanced International Studies, Johns Hopkins University. A specialist in international agricultural economics, his writings include "Adjustment in Agriculture and the Trade Act of 1974" in *Foreign Agricultural Economic Report No. 147* (1978), with B. L. Greenshields, "Japanese Agricultural Distortions and Their Welfare Value" in *American Journal of Agricultural Economics* (1978), and, with M. H. Cohen, the forthcoming U.S. Department of Agriculture report, *The United Kingdom's Agricultural Sector: A Study of Production, Consumption, and Trade.*

JOHN T. CUDDINGTON, Professor of Economics at Stanford University, has primary interests in international trade and finance, including integrated trade-finance models and adjustment dynamics, macroeconomics, money, and growth. His writings include "Estimating the Impacts of Property Tax Reform" in *Land Economics* (1978), and, with Jack Knetsch and Reed Johnson, *Evaluation of Amenity Resources and the Presence of Substitutes* (1977).

ALAN V. DEARDORFF is Associate Professor of Economics and Associate Chairman, Department of Economics, at the University of Michigan. His writings include "Trade Reversals and Growth Stability," *Journal of International Economics* (1974), "The Optimum Growth Rate for Population: Comment," *International Economic Review* (1976), and the forthcoming "One-Way Arbitrage and Its Implications for the Foreign Exchange Market," *Journal of Political Economy,* and "Weak Links in the Chain of Comparative Advantage," *Journal of International Economics.*

JOEL B. DIRLAM, Professor of Economics at the University of Rhode Island and editorial advisor to *The Antitrust Bulletin,* is Special Consultant to the National Economic Research Associates. He is the author of "The Process of Inflation in France" in *The Roots of Inflation* (1975), and has coauthored many articles with Alfred E. Kahn and others, including the following written with Walter Adams: "Import Competition and the Trade Act of 1974," in *Indian Law Journal* (1977), "Private Planning and Social Efficiency" in *Markets, Corporate Behavior and the State,* edited by A. P. Jacquemin and H. W. De Jong (1976), and "Import Quotas and Industrial Performance," a paper presented at the Nijenrode Conference on Industrial Organization in Breukelen, Holland (1976).

ROGER D. HANSEN is Jacob Blaustein Professor of International Organization at the Johns Hopkins School of Advanced International Studies and a member of the Board of Editors of *International Organization.* His many writings include *Beyond the North-South Stalemate* (1978), *The Politics of Mexican Development* (1972), and coauthorship with Albert Fishlow, Carlos F. Diaz-Alejendro, and Richard R. Fagen of *Rich and Poor Nations in the World Economy* (1978). He also wrote on "U.S.–Latin American Economic Relationships: Bilateral, Regional, or Global?" in *The Americas in a Changing World* (1975).

H. ROBERT HELLER is Vice President for International Economics at the Bank of America's World Headquarters in San Francisco, and former chief of the Financial Studies Division, International Monetary Fund, Washington, D.C. He is associate editor of the *Journal of Money, Credit, and Banking,* and a member of the executive committee of the Western Economic Association. The author of numerous articles in economic journals and of several books written for the IMF, his writings include *International Monetary Economics* (1974), *International Trade: Theory and Empirical Evidence* (1968, 1973), *The Economic System* (1972, 1977), and, with Emily Heller, *Japanese Investment in the United States* (1974).

D. GALE JOHNSON is Provost and Eliakim Hastings Moore Distinguished Service Professor, Department of Economics, University of Chicago. His work as consultant and economic advisor included a long association with the Rand Corporation, several U.S. commissions, the Agency for International Development (Brazil), and most recently, the U.S. Council on International Economic Policy and the Steering Committee for the President's Food and Nutrition Study, National Research Council, National Academy of Sciences. His writings include *U.S. Agriculture in a World Context: Policies and Approaches for the Next Decade* written with John A. Schnittker (1974), *World Food Problems and Prospects* (1975), *The Soviet Impact on World Grain Trade* (1977), and "Post-War Policies Relating to Trade in Agricultural Economics" in *A Survey of Agricultural Economics Literature,* edited by Lee R. Martin (1977).

ROBERT O. KEOHANE, Professor of Political Science at Stanford University, is editor of *International Organization.* He is the author of several articles, including "Not 'Innocents Abroad': U.S. Multinational Corporations and the U.S. Government" in *Comparative Politics* (1976), "American Policy and the Trade-Growth Struggle" in *International Security* (1978), "United States Foreign

Economic Policy toward other Advanced Capitalist States: The Struggle to Make Others Adjust'' in the forthcoming *Eagle Entangled: Contemporary Issues in American Foreign Policy,* edited by Robert J. Lieber, Kenneth Oye, and Donald Rothchild, and, with Joseph S. Nye, Jr., *Power and Interdependence, World Politics in Transition* (1977).

MICHAEL W. KERAN, Vice President and Director of Research of the Federal Reserve Bank of San Francisco, spent three years in the 1960s as Assistant Financial Attaché of the American Embassy in Tokyo, and in February 1978 was invited by the Saudi Arabian Monetary Authority to study Saudi Arabian money supply control procedures and make recommendations on their modification. He has written widely on financial and economic matters, including ''Inflation, Regulation, and Utility Stock Prices'' in *Bell Journal of Economics* (1976), ''Monetary Policy and the Business Cycle in Post-War Japan'' in *Varieties of Monetary Experience,* edited by David Meiselman (1970), and ''Is Gold a Good Private Hedge against Inflation?'' with M. Penzler, in *Business Review* (1975).

RACHEL McCULLOCH is Associate Professor of Economics at Harvard University and author of several discussion and working papers on marketing and international economics. Among her writings are ''United States Foreign Trade Policy: Emerging Issues'' in *Trade, Inflation and Ethics* (1976), ''Consequences of a Tax on the Brain Drain for Unemployment and Income Inequality in Less Developed Countries,'' written with Janet L. Yellen, in *The Brain Drain and Taxation*, edited by J. Bhagwati (1976), and ''Commodity Power and the International Community'' in *The New Economics of the Less Developed Countries,* edited by N. Kamrany (1978).

RONALD I. McKINNON, Professor of Economics at Stanford University, has been economic consultant to the governments of Colombia, Kuwait, and Chile, to AID in Korea, to the International Bank for Reconstruction and Development in Ethiopia, and to the Organization of American States concerning Latin American capital markets. The author of many articles on international trade, he has also written three books—*Money and Capital in Economic Development* (1973), *Money and Finance in Economic Growth and Development* of which he was editor as well as contributor (1976), and the forthcoming *Money in International Exchange: The Convertible Currency System*.

GORDON W. SMITH is Associate Professor of Economics at Rice University. He spent two years in Brazil as technical advisor to the Ministry of Planning in the field of applied economic research, and was consultant to the U.S. Treasury Department from 1975 to 1978. The author of *The External Debt Prospects of the Non–Oil-Exporting Developing Countries,* a monograph published in 1977 by the Overseas Development Council, his writings include "The International Tin Agreement: A Reassessment," with George R. Schink, in *Economic Journal* (1976), "The Choice of Technology: Multinational Firms in Brazil" written with Samuel A. Morley, in *Economic Development and Cultural Change* (1977), and "Commodity Instability: New Order or Old Hat" in the forthcoming *Challenges to a Liberal International Economic Order*, edited by Ryan C. Amacher and Thomas D. Willett.

ROBERT M. STERN, Professor of Economics at the University of Michigan, spent several years as consultant on trade agreements, negotiations, and international labor affairs with the U.S. State Department, Department of Labor, and the Treasury Department. He has written extensively on agricultural production, food exports, and commodity trade for publications in the United States and Europe. His article on "Tariffs and Other Measures of Trade Control: A Survey of Recent Developments," *Journal of Economic Literature* (1973), has been reprinted in *Recent Advances in Economics,* edited by R. Fels and J. J. Siegfried (1974) and, in part, in *Legal Problems of International Economic Relations,* edited by J. H. Jackson (1977). He is also the author of *The Balance of Payments: Theory and Economic Policy* (1973).

RICHARD JAMES SWEENEY is Associate Professor of Economics at Claremont Men's College in California. He was formerly Assistant Director of the Office of Policy Research in the U.S. Department of the Treasury, and Deputy Director of the Office of International Monetary Research. He was contributor and editor, with Ryan Amacher, of *The Law of the Sea: U.S. Interests and Negotiating Positions* (1976), and, with Thomas D. Willett, of *Exchange Rate Flexibility and the Stability of the International Monetary System* (forthcoming). His many articles include "On Some Relationships among Capital Theory, Growth, and the Theory of International Trade" in *Weltwirtschaftliches Archiv* (1976), and "Efficient Information Processing in Output Markets: Tests and Implications" in *Economic Inquiry* (1978).

ROBERT D. TOLLISON, Professor of Economics at Virginia Polytechnic Institute and State University, has been consultant to the U.S. Commerce and Treasury Departments, to the Office of Technology Assessment, and to the Council on Wage and Price Stability. His extensive writings include the forthcoming *Personal Liberty, State Action, and Economic Coordination: The Institu-*

tional Framework for Material Welfare, written with Richard Wagner, and "The Prospect for Liberal Democracy: Comment" in *Fiscal Responsibility and Constitutional Democracy*, edited by J. Buchanan and R. Wagner (1978).

THOMAS D. WILLETT, former Director of International Monetary Research at the U.S. Treasury, is Horton Professor of Economics at Claremont Graduate School and Claremont Men's College in California. He has given courses in international economics at the Fletcher School of Law and Diplomacy and at the School of Advanced International Studies, Johns Hopkins University. His writings include *Floating Exchange Rates and International Monetary Reform* (1977), *The Theory of Optimum Currency Areas and Exchange Rate Flexibility* with Edward Tower (1976), and, with Robert Tollison, "Internalizing International Externalities: A Public Choice Approach to the Law of the Sea Issues" in *The Law of the Sea: U.S. Interests and Alternatives*, edited by Ryan Amacher and Richard Sweeney (1976).

INDEX
(abridged)

PUBLICATIONS LIST
THE INSTITUTE FOR CONTEMPORARY STUDIES

260 California Street, San Francisco, California 94111

Catalog available upon request

THE CALIFORNIA COASTAL PLAN: A CRITIQUE
$5.95. 199 pages. Publication date: March 1976.
ISBN 0–917616–04–9
Library of Congress No. 76–7715
Contributors: Eugene Bardach, Daniel K. Benjamin, Thomas E. Borcherding, Ross D. Eckert, H. Edward Frech III, M. Bruce Johnson, Ronald N. Lafferty, Walter J. Mead, Daniel Orr, Donald M. Pach, Michael R. Peevey.

THE CRISIS IN SOCIAL SECURITY: PROBLEMS AND PROSPECTS
$6.95. 220 pages. Publication date: April 1977; 2d ed., rev., 1978.
ISBN 0–917616–16–2/1977; 0–917616–25–1/1978
Library of Congress No. 77–72542
Contributors: Michael J. Boskin, George F. Break, Rita Ricardo Campbell, Edward Cowan, Martin S. Feldstein, Milton Friedman, Douglas R. Munro, Donald O. Parsons, Carl V. Patton, Joseph A.Pechman, Sherwin Rosen, W. Kip Viscusi, Richard J. Zeckhauser.

DEFENDING AMERICA: TOWARD A NEW ROLE IN THE POST-DETENTE WORLD
$13.95 (hardbound only). 255 pages. Publication date: April 1977 by Basic Books (New York).
ISBN 0–465–01585–9
Library of Congress No. 76–43479
Contributors: Robert Conquest, Theodore Draper, Gregory Grossman, Walter Z. Laqueur, Edward N. Luttwak, Charles Burton Marshall, Paul H. Nitze, Norman Polmar, Eugene V. Rostow, Leonard Schapiro, James R. Schlesinger, Paul Seabury, W. Scott Thompson, Albert Wohlstetter.

EMERGING COALITIONS IN AMERICAN POLITICS
$6.95. 530 pages. Publication date: June 1978.
ISBN 0–917616–22–7
Library of Congress No. 78–53414

Contributors: Jack Bass, David S. Broder, Jerome M. Clubb, Edward H. Crane III, Walter De Vries, Andrew M. Greeley, S. I. Hayakawa, Tom Hayden, Milton Himmelfarb, Richard Jensen, Paul Kleppner, Everett Carll Ladd, Jr., Seymour Martin Lipset, Robert A. Nisbet, Michael Novak, Gary R. Orren, Nelson W. Polsby, Joseph L. Rauh, Jr., Stanley Rothman, William A. Rusher, William Schneider, Jesse M. Unruh, Ben J. Wattenberg.

FEDERAL TAX REFORM: MYTHS AND REALITIES
$5.95. 270 pages. Publication date: September 1978.
ISBN 0–917616–32–4
Library of Congress No. 78–61661
Contributors: Robert J. Barro, Michael J. Boskin, George F. Break, Jerry R. Green, Laurence J. Kotlikoff, Mordecai Kurz, Peter Mieszkowski, John B. Shoven, Paul J. Taubman, John Whalley.

GOVERNMENT CREDIT ALLOCATION: WHERE DO WE GO FROM HERE?
$4.95. 208 pages. Publication date: November 1975.
ISBN O–917616–02–2
Library of Congress No. 75–32951
Contributors: George J. Benston, Karl Brunner, Dwight M. Jaffe, Omotunde E. G. Johnson, Edward J. Kane, Thomas Mayer, Allen H. Meltzer.

NEW DIRECTIONS IN PUBLIC HEALTH CARE: AN EVALUATION OF PROPOSALS FOR NATIONAL HEALTH INSURANCE
$6.95. 277 pages. Publication date: May 1976.
ISBN 0–917616–00–6
Library of Congress No. 76 - 40680
Contributors: Martin S. Feldstein, Thomas D. Hall, Leon R. Kass, Keith B. Leffler, Cotton M. Lindsay, Mark V. Pauly, Charles E. Phelps, Thomas C. Schelling, Arthur Seldon.

NO LAND IS AN ISLAND: INDIVIDUAL RIGHTS AND GOVERNMENT CONTROL OF LAND USE
$5.95. 221 pages. Publication date: November 1975.
ISBN 0–917616–03–0
Library of Congress No. 75–38415
Contributors: Benjamin F. Bobo, B. Bruce-Briggs, Connie Cheney, A. Lawrence Chickering, Robert B. Ekelund, Jr., W. Philip Gramm, Donald G. Hagman, Robert B. Hawkins, Jr., M. Bruce Johnson, Jan Krasnowiecki, John McClaughry, Donald M. Pach, Bernard H. Siegan, Ann Louise Strong, Morris K. Udall.

NO TIME TO CONFUSE: A CRITIQUE OF THE FORD FOUNDATION'S ENERGY POLICY PROJECT *A TIME TO CHOOSE AMERICA'S ENERGY FUTURE*

$4.95. 156 pages. Publication date: February 1975.
ISBN 0–917616–01–4
Library of Congress No. 75–10230
Contributors: Morris A. Adelman, Armen A. Alchian, James C. DeHaven, George W. Hilton, M. Bruce Johnson, Herman Kahn, Walter J. Mead, Arnold B. Moore, Thomas Gale Moore, William H. Riker.

ONCE IS ENOUGH: THE TAXATION OF CORPORATE EQUITY INCOME
$2.00. 32 pages. Publication date: May 1977.
ISBN 0–917616–23–5
Library of Congress No. 77–670132
Author: Charles E. McLure, Jr.

OPTIONS FOR U.S. ENERGY POLICY
$5.95. 317 pages. Publication date: September 1977.
ISBN 0–917616–20–0
Library of Congress No. 77–89094
Contributors: Albert Carnesale, Stanley M. Greenfield, Fred S. Hoffman, Edward J. Mitchell, William R. Moffat, Richard Nehring, Robert S. Pindyck, Norman C. Rasmussen, David J. Rose, Henry S. Rowen, James L. Sweeney, Arthur W. Wright.

PARENTS, TEACHERS, AND CHILDREN: PROSPECTS FOR CHOICE IN AMERICAN EDUCATION
$5.95. 336 pages. Publication date: June 1977.
ISBN 0–917616–18–9
Library of Congress No. 77–79164
Contributors: James S. Coleman, John E. Coons, William H. Cornog, Denis P. Doyle, E. Babette Edwards, Nathan Glazer, Andrew M. Greeley, R. Kent Greenawalt, Marvin Lazerson, William C. McCready, Michael Novak, John P. O'Dwyer, Robert Singleton, Thomas Sowell, Stephen D. Sugarman, Richard E. Wagner.

THE POLITICS OF PLANNING: A REVIEW AND CRITIQUE OF CENTRALIZED ECONOMIC PLANNING
$5.95. 367 pages. Publication date: March 1976.
ISBN 0–917616–05–7
Library of Congress No. 76–7714
Contributors: B. Bruce-Briggs, James Buchanan, A. Lawrence Chickering, Ralph Harris, Robert B. Hawkins, Jr., George W. Hilton, Richard Mancke, Richard Muth, Vincent Ostrom, Svetozar Pejovich, Myron Sharpe, John Sheahan, Herbert Stein, Gordon Tullock, Ernest van den Haag, Paul H. Weaver, Murray L. Weidenbaum, Hans Willgerodt, Peter P. Witonski.

PUBLIC EMPLOYEE UNIONS: A STUDY OF THE CRISIS IN PUBLIC SECTOR LABOR RELATIONS

$6.95. 251 pages. Publication date: June 1976; 2d ed., rev., 1977.
ISBN 0–917616–08–1/1976; ISBN 0–917616–24–3/1977
Library of Congress No. 76–17444

Contributors: A. Lawrence Chickering, Jack D. Douglas, Raymond D. Horton, Theodore W. Kheel, David Lewin, Seymour Martin Lipset, Harvey C. Mansfield, Jr., George Meany, Robert A. Nisbet, Daniel Orr, A. H. Raskin, Wes Uhlman, Harry H. Wellington, Charles B. Wheeler, Jr., Ralph K. Winter, Jr., Jerry Wurf.

REGULATING BUSINESS: THE SEARCH FOR AN OPTIMUM

$6.95. 260 pages. Publication date: April 1978.
ISBN 0–917616–27–8
Library of Congress No. 78–50678

Contributors: Chris Argyris, A. Lawrence Chickering, Penny Hollander Feldman, Richard H. Holton, Donald P. Jacobs, Alfred E. Kahn, Paul W. MacAvoy, Almarin Phillips, V. Kerry Smith, Paul H. Weaver, Richard J. Zeckhauser.

TARIFFS, QUOTAS, AND TRADE: THE POLITICS OF PROTECTIONISM

$6.95. 330 pages. Publication date: February 1979.
ISBN 0–917616–34–0
Library of Congress No. 78–66267

Contributors: Walter Adams, Ryan C. Amacher, Sven W. Arndt, Malcolm D. Bale, John T. Cuddington, Alan V. Deardorff, Joel B. Dirlam, Roger D. Hansen, H. Robert Heller, D. Gale Johnson, Robert O. Keohane, Michael W. Keran, Rachel McCulloch, Ronald I. McKinnon, Gordon W. Smith, Robert M. Stern, Richard James Sweeney, Robert D. Tollison, Thomas D. Willett.

THE THIRD WORLD: PREMISES OF U.S. POLICY

$5.95. 332 pages. Publication date: November 1978.
ISBN 0–917616–30–8
Library of Congress No. 78–67593

Contributors: Dennis Austin, Peter T. Bauer, Max Beloff, Richard E. Bissell, Daniel J. Elazar, S. E. Finer, Allan E. Goodman, Nathaniel H. Leff, Seymour Martin Lipset, Edward N. Luttwak, Daniel Pipes, Wilson E. Schmidt, Anthony Smith, W. Scott Thompson, Basil S. Yamey.

WATER BANKING: HOW TO STOP WASTING AGRICULTURAL WATER

$2.00. 56 pages. Publication date: January 1978.
ISBN 0–917616–26–X
Library of Congress No. 78–50766

Authors: Sotirios Angelides, Eugene Bardach.